LB40450E

INCEST

*A Treatment Manual for Therapy with
Victims, Spouses and Offenders*

2nd Edition

D0008795

306.877
M468I
1993

Adele Mayer, Ph.D.

Lp LEARNING PUBLICATIONS, INC.
Holmes Beach, Florida

1/94

CUYAHOGA COMMUNITY COLLEGE
EASTERN CAMPUS LIBRARY   FEB 1 4 1993

ISBN 1-55691-054-1

© 1993 by Adele Mayer

All rights reserved. No part of this book may be reproduced or transmitted in any form or by any means, electronic or mechanical, including photocopying and recording, or by any information or retrieval systems, without permission in writing from the publisher.

Learning Publications, Inc.
5351 Gulf Drive
P.O. Box 1338
Holmes Beach, FL   34217

Printing: 5 4 3 2 1   Year: 7 6 5 4 3

Printed in the United States of America

Contents

Foreword.. vii

Introduction ix

PART I: STATISTICS: COMING OUT OF THE CLOSET

1   Scope of the Problem... 3

2   Review of the Literature.. 9

PART II: THE INCESTUOUS TRIAD

3   Family Dynamics.. 21

4   Personalities in the Incestuous Triad.............................. 27

5   The Family and the Law.. 33

PART III: THERAPEUTIC METHODS, MODELS
AND APPROACHES

Section A: The Victim

6   Facilitating Catharsis as a Major Therapeutic Goal for
the Victim of Incestuous Abuse 43

7   Avoiding the "Rescuer's Trap" with Teenage
Victims.. 61

8   Assertive Training for Child Victims............................... 67

Section B: The Wife

9   Strategic Therapy for Silent Partners in Incest
Families.. 75

10   Surrogate Mothering as an Initial Catalyst for Change
for the Wives of Offenders 79

11   Restructuring Clients' Self-Image Through Retaping 85

Section C: The Offender

12   Treating the Offender: Evaluation of Motives and
Potential for Change 95

13 Working Around Denial to Facilitate Change: Contingency
    Management as a Behavioral Control for the Offender.................. 107

14 Breaking Down the Components of Affective Reactions:
    Alternate Stress Management Techniques...................................... 123

Section D: The Family

15 A Behavioral Re-engineering Approach to Family
    Dysfunction and Social Isolation 131

16 Confrontation on Hidden Agendas in the Family 135

Section E: The Group

17 The Victim Group.. 143

18 The Wives Group... 149

19 The Sexual Enrichment Group 155

20 The Couples' Communication Group 163

Part IV: Innovative and Practical Treatment Techniques

Section A: General Approaches, Principles and
              Techniques for Children and Adults

21 Therapeutic Goals for Children, Adults and Family 199

Section B: Specific Methods for Use with Children and
              Adolescents

22 Art Techniques... 209

23 Writing Techniques 245

24 Sentence Blanks, Rating Scales, Check Lists and
    Sociograms... 249

25 Desensitization.. 255

26 Other Therapeutic Media.. 263

Appendix A: Suggested Books and Articles
Regarding Child and Sexual Child Abuse (Annotated)......... 273

Appendix B: References 283

Index 305

Foreword

This manual has been written for the practitioner who treats members of the incestuous triad either individually, as a family, or in group. The intention is to provide clinicians with treatment models and techniques for a client population that is increasing in numbers and that comes with specific characteristics requiring specialized expertise and knowledge. Secondarily, this manual has been written to heighten awareness about a topic that has had relatively little exposure until fairly recently.

In this revised edition of *Incest*, a number of changes have been made reflecting and updating both practical and empirical research in the last decade. First, increased awareness and reports of abuse have altered data regarding incidence even though there still are no reliable statistics on the prevalence of incest in the United States.

Chapter 2, "Review of the Literature," has been updated and condensed to reflect the proliferation of literature on dynamics and treatment. It would be impossible to provide an overview of the hundreds of first-person accounts, treatment manuals and prevention materials on the subject. Instead, the literature has been categorized into types of publications to provide an overall understanding of the focus of the last ten years. An annotated booklist and list of references and resources has been expanded in the appendices.

The changes are relevant and necessary as researchers and practitioners learn more about the devastating problem of incest and as this new information is shared through texts and trainings. This new edition of *Incest* reflects the growing state of knowledge in the field.

The manual is divided into four parts. Part I is an introduction providing an overview of the problem including data regarding the scope of incest in the United States, a review of the literature and didactic material on the dynamics of the family itself along with legal implications. Part II involves a consideration of the incestuous triad including family dynamics, personalities and legal implications. Part III contains general therapeutic methods, models and approaches related to the treatment of incest. Separate consideration is given to the treatment of individual members of the triad, the family as a unit, and the group. The material presented is largely original and where concepts have been modified or borrowed from authorities, due credit is given. Part IV is devoted to specific practical techniques useful in the treatment of children and adults. Here, too, the contents are original and hence should prove helpful to the therapist seeking innovative methods of treating the complex problems incest presents for all family members.

All names in case studies have been changed to protect the privacy of the individuals involved.

Introduction

When *Incest* was researched in the late 1970's, there were only a few pioneer works on the subject of intrafamilial molestation. The 1980's brought child sexual abuse out of the closet and with its emergence came a wave of literature covering virtually every aspect of the problem from prevention to the treatment of sex offenders and juvenile perpetrators.

The 1990's are bringing further refinements to the field. New studies on children's memories now are used routinely to determine credibility and competence, particularly in the courtroom. Male victims of all ages are overcoming hidden shame, disclosing early trauma and asserting their needs for validation and treatment.

Once thought to be a rare phenomenon, female sex offenses are being identified in shockingly large numbers, debunking the myth that perpetration is an exclusively male problem. Juvenile sex offenders as young as five or six now are in treatment with the realization that early intervention may be the only prevention for adult offenses.

Identification and treatment of ritual and satanic abuse have become aspects of new sub-specialties in the field of child abuse. Preschool-daycare abuse, like ritual abuse, involves its own set of dynamics, effects and prescriptions for recovery. Finally, MPD (Multiple Personality Disorder) and other dissociative states now have clearly been identified as sequelae of severe childhood trauma. Countless numbers of adults, some misdiagnosed for years, are finding appropriate treatment as sufferers of PTSD (Post Traumatic Stress Disorder) and its associated symptoms.

The unprecedented new awareness of incest and its devastating effects have resulted in a proliferation of the literature in the area of victimization. Yet it is important to maintain perspective and understand that the consequences of change in the field have been both positive and negative.

Change has resulted in increased reporting; new knowledge and awareness of child sexual abuse both by professionals and lay people; development and refinement in treatment techniques and modalities; massive, widespread prevention efforts; and the legitimacy of child sexual abuse as a specialty in behavioral health.

On the negative side, the past decade has seen a vicious backlash by powerful family rights proponents, particularly in the courtroom where experts are pitted against one another on a "for hire" basis. In protective services, fear of civil lawsuits for removal and non-removal of children in suspected abuse has resulted in fear-based interventions and a "damned if you do; damned if you don't" mindset.

The fact that child sexual abuse has become the sophisticated province of self-designated experts has resulted in attempts at exclusivity by professionals often motivated by self-aggrandizement and financial gain. This means that the role of trained paraprofessional survivors, often very effective in dealing therapeutically with child victims because of identification, validation, and empathy, is being diminished.

Child sexual abuse has become quantified as every disclosure is carefully examined and scrutinized for possible fabrication. Yet there still are a shockingly large number of behavioral health providers with limited knowledge in the field of child sexual abuse along with a continuing reluctance to notify authorities of cases of suspected abuse despite state mandates incorporating penalties for failure to report.

Reliable statistics regarding prevalence still are not available. Russell's work (1986), covering eight years of comprehensive research, is noteworthy as one of the few substantive research studies on prevalence. The numerous prevention programs, which were implemented before field tests, have come under scrutiny as costly and ineffective. Eager to meet the demand for educational materials on sexual abuse prevention, writers, film-makers and distributors flooded the market with games, books, pamphlets, audio, and videotapes, and cassettes, often without sufficient concern regarding content. For some children, for example, the use of the phrases "good touch" and "bad touch" generalize, resulting in the perception that the genitals inherently are bad.

Much of the new literature is valuable, especially in-depth studies of particular types of abuse such as juvenile sex offenders and female molestation. However, a number of recent studies are a rehash of the classics of the late 1970's and early 1980's. Walters (1975), Giarretto (1976), Forward (1978), Burgess and Holmstrom (1978), Finkelhor (1979), Justice and Justice (1979), Kroth (1979) and Groth (1979), among others were the original pioneers in the field and their works have become classics.

On balance, the single most important development of the last decade has been the growth of an unprecedented concern for sexually abused children and adults. Fortunately, that concern continues to grow with resultant efforts to alter dysfunctional aspects of the social fabric, in adult and child relationships in and out of the family and with the legal structure in the United States.

PART I:
Statistics: Coming Out of the Closet

1
SCOPE OF THE PROBLEM

Understanding incest is complicated by many befuddling and contradictory definitions. One source of confusion is the legal system which varies considerably among differing cultures, nations, states and provinces of the world. Further confusion arises when one attempts to identify and quantitate parental intent and degree of harm inflicted on children.

Therapeutic definitions of incest differ from carefully prescribed legal sanctions. Practitioners often consider subtle gradations of inappropriate verbal and non-verbal behaviors such as seductive eye contact between parent and child or inappropriately tight hugs.

In the 1980's, emotional incest which covers a broad spectrum of behavioral interactions was added to the definition of incest. Emotional incest has been identified as involving role switches where children become surrogate spouses for fathers or mothers.

Are we required by the nature of incest to be unclear in our definition? If we must consider laws, motives and social norms, we will always have great difficulty. If, however, we use incest to refer to a particular set of behaviors, regardless of norms or motivation, we can at least agree upon our subject matter. Clearly, incest need be no more than a term used to describe a set of behaviors, regardless of whether these behaviors are prohibited, condoned or exalted by a given society. The definition need carry neither moral nor legal proscriptions.

Definition

We can arrive at a satisfactory and clear definition of incest if we accept the premise that incest is, quite simply: any sexual contact or interaction between family members who are not marital partners.   This broad-based definition includes all stimulatory activities outlined in the table that follows.   It includes pornographic photography, sexual gestures, parental exposure of genitalia, fondling, petting, fellatio, cunnilingus, intercourse and any and all varieties of other sexual contact.

Incidence

Despite over a decade of research, there still are no reliable figures regarding the incidence of incest and available statistics show considerable variation.   The consensus among many authorities is that reported cases do not reflect reality and that for every incest case reported, countless others remain hidden.

Following eight years of thorough research on incest, Russell (1986) is a leading source of statistical data.   Along with Finkelhor (1979) and Geiser (1979) among other experts, Russell concludes that between three to five girls, and eight to eleven boys, will be sexually abused or assaulted (intra- and extrafamilially) before the age of eighteen.

Regardless of the figures cited, most authorities agree that child sexual abuse is more prevalent than present statistics indicate.   There are a number of factors affecting the inadequacy of reports and tabulations of statistics.

It is important to be aware of these conditions, some of which shed light on the nature of the problem and on the dynamics involved in child sexual abuse.   The main obstructions to adequate data-gathering are listed below.

1) *Police Reports:*   Most reports of sexual child abuse are based on inadequate police statistics.   Cases given directly to prosecutors are not reported in the statistics.

2) *Stereotypical Bias:*   The public equates sexual abuse with violent trauma.   Cases not involving forcible attacks are discounted.

TYPES OF INCESTUOUS ASSAULT AGAINST CHILDREN AND ADOLESCENTS

Sexual Molestation

- Non-coital sexual contact
- Results in sexual stimulation of offender
- Includes petting, fondling
- Includes exhibitionism (exposure of offender's sexual organs)
- Includes Voyeurism (watching victim undress, nude)

Sexual Assault

- Manual-oral and/or genital contact with genitals of victim
- Non-consent
- Includes masturbatory activities, fellatio, cunnilingus

Forcible Rape

- Forced sexual contact resulting in assault with penis
- Uses fear, violence, fraud, threats

LEAST DAMAGING

Involves different treatment plans, prognoses, ages time sequences, consequences (legal and psychological), and dynamics (homosexual, heterosexual, close relative, distant relative, related by marriage).

MOST DAMAGING

3) *Avoidance by Professionals:* Many professionals lack the knowledge necessary to identify child sexual abuse. In the absence of an understanding of the dynamics of incest, these professionals tend to suspect that victims are fabricating tales of sexual abuse as a result of anger or revenge related to family conflict. In addition, strong emotional reactions generate anxiety and denial among professionals. Anxiety and denial may result in avoiding the identification of cases of sexual abuse.

Some physicians have difficulty coping with the reality of adult-child sexual contact and, as a result, do not obtain the necessary corroborative evidence secured by physical examinations of the victims. Many physicians believe that the genital examination of a child-victim is intrinsically traumatic.

Finally, Freudian psychotherapists and analysts, de-emphasizing the distinction between real and fantasized childhood trauma and relying heavily on oedipal fantasy, may tend to discount patients' accounts of actual incestuous relationships.

4) *Reluctance to Report:* Child victims are reluctant to report sexual abuse for various reasons including shame, guilt, and fears related to family disruption resulting from disclosure. There might be fear of not being believed, and/or of reprisals by the offender. Some victims view removal from the home as a form of punishment. Others have enjoyed the sexual contact and view disclosure as a betrayal of the offender.

Mothers of victims also are frequently reluctant to report sexual abuse in the family. They, too, fear a disruption of family life with a resultant loss of financial and emotional security. Mothers also may fear social censure and the trauma that interrogations and court proceedings might cause their daughters.

5) *Age-Sex Factors:* Male victims of sexual abuse are proportionally less frequently reported than female victims. Finkelhor (1979) postulates a number of reasons for the discrepancy between male-female victim reporting including the fact that males are less frightened by sexual contact and therefore manifest fewer symptoms that might result in detection. Boy victims may be older, more self-reliant and less likely to arouse protective responses among adults. Younger offenders, too, seldom are reported due to parental reluctance and the belief that the offense can be handled within the home. Lew (1988) is one of the few authorities who has written an in-depth study on the dynamics involved in male victimization.

6) *Skewed Reporting:* Currently, there exists no sound methodology for ascertaining the frequency of incest in the various socio-economic strata. Disclosure is more likely among the lower classes (Slager-Jorne, 1978). The middle and upper classes have private means to manage the problem so that it does not come to the attention of reporting agencies.

7) *Prejudice, Emotional Impact and the Taboo:* In reality, the incest taboo is a defense against the natural experience of people living in close proximity and developing sexual relationships with one another. Instead, the taboo generally is perceived as a curse, forcing concealment of bestial acts. Viewed as such, it encourages guilt and non-disclosure of sexual abuse.

8) *Classification Confusion:* There is much confusion regarding which family members merit inclusion in the incest category. Step-relations, cousins and in-laws arbitrarily may be omitted from the incest taboo even though they may be living in relationships like those of natural parents.

Current Status

It is possible that sexual abuse of children has decreased over the centuries. In Europe in the 16th, 17th and 18th centuries, it was common practice to have sexual contact with youngsters (Finkelhor, 1979). There are no reliable figures, however, to determine increases or decreases in the problem during the past century. What we do know is that during the last decade there has been a significant increase in reporting and awareness, coupled with an interest in developing appropriate treatment methods.

Equally true is the increase in social isolation and alienation of the American nuclear family. Family members turn to one another for emotional nurture which might lead to an increase in incestuous acts (Justice and Justice, 1979).

The issue of child sexual abuse is quite complicated in a society where values are continually in flux and where social and moral values rapidly become politicized and polarized, with extremist views receiving most of the public attention. The women's movement and the children's rights movement, on the one hand, are demanding equality and the elimination of all exploitation of minorities. In opposition to these groups are the advocates of an increased tolerance for aberrant sexuality in our society. The ban on incest is being challenged with articles openly attacking the taboo. Instead of constituting a perversion, incest is perceived as beneficial (Time Magazine, 1980). Incest is being publicized in movies, television and novels.

Incest is a very serious problem and current trends toward exonerating sexual offenses against minors incapable of consensual relationships are possibly one indication of social and moral decadence in a society already expounding questionable and uncertain values. Moreover, dedicated professionals devoted to the principles of sound methodological research based on empirical evidence have collected sufficient data to indicate that incest results in serious short-term and long-term emotional and physical consequences for the victims. The clinician needs specialized expertise in order to treat families involved in incestuous abuse. The treatment of incestuous families involves, first, an understanding of what constitutes intrafamilial molestation and what motivates and determines this pathological manifestation. Second, it involves self-therapy on the part of the clinician, who must deal with her or his own bias, anger and identification before becoming involved in this area of treatment. Third, treatment involves knowledge of specific modalities to help families work through trauma and readjustment. Resolution may never be complete, but with sympathetic, humanistic and skilled professional expertise, families can reach more socially accepted modes of behavior.

2
Review of the Literature

When *Incest* first was researched in the late 1970's, the literature on child sexual abuse was criticized for its unreliable statistical, methodological errors, small sample sizes and biased data. Knowledge about incest in particular and child sexual abuse in general was limited. The same studies and the same authors were cited repeatedly in each new study.

Literature of the 1980's

There has been a proliferation of literature on child sexual abuse in the last decade partly because practitioners and the lay public have become more aware of the dimensions of the problem. It would be impossible to critique the voluminous number of books, articles, films, audio tapes, videotapes, television shows, school curricula, prevention games, dramas and dolls other than to note that there is much repetition. Particularly in the areas of prevention and treatment of sex offenders, innovation appears to have predominated over long-term field testing. For example, the penile plethysmograph (penile strain gauge) which measures genital responses to sexually explicit material was used in the assessment of perpetrators before being normed.

Anatomically-correct or natural dolls, used by therapists in the early 1980's to elicit disclosures in non-verbal or preverbal preschoolers, resulted in a number of (threatened) malpractice lawsuits. Though useful in therapy, the dolls are not an objective testing tool with measurements of validity and reliability. Thus, the clinician should use caution in evaluating new approaches since:

1. Theories regarding incest abound but often are not related to statistical observations.

2. Few studies measure changes over time and the effects of treatment interventions.

Conservative Versus Radical Bias

Bias and subjectivity pervade the literature because incest is an emotionally-laden issue that generates strong reactions — fear, anger, and revulsion. Unfortunately, this emotional climate precludes the likelihood of objective data gathering, as there is a strong tendency for defenses (reaction formation, denial, identification with the aggressor, projection) to operate among researchers and readers alike. Data is often distorted and used selectively to corroborate notions based on personal values and moral assumptions. The process snowballs as values and defenses influence the formation of initial assumptions and continue to serve as variables distorting the entire scientific inquiry. (For clarification of this position, see the chart that follows.)

There is a radical-conservative continuum involved in the incest controversy. On the radical side is the Rene Guyon Society whose members openly espouse the view, "Sex before eight or else it is too late." They call for a ban on the incest taboo, believing that the taboo causes sexual repressions, inhibitions, guilt and perversions (Finkelhor, 1978). On the conservative side are the extremists who view offenders not as emotionally disturbed individuals but rather as vicious rapists. Each of these groups can use the data found in the literature subjectively to substantiate their biased positions.

Another powerful group located on the radical-conservative continuum is comprised of feminists who view incest as a subcategory of rape--a manifestation of male power and oppression of the female (Rush, 1974). Finkelhor (1979) believes sexual abuse of children has become a pre-eminent issue because of the political power of the women's movement combined with that of the child protection lobby. However, each constituency views the problem differently. The National Committee for Prevention of Child Abuse and the National Center for Child Abuse and Neglect (DHEW) categorize sexual child abuse as a sub-category of child abuse while members of the women's movement view the act as rape.

DISTORTED DATA GATHERING AND SELECTIVE PERCEPTION IN THE INQUIRY INTO INCESTUOUS ABUSE

Fallacious Assumptions Based on Value-Moral System and Operation of Defenses		Cognitive Dissonance		Variables Adversely Affecting Data Gathering		Data Gathering
1. Incest is beneficial and no one is harmed or emotionally disturbed. 2. Incest is harmful and someone (the "bad guy") is responsible (Mom, Dad, Child).		Need to prove assumptions based on need to find closure and definitive answers; inability to tolerate cognitive dissonance.		Interference of value system and emotional bias (hidden moral and religious agendas; subjectivity; operation of defenses; emotionally charged reaction to the issue).		Selective data gathering and generalizations to prove initial assumptions.

Numerous other powerful groups have influenced the political and social climate through their bias and distortion of available data. VOCAL (Victims of Child Abuse Laws), a group organized in Minnesota in 1984, has over 3,000 chapters nationally to provide support, advocacy and advice for parents accused of incestuous abuse.

Child Participation

One very controversial issue still reflected in the literature involves the role of the victim in incestuous abuse. From the 1930's to the 1950's, researchers accused victims as young as four years of age of unusual attractiveness, seduction and outright instigation of incest in the home (Bender and Blau, 1937; Weiss, 1955). Public sentiment continues to reflect this bias. The strength of conviction of male authorities such as Weiss, Bender and Blau, whose samples were small and whose studies were retrospective, again lends credence to the notion that defenses and emotional biases operate strongly in data gathering and interpretation.

Objective, relevant issues should be considered when carelessly tempted to cast blame on mothers and daughters in incestuous families, including the following:

1. Children do not share the adults' perception of sexuality and their alleged precipitating actions might stem from quite different motives from what the offender interprets as sexual gestures or overtures.

2. Sexually victimized children often are conditioned and trained to seek affection through "seductive" behaviors and to sexualize all relationships.

3. According to our laws, no minor is capable of consensual sexual relations regardless of the degree of seductive behavior on her or his part.

4. Adult offenders ultimately bear responsibility for incestuous abuse. It is they who, at the expense of their victims, act out sexually with all of the power that their adult and parental roles convey.

5. In homes where incestuous abuse occurs, psychopathology exists and affects all members. The children are not emotionally healthy. Raised in a climate where needs are met in distorted

and pathological ways, they learn to meet their needs in similar fashion. Their behavior is learned and perhaps necessary for personal survival or for survival of the family unit. However, to recognize the fact that each individual in the family has a role in incestuous abuse is not equivalent to removing final responsibility from the offending adult member.

The Male Dominated Society

Feminists argue that sexual abuse of children is a by-product of a male dominated society. Men have the power which is exercised by strong sanctions and taboos on female sexuality, along with covert tolerance for their own behavior (Finkelhor, 1979).

Butler (1978) stresses the socialization process as a major causative factor in incestuous abuse. She believes that women are raised to be victims—passive, emotional, weak and dependent on the male. The female role, essentially masochistic, leads women to identify with their daughters and feel powerless to help them in inescapable and inevitable incestuous situations. The male, on the other hand, is socialized to feel contempt for the female. Wives and children are viewed solely as possessions to be conquered.

Freudians explain the dynamics of incestuous abuse by relying heavily on theories of infant sexuality. The oedipus-electra complex places the onus of responsibility not on the male but on the child victim whose unresolved sexual conflicts lead her to yield to forbidden temptations--albeit with resultant guilt (Butler, 1978). The Freudians also explain the origin of the incest taboo by starting with the primal horde and continuing on to the oedipus complex. Heavy reliance is placed on the patriarchal society where mother-son incest is abhorred as an insult to male supremacy while the notion of father-daughter incest is less threatening and more sanctioned with the result that the taboo is violated more frequently (Herman & Hirschman, 1980).

It should be emphasized that psychoanalytical theories are still widely read but lack empirical confirmation. Theory overshadows sound methodology and the Freudians tend to be used for propaganda and political ends.

The Traumatization Controversy

Like the dichotomies evident in the conservative versus radical controversy and the child victim versus the child participant controversy, polarity exists among followers of the pro-trauma versus anti-trauma controversy. One side considers long and short range effects of child sexual abuse to be non-existent; the other claims they are extremely damaging. In my view, these differing attitudes involve important implications regarding treatment and, therefore, the polarity merits considerable attention.

In general, those who believe resultant trauma is minimal seem to trust the innocence of children to serve as a natural protection against long-term effects. They believe that, with their dim sense of mature sexuality, children are not aware of the implications of incestuous abuse.

At the other end of the continuum are authorities who cite numerous retrospective studies of adults who were victims as children and who suffer from depression, guilt, shame, interpersonal difficulties and sexual dysfunction. Among the numerous and notable authorities who claim that there are serious long-term effects resulting from childhood incest are Benward and Densen-Gerber of Odyssey House in New York City (1975), Fontana (1978), De Francis (1969, 1978), Giaretto (1980), Yorukoglu and Kemph (1980), Russell (1986), Maltz and Homman (1987), and Courtois (1988). Each of these researchers cites cogent empirical evidence of damaging personal and sexual disorders occurring directly as a result of early trauma.

The long-term effects of incest are not immediately evident and therefore often minimized, but they are nonetheless devastating.

The anti-alarmists are equally convinced of the validity of their stance. Landis (1965), Schultz (1980), Peters (1976), Bender and Blau (1937), and Burton (1968) all minimize the traumatic effects of incestuous abuse. Schultz is rather adamant in his assertions that the literature does not support a casual relationship between incest and pre- or post-incest behavior and that trauma can result from how incest cases are processed by the law and by mental health professionals rather than from the abuse itself.

Thus, one side of the controversy collects data to corroborate the notion that the dangers of incest are exaggerated. The radicals deny any serious effects, demanding absolute and empirical proof of trauma. The conservatives, on the other hand, believe that there is a substantial body of irrefutable evidence to the effect that incest is extremely damaging to personality development and results in a variety of affective and behavioral disturbances.

CURRENT LITERATURE

In general, the literature of the past decade can be divided into three broad categories: materials for survivors; studies (prevalence, etiology, dynamics, effects and treatment); and prevention materials.

Materials for Survivors

The market has been glutted with audio- and videotapes, poetry, newsletters, first-person accounts, and self-help manuals for survivors of child sexual abuse. Even prominent personalities such as Senator Paula Hawkins (1986) are detailing their traumatic childhoods involving sexual abuse and exploitation. Many of the self-help manuals are repetitious, rehashing already-published materials. One of the most all inclusive self-help books, *The Courage to Heal* (1988) by Bass and Davis lists nearly thirty pages of books, clubs, newsletters and groups for all ages and is an invaluable resource for both survivors and therapists.

Professionals should review all tapes and literature before recommending or assigning them to clients. For example, *If I Should Die Before I Wake,* a novel by Michelle Morris (1976) ends with murder. Powerfully explicit and graphic in its depiction of abuse and its aftermath, the book has considerable impact on suggestible and vulnerable victims and should be screened before assignment to clients.

Self-help manuals and first-person accounts can be helpful for victims needing validation, working through the trauma of abuse, and dealing with early, blocked memories. There continues to be a need for materials by and for male survivors, and for non-offending mothers and fathers of victims of in- and out-of-home molestation.

Studies

In recent years, there has been considerable progress in research into the etiology and dynamics of incestuous abuse. Factors related to the victim (sex, age, personality, past victimization, developmental and psychosexual stages, and level of mental functioning); offender and non-offending spouse (relationship issues); and the offense (type, onset, duration, and frequency) now routinely are considered when assessing the needs of victims.

The dynamics of incestuous abuse have been summarized in the early classics (Butler, 1978; Forward and Buck, 1978; and Finkelhor, 1979). Finkelhor (1986) has updated and refined existing information with a focus on prevalence, abusers and effects. Some of the recently published self-help manuals provide comprehensive coverage of short- and long-term effects (Blume, 1991; Gomes-Schwartz, Horowitz and Cardrelli, 1991). These manuals also are useful in providing suggestions for recovery and often include specific techniques and exercises for client use outside of the therapeutic setting.

A decade ago, Giarretto's Parents United-Child Sexual Abuse Treatment Program in Santa Clara, California, offered one of the only nationally-known integrated models to treat intrafamilial molestation. In recent years, new treatment approaches earmarking adult and child survivors have proliferated throughout the United States.

By 1990, every major city in the nation boasted programs for the treatment of incest perpetrators. Knopp (1984) summarizes the components of ten of these programs. Models vary but current thinking in the field relates heavily on the addiction model with a major therapeutic focus on relapse prevention (Carnes, 1983; Laws, 1989).

As in the past, experts tend to advocate family therapy if:

1. Offenders have admitted the abuse, served jail time, been in treatment and apologized to victims.

2. Mothers have demonstrated support and a strong protective bond for child victims through individual and dyad therapy with daughters or sons.

3. Victims have worked through the trauma and clarified their feelings about the abuse and their parents.

Treatment approaches for mothers of victims are limited both in number and scope. Byerly (1985) and Crowley (1990) focus on the needs of mothers in in- and out-of-home molestation, respectively. There is a need for treatment that addresses denying, collusive mothers, who, in many cases, were victimized as children. Subtle dynamics involving emotional misuse of children by women who have not resolved their own issues should be thoroughly explored in the literature along with suggestions for treatment and resolution of underlying dynamics.

In contrast to the dearth of treatment approaches for mothers has been the proliferation of material for child and adult victims. Many of the recent publications provide invaluable suggestions, techniques and therapeutic models (Sgori, 1982; Mann and McDermott. 1983; Baxter, 1986; MacFarlane and Waterman, 1986; Bear, 1988; and Lew, 1988).

Prevention

Games, books, school curricula, films, dramas, puppetry, audio tapes, videotapes and coloring books on preventing child sexual abuse literally have glutted the market in recent years. These materials generally are designed for specific populations such as preschoolers, teenagers or parents and focus on specific types of sexual abuse including incest, extrafamilial molestation or rape.

Many of the materials are useful, particularly in therapy with child victims who need validation in order to disclose abuse, values clarification, and training in assertiveness. In general, prevention resources should be reviewed with caution. Approaches that are innovative and marketable have not necessarily proven to be effective. Among the concerns are the following:

1. Young children are not able to generalize appropriately. Hence, concrete examples are useful only in a specific setting involving specific individuals and behaviors.

2. Young children may not be capable developmentally and behaviorally of discriminating between appropriate and inappropriate touch especially in situations involving manipulation and control.

3. Young children should not bear the onus of preventing crimes. The focus of publicity, awareness and expenditures should be on preventing perpetration through rigorous pursuit of offenders.

Comment

The literature of the past decade has reflected positive change. Heightened awareness of incest resulted in anecdotal and empirical studies on etiology, dynamics and effects. New programs involving a variety of modalities for treatment of members of the incestuous triad have proliferated along with efforts to deter the alarming rise in incidence.

PART II:
The Incestuous Triad

3
FAMILY DYNAMICS

Incest cannot be considered an isolated problem but should be understood as a manifestation of family dysfunction. Different authorities stress different aspects of family pathology. However, similar patterns of dysfunction emerge in a review of the literature. These patterns should be understood and evaluated before appropriate therapeutic intervention is attempted.

The Family Profile

It is primarily in father-daughter incest that family dysfunction plays the most significant role. In other forms of incestuous relationships, individual pathology assumes greater importance as a motivating force. For example, in father-son incest, homosexual conflict often underlies the offender's behavior. In sibling incest, individual pathology also dominates the picture. Especially with older offending siblings, unconscious needs and conflicts are expressed covertly through incestuous behavior.

In mother-daughter incest, the offender is often extremely disturbed, manifesting infantile and/or psychotic behavior. By turning to her daughter for emotional nurturance, she may effect a total role reversal in their relationship. In mother-son incest, the father often is absent or out of the home and the mother seeks substitute gratification with her son. In grandfather-granddaughter incest, in cases where the grandfather is much older, the victim is used to bolster the offender's ego and to help him assert his manhood; however, when the grandfather is younger, the dynamics are similar to those of father-daughter incest (Forward and Buck, 1978).

Type of Incest	Motivations (Individual Psychopathology)
Father-son	Homosexual conflict
Sibling (older)-sibling	Expression of unconscious conflicts
Mother-daughter	Psychosis/Infantilism
Mother-son	Substitute gratification for absent father
Grandfather (older)-granddaughter	Assertion of manhood

In father-daughter incest, the entire family is involved and each member is active in perpetuating the abuse. In the late 1970's, Dr. Roland Summit, UCLA, Harborview, described the Child Sexual Abuse Accommodation Syndrome involving incestuous families in which victims helped to maintain the family status quo by serving the fathers while protecting the mothers. Incest is motivated largely by urges to satisfy underlying emotional needs rather than by a need for sexual gratification (Slager-Jorne, 1978). The success of therapeutic intervention depends on understanding the complexity of the relationships involved, the results of blurring generational boundaries, and the effects of violating the taboo. Stereotyping and generalizing, however, should be avoided as each family is unique. Therapy must be adapted to conform to the particular characteristics of the family in treatment.

A. Isolation

One of the striking characteristics of the incestuous triad is social isolation. Members depend upon one another for satisfaction of both emotional and sexual needs. Emotional constriction results in these families where needs are unfulfilled or only partially met, where interdependence cripples members and where there are few outlets for anger, tension and aggression.

The term "enmeshed" is used to describe these rigid, secretive families in which members provide one another with little genuine support but, because of insecurity, are very dependent upon one another. Communication is lacking or seriously impaired. Messages often are indirect or nonverbal. Hidden agendas abound and denial becomes a major coping mechanism. Incest is one result of this inability to obtain needed gratification. After incest occurs, the family becomes even more isolated because of fear of disclosure. Controls become stronger as the children reach the teen years and begin to expand their social horizons for needed fulfillment.

B. Marital Discord

Sexual incompatibility and dysfunction between a male offender and his wife are primary causes of incest. Anger toward the spouse results from sexual problems and motivates the offender to engage in incest. The development of anger is related to a number of factors. In some cases, the offender reacts with anger to a passive, dependent wife (Peters, 1976). Sexual abuse of offspring is the ultimate act of anger toward the wife and repudiates her worth as a person, wife and mother. Forward and Buck (1978) believe that the offender seeks tenderness unavailable from his wife and wants revenge against her for what he considers an emotional crime against himself.

The wife may withdraw from sexual relations for a variety of reasons. She may find sex distasteful and/or she may have been sexually victimized as a child. Often, the wife "sets up" her own daughter for a repetition of her own experiences involving sexual abuse. Butler (1978) believes that both parents have unresolved conflicts related to childhood. Many perpetrators and non-offending spouses were sexually victimized as children. They turn to their children to act out these conflicts. Some wives are chronically ill and unable to function sexually while others use psychosomatic symptoms as a pretext for avoiding marital responsibilities. Peters (1976) has found that in some families the wife assumes the role of the husband's mother and thus becomes unapproachable sexually.

It has yet to be explained satisfactorily why some similarly dysfunctional and sexually disturbed families are not incestuous. Gottlieb (1980) hypothesizes that incestuous fathers are insecure and so dependent on the family that they are unable to seek extra-familial sexual gratification. Lustig (1966) characterizes incestuous fathers as unwilling to seek sexual satisfaction outside of the home because of a need to maintain a facade of stability and respectability. Explanations such as these are too simplistic and exclusive. Many factors merit consideration including the nature of the interactions between the parents, their past experiences and socialization, their particular needs and the unique way that the marital relationship has evolved through the years.

The child forms the third member of the triad. Children become aware of marital discord very early. Fear of abandonment and of family disintegration make them particularly vulnerable. They sense the parent's need for sexual gratification and they may try to keep the family together even at the cost of victimizing themselves. In some cases, the child has been neglected or rejected and might accept or even encourage incestuous relationships in an attempt to obtain affection, especially if the offender insists that such behavior is proper. Some child victims regard unusual sexual behavior as partially acceptable. Frequently, the mother unconsciously or even consciously condones seduction of a child.

c. The Mother's Role: Role Reversal and Generational Blurring

The mother often consciously or unconsciously forces her daughter into a maternal role. Her actions may be motivated by frustration because of discord and sexual incompatibility, unmet dependency needs, feelings of inadequacy or illness. The mother may retreat into passivity to avoid friction in the home and covertly encourage and allow incest in order to keep the family intact (Butler, 1978). In some cases, women who seek employment for self-realization and/or additional income inadvertently force their daughters into pivotal roles in the household. In almost all cases, the daughter is placed in the position of wife, where she feels that she has to satisfy her father's emotional and sexual needs.

Some authorities feel that the mother is the more culpable member of the incestuous triad. For example, Forward and Buck (1978) admit that the father is ultimately responsible but they state that it is the mother who creates the home atmosphere in which incest is likely to occur. Lustig (1966) is even stronger in his condemnation of the mother, asserting that despite the overt culpability of the fathers, it is the mothers who manifest the psychological passivity that results in incest.

Thus, father-daughter incest involves role reversal in a blurring of generational boundaries. The child assumes the role of spouse in which she satisfies the father's needs and takes a protective role toward her mother. In many cases, however, the victim suffers from extreme ambivalence. She wants to shield and protect her mother but at the same time feels angry and betrayed because she has not been protected from abuse.

Stepfather-stepdaughter incest is common and thus merits some attention. In the case of the young child who has not known or who has little memory of her natural father, the dynamics are similar to those of father-daughter incest. However, when the stepfather enters a family where the daughter is older, the situation differs from that of natural father-daughter incest (Finkelhor, 1979). The stepfather is a stranger to the girl and, therefore, is more likely to respond to her sexually. In addition, in some families, the daughter may compete with the mother for the affection of her stepfather.

Summary

Father-daughter incest most often occurs in dysfunctional, socially isolated families. Its principal function seems to be to ward off family disintegration. To achieve this end, the following typical patterns emerge which might be considered indicators of the probability that incest may occur or has occurred.

1. Marital discord and a poor sexual relationship between the parents.

2. Unwillingness of the father to seek sexual relationships outside of the family.

3. Role reversal between mother and daughter which makes the daughter the central female figure in the home with the responsibility of satisfying the needs of the father.

4. Conscious or unconscious condonation on the part of the mother of the relationship between father and daughter.

4
PERSONALITIES IN THE INCESTUOUS TRIAD

There are a number of opposing characteristics of the personality types involved in incest. Offenders variously are described as psychopathic, paranoid, bright, of average intelligence, pedophilic, insecure, power-seeking, symbiotic introverts (Justice, 1979), alcoholic-dependent, authoritarian tyrants, timid, passive and passive-aggressive.

There seems to be more agreement concerning the personality traits of the mother but there is also a greater tendency to stereotype and characterize her in superficial terms.

Finally, authorities have been unable to present a consistent personality profile of the victims partly because they still are in the process of development. Moreover, many victims come to the attention of therapists and helping agencies after years of incestuous relations with their fathers, so that what might have been normal personality development now is damaged. Conclusions drawn about the pre-incest personality would most likely be based on false premises.

Approach to Characterizing the Triad

Because of diametrically opposing characterization of personality types by authorities, it seems logical that we should be cautious in our generalizations about the incestuous triad. It is possible that no single personality type is involved and that it is the researcher's need for closure and definitiveness that causes him or her to seek simplistic personality profiles. Many factors, some extra-familial, such as stress and social isolation imposed by a mobile society, contribute to the onset of incest and lend credence to the notion that personality types involved in this form of pathology may be multiple.

In view of the above, the focus here will be on general traits commonly found in members of the incestuous triad. I have drawn conclusions not from hypothetical personality constructs but rather from behaviors and facts. For example, in his behavior the male offender manifests low impulse control; also it is a fact that a large percentage of offenders and their wives were sexually abused as children. Information presented by this study should be useful to therapists in evaluating families, planning appropriate treatment strategies and (cautiously) assessing high-risk families.

The Father

Most offending fathers are in their thirties, with a teenage child or stepchild whom they have been sexually abusing for some time. They share several striking traits. First, the offenders demonstrate poor impulse control, with acting-out behavior sexually and in other areas of their lives. Poor impulse control clearly is linked to low frustration tolerance. Second, their behavior is regressed as they demonstrate a need for immediate gratification. The conscience which monitors adult behavior and facilitates appropriate reality-testing is in abeyance for these males when they sexually act out with their daughters.

This combination of poor impulse control, low frustration tolerance, need for immediate gratification, and regression, often contributes to substance abuse (alcohol or drugs). Substance abuse has been linked to frustrated dependency needs and is consistent with the need to avoid pain at all costs for the emotionally, sexually and behaviorally immature individual.

Sexual acting out in these men is a passive-aggressive, covert means to express underlying affect whether it be anger, frustration, thwarted dependency needs or fear of inadequacy. These men tend to have low ego strength and low self-esteem, compensated for by aggressive acts against powerless children. Often the offenders are quite passive outside the home.

Many offenders appear to have antisocial personalities with the absence of guilt or remorse. Whether they are socio-psychopaths or not, almost all of these men rationalize or openly deny their acts to absolve themselves either of responsibility or of guilt. They project blame on everyone and everything (alcohol, a seductive daughter, an indifferent wife, etc.) in order to avoid responsibility for their acts. Thus, these men tend to be highly manipulative.

COMMON CHARACTERISTICS OF OFFENDING FATHERS

1. Poor impulse control

2. Low frustration tolerance

3. Regression, i.e., sexual and emotional immaturity

4. Need for immediate gratification

5. Suspended or faulty super-ego operation (i.e., absent or questionable degree of guilt or remorse)

6. Substance abuse (alcohol or drugs)

7. Frustrated dependency needs

8. Passive-aggressive expression of affect (anger, frustration, thwarted dependency needs, fear of inadequacy)

9. Low ego strength

10. Low self-esteem compensated for by the sexual abuse of a child

11. Powerlessness and passivity outside the home

12. Rationalization and denial of acts, i.e., projection of blame

13. Manipulation

The Mother (Silent Partner)

Silent partners, like their spouses, often have a history of abuse, either physical, emotional or sexual, in their backgrounds. Possibly because of this history, many of them possess characteristics similar to those of battered wives, i.e., very poor self-image, with feelings of inadequacy as a wife and mother; strong dependency needs, with the inability to take responsibility and cope with everyday problems; and passivity, where they will tolerate any abuse to placate their husbands (Forward and Buck, 1978).

Like their husbands, these women are emotionally immature and often engage in infantile behavior. They readily cross roles with their daughters, who become their protectors as well as surrogate wives and homemakers to their husbands.

The wives of offenders have sexual problems and often are sexually naive and unable to understand their own types of sexual dysfunction. Some of them perceive sex as disgusting and, as a consequence, they may withdraw from all physical contact with their husbands.

Again, like their spouses, silent partners characteristically use denial as a defense. At some level, they are aware that incest is occurring but, to ward off guilt or to avoid facing the potential dissolution of their marriage, they deny its existence in the home.

As with all members of the triad, generalizations have been made about silent partners. The important point to remember is that all of the traits cited are shared by only some women in these triads. Butler (1978) notes that depression and withdrawal are characteristics of these women. MacDonald (1971) believes that jealousy of the daughter's developing sexuality plays a role in motivating the mother to "set the stage" for incest. Zaphiris (1978) characterizes silent partners as cold and frigid while Gottlieb (1980) finds them to be masochistic and passive-aggressive in their behavior towards their daughters.

COMMON CHARACTERISTICS OF SILENT PARTNERS

1. Poor self-image

2. Feelings of inadequacy as wife and mother

3. Strong dependency needs

4. Inability to take responsibility and cope with everyday problems

5. Passivity

6. Emotional immaturity with infantile behavior

7. Sexual dysfunction

8. Denial as a defense mechanism

9. Guilt

The Daughter

As explained earlier, it is difficult to describe the personality of the victim, due to age variations at the time of disclosure and lack of knowledge of pre-incest characteristics. At the time that incest is disclosed, the victim often suffers from a variety of physical and emotional problems. She may have school phobia, nightmares, fear of the dark or of being alone, and various somatic complaints including enuresis, headaches and gastric complaints. Older victims often are found to be promiscuous and to suffer from a variety of acting out behaviors, including truancy, and alcohol and drug addiction. They appear depressed and confused and are blocked on an affective level.

It is difficult for these girls to trust adults, a fact that is understandable in view of the betrayal that has occurred in the home. They have little insight or understanding of the psychic forces operating within and motivating their behavior. Some are fixated emotionally at a very early age, possibly at the age when trauma began. Emotional constriction characterizes their mode of affective behavior.

Victims generally have low self-esteem, believing that they are not or cannot be loved unconditionally. Therefore, they submit to sexual abuse for love and affection. The equation of "love equals sex" is firmly rooted in their psyches.

Often these youngsters feel very responsible for the welfare of their families. They express little, if any, overt anger toward their mothers whom they feel they must protect from hurt. They express ambivalence toward the father, alternately expressing warmth and anger. Many of them experience guilt of which they are not fully aware and they internalize blame and responsibility for being victimized. Because these girls express little genuine affect of any kind they appear confused and ambivalent.

Some authorities believe these victims are seductive (Gottlieb, 1980) and others feel that their behavior is a reaction to cues from the offender. More likely the behavior is learned, by a child who feels rejected and unloved, as a means to receive attention from her father. Other authorities describe the victim as passive because she offers little or no resistance to sexual abuse. It must be remembered, however, that incest is covertly accepted at home and that many of these children have been threatened or bribed.

COMMON CHARACTERISTICS OF VICTIMS

1. Somatic problems ranging from enuresis to gastric distress
2. Emotional and acting-out problems including school phobia or truancy, promiscuity and substance abuse
3. Emotional constriction
4. Fixation
5. Block affect
6. Lack of insight
7. Low self-image
8. Internalized guilt and blame
9. Ambivalence regarding parents
10. Pseudo-maturity, related to assuming maternal and spousal role in the home

5
THE FAMILY AND THE LAW

Since our focus is on treatment of incest, it is not the purpose of this manual to provide extensive details regarding the court process. Because legislation concerning child abuse is not the responsibility of the federal government but of the individual states, there is much variation in definition as well as in legal and criminal procedures. Moreover, although every state has a statute requiring that child abuse be reported, not all require that sexual abuse be reported as distinguished from general child abuse.

Even when a complaint is signed against the offender, often little if any action results. Once the victim signs a complaint, she become a witness for the state and if she refuses to testify the state loses its case. In many instances, the victim will not testify against her father because of guilt, fear, embarrassment or family pressure. The victim sometimes is accused of lying. In some states a child's testimony has to be corroborated by a witness or charges will be dropped, while in others, testimony of preteens is not acceptable. Hence, the court process is complicated and merits separate, detailed, state-by-state consideration.

What concerns us here is the trauma involved in the criminal and legal proceedings—trauma for all members of the incestuous triad. In these cases, the assistance of the therapist is of utmost importance to help counteract the negative effects of the court process. It should be borne in mind that the criminal court is not concerned with the needs of the child and her family, since its purpose is to determine whether or not a crime has been committed and to punish if guilt has been established.

Need for Information

It is advisable for all therapists involved in the treatment of incest to be cognizant of state and local laws and to have a thorough knowledge of the resources in her/his jurisdiction. Some states have a victim-witness program working out of the county attorney's office, which is designated to facilitate the court proceedings. It provides the victim and her family with information on the process and accompanies them step-by-step through the court hearings. This service is, on the whole, informational and should not be equated with the specialized services offered by the therapist.

The therapist should also be aware of the pitfalls inherent in reporting cases of abuse. As a protection against being sued for slander or libel, many states have a law indemnifying the professional reporter against all liability (Forward and Buck, 1978). In any case, complete, accurate and precise records should be kept not only to facilitate the court process but also for the protection of the therapist.

Therapists often face confused families with a low trust level for any authority figure. If the therapist is honest and knowledgeable in interpreting the court proceedings, respect and credibility will be established, thus building trust and confidence necessary to the therapeutic relationship.

The Court Process and Its Effect

The court process often involves at least two hearings, sometimes open to the public, one in district court and one in superior court. The child may have been subjected to a painfully embarrassing physical examination and lengthy detailed interrogation by police, social workers, judge, district attorney and defense counsel. The entire process may involve many grueling months. The defense attorney will often manufacture reasons for postponement in the hope that the victim will renege under intense pressure. In other cases, the defendant might not appear because he has been advised by his attorney of probable adjournment.

This process is extremely painful and damaging for both victim and family. Court delays disrupt family life, result in lost work time, and increase already existing anxieties regarding outcome and future. However, the court process is most damaging to the victim, who is forced to relive the original abuse over and over again. She fears facing the offender in court because of ambivalence plus painful and unpleasant associations. There is the embarrassment of testifying in open court and the likelihood of one-sided cross-examination by a defense attorney who make every effort to discredit her testimony. The victim often feels betrayed by the very people she previously deemed supportive.* Symptoms often recur or are exacerbated for the child, who once again begins to experience school phobias, enuresis, or nightmares. It is at this time that the therapist becomes a major support and is often a primary link or buffer for the family facing insensitive legal authorities.

Testifying or Not

In some instances the victim and her family, reacting to crises, request that the therapist decide for them if they should file a complaint against the offender. It is imperative that the therapist resist temptation to give direct advice that later could be misconstrued or resented. Instead, all consequences and alternatives should be presented in order to help the child decide. In the end, it is the child who has to testify and, therefore, (if possible) it is she who should make the decision, with the support of her family and therapist.

Considerations to present to the child include the fact that: 1) she might feel relieved once she has publicly stated her case; 2) she will have to face the offender in court; 3) delays in the proceedings are possible; 4) whether she testifies or not, she is responsible neither for the outcome in terms of sentencing or for future stability of her family; and 5) no one has the right to blame her if she testifies or does not testify.

Therapists should be aware of the fact that many children initially do decide to testify and later renege following the preliminary hearing. Clinicians should be aware of inconsistencies and ambivalence in victims and their families in order to guard against reacting unprofessionally with anger or resentment, in the case of unanticipated changes in what may have appeared at first to be a straightforward legal process.

Punishment or Treatment

There is much controversy regarding the best approach to the offender. Since incest carries criminal penalties in every state there are people who advocate a purely punitive approach. Additionally, some

---

*All too often, secondary victimization results from the court process.

authorities assess the offender as a poor candidate for rehabilitation, since he often is characterized as a psychopathic personality who does not experience guilt or remorse for his actions.   On the contrary, many therapists and professionals in the helping fields advocate a humane treatment and family-oriented approach to the offender, one that focuses on rehabilitation coupled with attempts to reunite the family.

It seems logical that therapy ideally should be based on accurate diagnosis and prognosis. Clearly there are some offenders who have been severely damaged psychologically and/or are antisocial personalities. Rehabilitation simply is not effective with these men. On the other hand, a large proportion of offenders who receive no counseling or therapy could be helped. It is unfair to them and to their families simply to incarcerate them without treatment, as usually happens in our justice system.

In the absence of a cooperative alliance between the helping processions and the courts, the best system might involve the dual approach of incarceration plus therapy. Incarceration in itself can be therapeutic by helping offenders to recognize the severity of their crimes and to accept responsibility for their acts.   Once the offender begins to face his culpability, he might be amenable to proper therapeutic intervention.

Comment

It is criminal that innocent child victims are subjected to the rigors of a traumatic court experience, all in the name of providing justice for offenders.   The average child suffers immensely and sometimes is permanently damaged. Moreover, it is often she and not the offender who is removed from the home.

Thus far, states have resisted instituting procedures that could alleviate the strain for traumatized children. Two such procedures are the use of videotapes in open court, so that the child would not have to appear, and the use of surrogate witnesses for the child, such as psychologists and psychiatrists.

Unfortunately, resistance to change seems predicated on the perception of the victim as culpable and as a willing participate in incest, a participant capable of adult consent. Hence, she, too, is punished by the legal system. Until our national perception changes and we realize that sexual abuse of a child involves a victim and an offender, it is unlikely that the courts will be more humane to the powerless.

PART III:
Therapeutic Methods, Models and Approaches

The therapist working with incest families has a difficult task. She or he is dealing with both individual and family needs in circumstances involving deeply entrenched pathology within and between all members. Differing situational as well as individual factors preclude the possibility of formulating set approaches to working with such families. The victim may be removed from the home; the parents may divorce, separate temporarily or wish to work toward reconciliation; or the offender may be serving time in jail. To simplify a complicated environmental and family picture, this part of the manual is divided into sections that will be helpful to the therapist whose clients are in a variety of life situations. The approaches and models presented have general applicability.

The first section considers common therapeutic needs of the victim, whether or not she is in the home, and whether or not her family is planning to reunite. The general assumption for working with victims is that individual, group and family therapy are all required. The victim needs a one-to-one trusting relationship with a therapist. Issues related only to her particular situation also require individual intervention. On the other hand, a number of therapeutic issues common to all incest victims are worked through most effectively in group. In general, the victim is seen on a one-to-one basis first; then she enters group and/or family work.

The second section concerns the silent partner and again outlines certain problems common to most wives of offenders, with specific strategies for resolution. The same principles apply to the mother as to the child, i.e., individual work precedes group work. The issues considered in this section apply whether or not the wife plans to return to her husband.

The section dealing with the offender focuses on three important aspects of treatment. First, with offenders, it is critical to determine whether or not they are treatable and then to learn to recognize and deal with denial. Stress management is a vital part of the treatment process for all family members; however, it is particularly important for the offender to learn to recognize stress and to use helpful coping strategies for exerting more control over impulsive behavior.

Partly to highlight key issues related exclusively to the nuclear unit, the family is dealt with separately from group therapy. Dealing with the family as a separate entity in no way precludes the possibility of considering members as a group, of grouping several families together, or of including mothers and daughters together in group work. Again, the rule is that individuals are seen privately first and then are prepared for work in dyads, triads or group.

The final section deals with the group. Group work is both powerful and productive. For incest families, there is an immediate bond among members, almost instant identification, and a strong contagion factor that operates throughout the duration of the group experience. Sponsorship often results spontaneously among group members. The types of groups that can be facilitated are numerous and can include different ages, sexes and combinations of members.

The focus of this section is on groups involving victims, wives and couples because these groups are frequently facilitated. Moreover, they are easy to establish in agencies that do not necessarily specialize in therapy with incest families and that are not necessarily accountable to the legal system for diversionary therapy for offenders. The therapist, however, should be aware of other types of groups currently being used with success by sexual assault and incest treatment centers nationwide. These include offender groups (often diversionary), sons and daughters groups (on-going victim groups, usually for intact families), parents' groups, family groups and mother-daughter groups.

Frequently the group is the final aspect of therapy and groups that focus on education or training in communication or other skills are short-term. With incest families, however, long-term group work is often deemed appropriate since therapeutic issues are complicated (and perhaps never fully resolved) and also since support is needed for isolated families and their members. Typically, behavior of incestuous family members is regressed, with mothers abdicating adult roles and fathers dealing immaturely with stress and dysfunction. Hence, the long-term group serves the function of meeting the needs of regressed individuals by providing nurturance, support and confrontation when needed.

SECTION A:
The Victim

6
FACILITATING CATHARSIS AS A MAJOR THERAPEUTIC GOAL FOR THE VICTIM OF INCESTUOUS ABUSE

Inducement of spontaneous catharsis for victims of incestuous abuse is a very important aspect of both individual and group therapy. Prior to entering therapy girls as young as ten and adult women abused as long as a quarter century prior to entering therapy need release from two major affective results of incest: guilt and anger.

However, I concur with Dollard and Miller (1950) that classic psychotherapeutic catharsis alone is ineffective. Confession per se is not necessarily therapeutic for it needs to be linked to permissiveness in order to lower guilt or anxiety. A punitive or even neutral atmosphere conceivably could heighten painful affective states. Being forgiven, on the other hand, reduces separateness, indicates acceptance into a larger community and foreshadows future rewards for new solutions to problems.

Thus, the process is two-fold, first involving techniques designed specifically to induce catharsis and second involving appropriate therapeutic responses from the clinician. Sympathetic responses from the therapist during and following catharsis are especially important, since confrontation often is necessary in the induction process. An attitude on the part of the clinician that conveys empathy and unconditional positive regard, coupled with reflection, clarification and direct reassurances is most effective.   Before presenting several specific approaches for stimulating catharsis, I want to emphasize one additional point.   Inducing catharsis should be attempted only under certain conditions.   Principally, these are as follows.

1.   A trusting relationship must have been firmly established with the therapist.

2.   The client must be able to expect sufficient time and commitment on the part of the therapist for follow-up and closure.   (Induction of catharsis by a well-intentioned but overworked child protective services caseworker during a home visit can prove destructive rather than therapeutic.)

3.   The time and setting must be neutral to diffuse the expected heightened anxiety level that catharsis produces.

One teenage girl in residential care following a six-year incestuous relationship with her father was encouraged erroneously to "face her abuser" using the gestalt empty-chair technique one day prior to a home visit.   Fortunately, her defenses were intact and she resisted the simulated encounter. Another pre-adolescent girl was given a "Rape Diary" during her wait at the preliminary court hearing where she was to face her offender-father.   She wrote feverishly in the diary and subsequently broke down, refusing to testify.

4.   Dissonance and anxiety as manifested by specific behavioral and neurotic symptomatology should be clearly evident in the client. A frigid woman, a teenager with chronic migraine headaches or an 11-year-old girl who suffers from nightmares are possible candidates for inducing catharsis.   On the other hand, when blocking occurs as a necessary defense to ward off decompensation or panic, the client should be approached with extreme tact and gentleness.   This is especially applicable in cases of young children whose homeostasis needs preservation. Stimulation of catharsis can produce additional trauma or overwhelming anxiety with which such victims are not ready to deal.

Methods to Stimulate Catharsis

A. Writing Techniques

Using a vehicle besides the therapist and client can be extremely effective in stimulating various affects. Different psychological mechanisms operate when a client is called upon to by-pass verbal communication and to substitute writing, drawing or modeling in clay in order to project certain of her conflicts or experiences. The usual defenses are not operating and significant material linked to powerful emotions may emerge quite rapidly.

A common technique borrowed from gestalt therapy involves asking the client to write a letter to the offender or to the mother in the incestuous triad. The victim is directed to say, in writing, anything that spontaneously comes to mind without censorship, regardless of how vulgar she judges her feelings and thoughts to be. Assurances are given that the letter will not be seen by anyone other than the therapist or members of the group in which she is involved. It is interesting how often the victims later express a desire to hand-deliver their letters to the very persons to whom they are addressed.

A very important part of this therapeutic process is to encourage the client to stand assertively before the therapist or group and read her letter with the verbal and tonal expression required. She is directed to stand erect and to make frequent eye contact with her audience whenever possible as she reads. If a catharsis is not forthcoming, the victim repeatedly is confronted by the therapist or group members to re-read her letter loudly and with more genuine expression of affect, or to repeat loudly certain significant phrases expected to elicit strong feelings. Following the reading, the victim is given verbal and contact support from the therapist and/or group. Legitimatizing and empathizing with her feelings provide relief and reassurance and has a deconditioning effect on the victim. This technique can prove to be extremely powerful. Many victims, like the one whose letter appears below, initially are disturbed, shocked and embarrassed by the intensity of the emotions they express.

Dear Joe:

There are a few things I want to tell you. Why were you a sex pervert with me? Why bring it home? Why not someone else? You are a fucking idiot—worthless, an alcoholic bum. I feel like you should be out with the animals—fondling all the sheep you want. I feel disgust. Pick on someone your own size. I hate you for what you did, for fingering me and making me feel that way I feel. I would like to tie you up and get a rubber hose, a catheter, and stick it up your dick and I would blow into the catheter with alcohol, gas and turpentine. Then I would cut off your nuts and let you lie there and remind you of all the things you did to me.

Journal writing is a second valuable tool to stimulate catharsis. The journal, however, should be a directed activity. Without guidance, it can become a fruitless endeavor as victims of all ages seek to avoid a direct encounter with their own underlying affects. In the absence of direction, one woman faithfully kept a journal recounting ongoing feelings about current events in her life, events totally unrelated to the incestuous abuse she had experienced years earlier. Another victim, a child, also diligent about the assignment, wrote pages detailing school progress, hobbies, television programs and the like.

The emphasis must be on remembering and recounting details of the incestuous abuse along with associated affects. At the end of this chapter is an example of extreme direction in the form of a fill-in questionnaire called, "A Page in My Journal," to be used in session with very resistant clients for whom focusing is difficult.

With children especially, sometimes it is helpful to limit journal writing to therapeutic sessions where the clinician can monitor progress and content and in addition can explore reactions during and following the time of writing. With very young children it is useful for the therapist to do the actual writing as the child speaks, and to legitimatize the entire experience by giving a name to the journal, such as, "My Personal and Private Molest Book."

Whether done at home or in session, the content of the journal should be read aloud and processed in a fashion similar to that used in the letter-writing exercise. Especially in a group setting, this technique is quite powerful, as contagion operates strongly. Group members support and enhance the intensity of one another's experiences, thus providing needed validation. For this reason, in the absence of an ongoing group, sometimes it is helpful to invite two or three women (or children) who have experienced incestuous abuse to partake in short-term sessions designed to work through trauma.

Allied to spontaneous writing is the use of sentence blanks and questionnaires. In The Disowned Self, Branden (1979) shares a list of items he uses with clients, who often become deeply emotional during the exercise. Pre-structured questionnaires such as the one at the end of this chapter can be used with victims, bearing in mind that each situation is different and invites improvisation.

Some clients have extreme difficulty talking about the incest experience. A number of avoidance tactics—the use of circumlocution, nonsequiturs and direct blocking—alert the therapist to the need for a less confronting approach to encourage catharsis. For such clients the induction of emotional release may proceed in stages beginning with the use of a questionnaire similar to the one at the end of this chapter which functions to assist with recall and to begin the deepening process. By reading such a list of questions aloud to a client, then writing or recording each response, the therapist provides a comfortable distance between client and clinician while adding an air of formality that defensive victims find reassuring.

The therapist may find unanticipated and secondary benefits through the use of formal questions. Specific data is obtained that often is necessary for later court testimony. In addition, responses may set a direction for the treatment process. For example, one woman I treated had a presenting complaint of frigidity. She gained valuable insights after completing the questionnaire. First, in forcing herself to recall details of the molestation, she learned that a major area of aversion in the sex act for her was any form of manual stimulation. Second, she understood that her aversion to her husband was partly related to the onset of nausea whenever he drank. While completing the questionnaire, she remembered that her stepfather had molested her only when he was drunk and that she had reacted to the smell on his breath with extreme distaste.

The questionnaire on molesting should be modified for relevance to particular situations or age groups. Rarely is it applicable in entirety. It is presented at the end of this chapter as a guide rather than as a definitive tool for use in all cases.

B. Art Techniques

Children in particular respond readily to pictorial and visual expression. They can be encouraged to depict various aspects of the incestuous experience, and various affects associated with incest, in their drawings and clay work. Specific techniques for use both with adults and children, individually and in groups, are outlined in the final part of this book. The important point here is to stress the fact that art media are valuable for use in concretizing expression of suppressed and repressed material.

With art media, victims are denied use of their usual defenses; consequently unconscious conflicts find rapid expression. In addition, visual expression readily helps make implicit feelings explicit—especially for individuals who are blocked or who are suffering from emotional difficulties. Art media allow victims to give symbolic expression to conflicts and impulses. Forbidden feelings are released in a socially acceptable, non-threatening manner. Insights often emerge suddenly from art work, insights that can be hinged to verbal expression to stimulate cathartic release. Finally, art work is very useful in group settings where secondary benefits include enhancement of group cohesiveness and unity. A stimulating dialogue often occurs spontaneously, thus combining verbal and nonverbal expression—a combination which has particular impact in stimulating emotional release.

C. *Poetry Therapy*

Poetry has a value similar to that of art therapy in stimulating emotional release. A relative newcomer to projective therapy, poetry therapy is a category of bibliotherapy. It involves the writing, memorizing, and reciting of, and listening to poems (of the client or of other patients) appropriately selected for individual and group settings. Poetry therapy is being used with schizophrenics, psychoneurotics, drug addicts and troubled adolescents, and in encounter group settings.

A variety of principles applies to the recitation of poems. Among the most important are:

1. The poem must be read word for word so that rhythm, rhyme, assonance and alliteration are appreciated.

2. The poem must be clearly heard.

3. The isoprinciple must be applied, i.e., the feeling of the poem must be the same as the feeling of the person hearing the poem (Leedy, 1973).

Numerous principles, still being evolved, are an outgrowth of experiential and experimental work currently in practice. Some of these principles are summarized below.

1. Poems with regular rhythms (those that approximate the beat of the human heart) often affect clients very deeply (Leedy, 1969).

2. Poems where the focus is on sound rather than content (Coleridge's "The Ancient Mariner") sometimes overcome resistance more readily that non-mood poems (Parker, 1969).

3. The Psalms are of particular value with depressives. The Psalmist refers to the problems of existence, seeks a sense of identity, but almost always ends with a note of victory (Gelberman & Komak, 1969).

4. Nonsense poetry, similar in content and style to dreams, calls forth forbidden and aversive affects and is apt to be expressed in an emotional (rather than a logical) frame of reference (Pietropinto, 1973).

With each of the art therapies, rapport and a sense of trust must be developed by the therapist to encourage free and spontaneous expression of feelings. In writing poems, one main condition should prevail: that the poems be written spontaneously, thus allowing for free play with words and images and for the expression of strong feelings (Leedy, 1973).

It helps for clients to read or learn poems written by troubled or emotionally disturbed people. Not only is a sense of identification enhanced but the inhibited client feels less reluctance to reveal and express himself in poetry when he knows his peers have done so in a similar fashion. Providing clients with a list of song titles—"Moody Blue," "My Life," "Feelings," "My Way"—or book titles—Surviving the Loss of a Love, Kiss Daddy Goodnight, Daddy's Girl—sometimes stimulates the creative process. In general, writing is stimulated if it follows recitation.

Authorities have noted that one of the most valuable therapeutic effects of poetry is to provide creative release and ventilation for the depressed, alienated, lonely and angry. Poetry reduces resistance and, as with art, circumvents customary defenses through the use of condensation and symbolization. Catharsis, unburdening, reduction of anxiety and the sharing of common experiences are facilitated in groups using poetry therapy as a catalyst for movement.

The therapist should be imaginative in the directing of poetry therapy and in selecting appropriate poems for recitation. A partial list of poems suitable for poetry therapy is provided at the end of this chapter.

An example of the potency of art and poetry therapy occurred among a group of sexually victimized teenage girls in treatment in a residential center. During the first session, the ten girls, aged 13 to 16, were hostile, sullen and unwilling to self-disclose. I combined verbal and non-verbal methods by first asking each girl to depict, "the worst thing that ever happened to me." The drawings then were passed around. Each girl had before her someone else's drawing. Next, group members were directed to make a group poem, by having each girl respond to the drawing before her with one or two descriptive phrases. The exercise unified the group and resulted in the following poem that served as a catalyst for release for one group member:

> "Death.
> Beauty locked away in a different world.
> A fatal blow that ended the show,
> Shot with a black-hearted knife.
>
> Sex is torture...
> As the old world ends a new life begins.
> (Man created Hell.)
>
> Love never parts...
> A fat man,
> Being along and frightened and confused,
> Not caring and unreal and uncertain.
>
> All different sorts of feelings — happy, sad...
> A broken thing between two people.
> They are trying to break through and meet again.
>
> I'm trapped and my heart is broken.
> A Hallucination.
>
> A house with two doors.
> I'm caught in your pain...I'm drowning,
> Murdered by evil.
>
> Unlatched strings.
> Death strikes again."

D. Gestalt Techniques

Gestalt therapy is very useful in stimulating catharsis because techniques are experiential and because the focus in on here-and-now awareness. Among the most valuable techniques are "empty chair" confrontations and written dialogues with parts of the self or with the offender.

Before beginning gestalt work either individually or in group, it is important to create a tension-free atmosphere and to induce a state of relaxation for the victim with simple breathing exercises, autogenic techniques or deep muscle relaxation. For clients unfamiliar with gestalt, the awareness continuum provides a good introduction to experiential work and to the "how," not "why," of experience. The client is asked to close her eyes and begin by responding to the question, "What are you aware of now?" The client then proceeds to deep awareness by answering the question with a succession of responses related to her here-and-now experience. The clinician may intercede therapeutically at any point by having the client focus on a single area of awareness. For example, if the victim is aware of being nervous, the therapist might facilitate a deepening process by asking her to become aware of where, in what way and with what physical manifestations she is experiencing tension.

The most obvious empty chair exercise involves asking the victim to face the perpetrator or her mother. Role plays involving the therapist or a group member and the victim are effective, but the empty chair technique is more potent in deepening awareness because it allows and directs focusing upon the self. A variation of the technique is to have the victim alternate sitting in each of the two chairs and speaking first as herself and then responding as the offender or mother.

Written dialogues also can be helpful. One victim wrote a dialogue between the "controlled" part of herself (identified as anger and sexuality) and the part of herself that felt "out of control" (identified as fear and anxiety). Another young woman who felt a genuine aversion to her breasts (related to incidents of fondling by her offending father) worked through an area of conflict by using the dialogue method. First I asked her to draw her breasts in detail and describe them for her group. She then wrote a dialogue between herself and her breasts, viewed by her as detached appendages. Part of her ten page dialogue is reproduced below.

Self: I don't know how to feel good about you.

Breasts: Why?

Self: Because I was molested and you were the part that was molested.

Breasts: Then you see me as the bad guy.

Self: I don't know. I don't know if I see you as anything.

Breasts: Are you afraid of me?

Self: I don't know

Breasts: You don't know anything.

Self: When I was molested I know I turned you off and now I can't turn you back on.

Breasts: You don't.   We are not light switches.   We have feelings.

Self: I don't feel your feelings.

Breasts: Damn it I'm part of you.   You won't acknowledge us. Shit.

This same woman worked through additional trauma involving alienation of bodily parts through self-collages and dialogues between dream parts.

E. Other Methods

There are a wide variety of visual and auditory aids that can be used to stimulate dialogue and affective reactions, particularly among group members. One technique involves recording interviews with incest victims and with the offenders, to be played back in group and individual sessions. For ongoing groups, therapists should consider obtaining a file of materials from the American Humane Association, materials which heighten consciousness and awareness as they detail statistics on the enormity of the problem of incestuous abuse.

The film *The Victim No One Believes* involves the plight of three victims of molest. It is available through university libraries, rape crisis centers and sexual abuse treatment centers. It presents a profound catalyst for group discussion and involvement.

Conclusion

Traditional psychotherapy involves verbal communication alone, which, because of the complexity of psychological defenses following years of trauma, may not be effective in inducing needed catharsis among incest victims. Tools and specialized techniques usually are needed to release deeply embedded anger and guilt. All of the methods presented here are designed for that single end, i.e., to heighten emotional responses and to follow up with opportunities for release through catharsis in a warmly supportive setting where the victim can experience a genuine sense of validation.

A Page in My Journal

At (time, date)_____, I was (tell where you were)_____.

I was (tell what you were doing) _____

_____.

I was feeling _____ and I

was thinking _____ and I

was wondering _____ and I

was hoping _____. Dad

was (tell what he was doing) _____.

He came to me and said _____

_____. Then he (tell exactly what he

did to you) _____

and he also_____

and he also_____.

While he was (tell what he did) _____

_____, I said to him _____

_____, and I pretended _____

_____, and I thought _____

_____, and I felt _____

_____, and I wanted to _____

_____, and I wanted him to _____

_____. The place we were in was

(describe) _____.

The rest of the family was _____.

Dad stayed (how long?)_____. When he left, I

(tell what you did)_____, and I

thought _____, and I wondered _____

_____, and I felt _____.

And now I think _____, and I wonder _____

_____, and I feel _____, and I want

to say this to dad: _____

_____.

VICTIM SENTENCE BLANK

1. Right now I am feeling
2. And I expect
3. When I think I am here I wonder
4. And I remember why I came and I think
5. When I remember Dad I think
6. And I wonder
7. And I feel
8. What happened between us was
9. What Dad actually did
10. And what I did
11. Dad said to me
12. And Dad also said
13. And Dad promised
14. And I remember thinking
15. And I remember feeling
16. Remembering now makes me feel
17. What I really wanted from Dad was
18. What I really want from Dad now
19. If Dad really loved me he would have
20. Someday Dad
21. Mother
22. I remember Mother saying
23. If Mother knew what Dad did
24. Mother never knew because
25. What I really wanted from Mother was
26. If Mother really loved me she would have
27. I need Mother to
28. I need Dad to
29. If only Dad
30. If only Mother
31. I see myself as
32. Dad helped me understand that men
33. Mother helped me understand that women
34. Men should
35. Women should
36. Incest
37. Sex
38. Life
39. I want to tell Dad
40. I want to tell Mother
41. I feel

QUESTIONNAIRE ON MOLESTING

Date: _____

Length of Interview: _____

Person Interviewed:

    Victim: _____

    Relative of Victim: _____

Present Age of Person Interviewed: _____

Sex of Victim: _____ Of Person Interviewed: _____

Occupation of Person Interviewed:_____

Part I: The Molester

1. Who was it who molested you/your relative? _____
2. How close was he to the family? _____
3. Did he live with the family? _____
4. How old was he at the time? _____
5. Can you describe him physically? _____
   _____
6. Was he married at the time? _____ Previously? _____
7. Did he have children? _____ Living with him? _____
   What were their ages and sexes? _____
8. What was his relationship with his children? _____
   _____
9. Did he prefer one of his children over another? _____
   Which? _____
10. In what ways was he a good/bad father? _____
    _____
11. How did he punish his children? _____
12. How did he show affection? _____
13. How many years was he married? _____
14. What was his wife's age? _____
15. What was his relationship with his wife? _____
    _____
16. In what ways was he a good/bad husband? _____
    _____
17. Do you know anything about his sexual relationship with his wife?
    _____
18. Use three adjectives to describe this man: _____
    _____

19. Use three adjectives to describe his wife: _____
    _____
20. Was he/had he ever been involved in criminal activities? _____
    If so, what were they? _____
21. Did he have a police record? _____
22. Did he use alcohol or drugs? _____
23. What job did he have at the time? _____
    In the past? _____ What was his income? _____
24. What grade level in school did he complete? _____
25. Did he have a religious affiliation? _____
26. What was his nationality? _____
27. What was his regional origin? _____
28. As a person, which, if any of the following adjectives describe him?
    ❑ Seductive   ❑ Affectionate   ❑ Aggressive
    ❑ Rigid   ❑ Cold   ❑ Hostile
    ❑ Loving   ❑ Impulsive   ❑ Immature
    ❑ Inadequate   ❑ Serious
29. Do you know if he had psychiatric problems? _____
    Was he ever seen at a mental health agency for therapy? _____
    _____
30. Do you know if he was abused, molested or neglected as a child?
    _____
31. Were his parents divorced? _____ Separated? _____

Part II: The Act

1. What did he do when he molested you/your relative? **Can you de-**
   scribe the details? _____
2. Was this a single act or one repeated over time? _____
   If repeated, for what length of time? _____
3. How did he approach you/your relative? _____
4. Before he molested you/your relative, did you ever feel **uncom-**
   fortable in his presence? _____ If so, why? _____
5. During the act, how did he behave? _____
   Was he persuasive? _____ Threatening? _____
   Sadistic? _____ Did he offer bribes? _____
6. If the molesting occurred over a period of time, how **did his be-**
   havior change? _____
7. Were you passive or required to participate actively? _____
   _____
8. Where did the molesting occur? _____

9. What details regarding setting, clothing, time of day, appearance do you recall? _____

10. What words did he say to you? _____
11. Was anyone else present? _____

Part III: The Victim

1. How old were you/your relative when the molesting occurred? ____
2. What was your family constellation? _____
_____ Age and sex of sibling(s)? _____
_____ Were your parents married? _____
Separated? _____ Divorced? _____
3. Would you describe your family as close? _____
4. Were you closer to your mother or father? _____
5. Was any other member of your family molested? _____
By whom? _____
6. Use three adjectives to describe your mother. _____
_____ Your father. _____
7. Did your family know about the molesting? _____
Which members knew? _____ How did they react?
_____ Do you remember what was said to you?
_____

8. How did you feel after the act?
   ☐ Angry?   ☐ Guilty?   ☐ Worthless?
   ☐ Hostile?   ☐ Used?
   ☐ Scared?   ☐ Responsible?
   Did your feelings change with the passage of time? _____
9. How do you feel now, talking about the molesting? _____
_____

10. Did you see a counselor or physician at the time? _____
Is so, what occurred? _____
11. Were the police involved? _____ If so, what occurred and when were they informed? _____
_____

12. Whom in your life have you told about the molesting? _____
_____

13. If you could say two or three sentences to the molester now, what would they be? _____
_____
_____

14. How do you feeling the molesting has affected your relationship with men? _____

Sexually? _____

How did/does it affect your marriage? _____

_____

15. Were you very active sexually before/after marriage? _____

_____ How active? _____

16. Have you experienced any of the following difficulties:
    - ☐ School drop out?   ☐ Excessive use of
    - ☐ Criminal activities?   drugs or alcohol?
    - ☐ Delinquency?   ☐ Suicidal attempts?
    - ☐ Serious depression/   ☐ Thoughts of "going crazy"
      anxiety?   or "being out of control?"

17. How do you handle anger? _____

18. At what age did you marry? _____

    Have you been married more than once? _____

19. Use three words to describe the man you married: _____

    _____

20. What mental health services have you sought in life? _____

    _____

21. Have you ever been active sexually with a member of your own
    sex? _____ Attracted to a member of your sex? _____

22. Use three adjectives to describe yourself: _____

    _____

23. Do you have children? _____ Age and sex? _____

    Have they been molested? _____ If so, by whom? _____

    _____ What do you tell them about sex? _____

    _____ Are you affectionate with them? _____

24. Give your first reaction to the following: Nudity: _____

    Group sex: _____ Heterosexuality: _____

    Homosexuality: _____ Bisexuality: _____

    Sexual perversion: _____

    Oral sex: _____ Anal sex: _____

25. How are you feeling now? _____

Comments:

A PARTIAL LIST OF POEMS SUITABLE
FOR POETRY THERAPY

1. BELLOC, HILAIRE
    The Night

2. BLAKE, WILLIAM
    The Tiger

3. BURNS, ROBERT
    My Luv

4. COLERIDGE, SAMUEL
    The Quarrel of Friends

5. DICKINSON, EMILY
    I'm Nobody

6. FROST, ROBERT
    The Sound of the Trees

7. HOLMES, OLIVER WENDELL
    Contentment

8. HOUSEMAN, A.E.
    When I was One-and Twenty

9. HUNT, LEIGH
    Abou Ben Adhem

10. MILLAY, EDNA ST. VINCENT
    The Return

11. MILTON, JOHN
    On His Blindness

12. MOORE, THOMAS
    'Tis the Last Rose of Summer

13. POE, EDGAR ALLAN
    Annabel Lee

14. ROSETTI, CHRISTINA
    Uphill

15. SHELLEY, PERCY BYSSHE
    To A Skylark

16. STEVENS, WALLACE
    Tomorrow

17. TENNYSON, ALFRED LORD
    New Years Eve

18. WHITMAN, WALT
    O Captain! My Captain!

19. WORDSWORTH, WILLIAM
    Daffodils
    The Rainbow

20. YEATS, WILLIAM BUTLER
    Three Things

21. MASEFIELD, JOHN
    Sea-Fever

7

AVOIDING THE "RESCUER'S TRAP" WITH TEENAGE VICTIMS

It is important that the therapist become aware of certain pitfalls and inevitable failures in counseling teenage incest victims. Victims may vary in their emotional and behavioral reactions to the offenders, depending on a number of factors. These include the duration of incest, age at onset, time of reporting, circumstances surrounding disclosure, severity and type of abuse, personalities of the child and of the offender, and relationship between offender and victim. Certain victims have a strong emotional investment in the father or father figure. For some victims, incest has had pleasurable aspects. In such cases, despite social and emotional ambivalence, the bond between victim and offender is strong, representing perhaps the only genuine attachment either ever has experienced. This category of victim is the focus of our concern here.

Before elaborating on the pitfalls of treating this specific group, it must be noted that some younger children, too, feel a strong and often unbreakable bond with their fathers or father figures. Children under fifteen or sixteen, however, being still under domination of external authority, exercise less self-determination than is found in older youngsters. Legal constraints involving young child victims are strong. Maternal pressure, also, often is influential in resolving issues related to filing charges and participating in the court process. Finally, child protective services makes a concerted effort toward separating the offender and victim. Hence, situational failures, i.e., acts of recidivism, may not be as frequent with young children as they are with teenagers.

Pitfalls

Counseling teenage victims can be extremely frustrating to the novice therapist who makes the assumption that incest is patently unhealthy and that therefore all victims require, need and want to be "rescued" — or that all victims basically believe incest has a deleterious effect on them — and they want the abuse stopped.

Clearly, incest is unhealthy and the consequences are not only deleterious but often disastrous. It is precisely because incest is unhealthy that victims emerge from sustained abuse in a vulnerable, emotionally precarious and deeply ambivalent condition. Thoughts, feelings, and behaviors are distorted. Unfortunately, some victims do not want help and some are so ambivalent that their desire for change alters soon after disclosure. Therapeutic intervention is possible only in certain circumstances.

In the first place, motivation for accepting help must be stronger than motivation to continue the incestuous bond. The approach-avoidance conflict regarding therapy must be resolved by the client's desire to be free of painful symptoms in the face of her fears regarding social ostracism, removal from the home, rejection or retaliation by the offender and the possibility of pregnancy. Any of these motivating factors may be present; several or all may co-exist. Hence, the situation is complicated and even if factors weighted in favor of therapeutic intervention are numerous, they still may not carry sufficient strength to counteract the attachment that a teenager feels for her assaulter. To counteract the effects of the offender-victim bond, it is imperative that a trusting client-therapist relationship be established prior to the time of disclosure. Once a report that initiates the therapeutic process has been received, the therapist should be particularly aware of patterns of teenage incest victim behavior concerning therapy. This is, in general as follows.

1. The victim willingly and sometimes enthusiastically participates in the crisis phase of therapy.

2. Despite ambivalence regarding therapy, separation from or of the family, or court involvement, therapy proceeds uninterrupted up to or into the crisis stage.

3. The victim terminates therapy following or during the latter stages of crisis work.

Therapy is terminated for several reasons. The confessional, cathartic aspect of therapy may relieve guilt and give the victim the needed reassurance to return to her usual pattern of behavior. Secondly, the reality of life changes (separation from her father, court involvement, financial stress, or estrangement from her mother) may be too painful for the victim to face. Finally, once the crisis is resolved, the victim realizes that she will be working through underlying trauma, and the prospect of deeper therapy is too threatening for her.

When a victim is coerced into therapy, or refuses altogether to participate, therapeutic efforts fail immediately or during the crisis phase.

Avoidance of Pitfalls

Even the most conscientious therapist will not be able to avoid totally the pitfalls involved in counseling incest victims. Losing a young victim who clearly needs intervention can be painful to the clinician who has a high degree of awareness and understanding of the dynamics of incest. To some extent, however, pitfalls can be avoided if the therapist is aware of the following mitigating conditions.

1. Therapists are not police who operate from an unambiguous position of right and wrong. Client self-determination is a key aspect of effective therapeutic intervention, even in an area that involves illegal activities. The therapist must be clear about where her/his legal obligations begin and end and how these legal obligations are separate from the therapeutic process. Above all, the personal values of the victim must be recognized, in light of her individual circumstances, separately from the therapist's personal values. The therapist's view of incest as wrong must be tempered by the realization that a client may perceive it as right for her — or at least as necessary to her well-being. The therapist's respect for the client's point of view will not only help the therapeutic relationship; it will also minimize any sense of self-blame that results from alleged failures.

2. The therapist must understand that often timing is a crucial factor in therapeutic intervention. A teenager initially frightened by therapeutic contact may well return for help within a relatively short time, possibly during a period of exacerbated conflict.

3. The therapist who becomes too deeply involved emotionally
    with the teenage incest victim by assuming a nonproductive
    "rescuer" role can become subject to possible hurt and
    disappointment for two reasons. FIrst, incest victims emerge
    from homes where the ability to relate has been impaired and
    distorted and where trust and communication are lacking.
    Hence, building relationships and genuine trust with teenage
    victims is a precarious, difficult and sometimes impossible task.
    Second, often it is virtually impossible to assess true from
    feigned motivation for help with teenage victims, partly because
    they themselves are unaware of what inner forces are operating.

Many teenage victims who self-disclose about long-term
father-daughter incest have suspect motivations for doing so, motivations of
which they themselves are not aware and which may preclude the
possibility for effective therapeutic intervention. For example, a teenager
may report incest ostensibly because she fears her father will abuse younger
siblings. In reality, she has a boyfriend of whom her father is jealous.
Shortly after the commencement of therapy, she loses interest in her
boyfriend and strong positive feelings for her father begin to re-emerge.
Along with the renewed bond with her father is a declining interest in
therapy. Another teenager may report incest allegedly because she fears
pregnancy. Still, she has feared pregnancy several times previously but not
reported the occurrence of incest. In reality, the girl may resent new
parental restrictions and be acting out revenge against her father. The father
then becomes aware of her resentment and, in an effort toward
appeasement, loosens restrictions in the home. The victim, in turn, no
longer feels the need for therapeutic intervention. Clearly, to the extent that
it is possible, therapists should assess the true motivations of these
teenagers when they report incestuous abuse in the home.

Case Illustrations

1. Mary, aged 12, lived with her natural father and 17-year-old
    sister, Carole, in a small apartment. Carole and her father shared
    a double bed and, according to Mary, had been involved in an
    incestuous relationship since the sisters moved into their father's
    apartment four years before. Following a single incident
    involving her and her father when Carole was out of town on a
    camping trip, Mary reported to her school counselor that there
    was incest in the home. However, Mary refused to file charges,

moved into her mother's home immediately and had short-term therapy followed by group work.

Carole agreed to be interviewed by me, Mary's therapist. She adamantly refused to acknowledge any illicit activities involving her father and accused her sister of "lying about Dad's touching her." She admitted sleeping in the same bed with her father and going to bars "socially" with him. Carole stated that she did not date although her father had occasional girlfriends. She claimed that she "took care of Dad" and that their relationship was natural and "innocent." Neither therapeutic nor legal intervention was possible in this case.

2. Sherry, aged 15, reported the existence of incest with her natural father following his marriage to his third wife. Sherry, who told her friend's mother about her eight year liaison with her father, immediately was removed from the home by the authorities. Twenty-four hours following disclosure, she attempted suicide by overdosing on 100 assorted non-prescription pills. She was hospitalized in a psychiatric facility for four months before being placed in a therapeutic residential care for two years. For the duration of her therapy, Sherry steadfastly claimed that her only interest was in renewing her relationship with her father, whom she said she had reported "out of jealousy" because he married again. She claim that her suicide attempt was precipitated by guilt and regret "over telling on him." She ran away from residential care innumerable times and each time she was located in her father's home. After two years, her father divorced his wife and moved out of state. Sherry, who ran from the residence for the last time, presumably returned to her father's care.

3. Casey, 19, telephoned my counseling agency to report a ten-year incestuous relationship with her father. During the initial interview, she claimed that she was disclosing the existence of incest "to save my seven-year-old sister." Casey said that she was joining the Army and she feared her father would begin to abuse her sister. She claimed that she was angry and guilty regarding the relationship with her father and she began the initial process of filing charges.

Crisis counseling proceeded as Casey began to unravel her complicated feelings for both parents. Her mother, who was cooperative and willing to participate in therapy, immediately moved into an apartment with the three younger children and began divorce proceedings.

Several weeks after the commencement of therapy, Casey told her mother that she did not need help anymore, that she forgave her father, and that she did not intend to complete the process of filing charges. She immediately married her boyfriend with whom she had been unable to have sexual intercourse "out of fear." The couple moved into her father's studio apartment. Within two weeks, her new husband joined the Marines and left the city, leaving Casey alone with her father. Her mother, stunned, surmised either that Casey originally had reported the incestuous abuse "to get rid of me so that she could have her father all to herself" or "because she was jealous that he might be more interested in Christy (the seven year old sister) than in her."

8
ASSERTIVE TRAINING FOR CHILD VICTIMS

Nonassertiveness has been linked to a number of psychological difficulties including excessive shyness, withdrawal, low self-esteem and fearfulness. Hence, assertiveness is a valuable skill for everyone to master. Since the publication of *Your Perfect Right: A Guide to Assertive Behavior* by Alberti and Emmons in 1970, numerous books and articles have been published on the subject. Most if not all of the literature, however, has been oriented to the adult population. I have found, however, that even a young child can learn skills of assertiveness if the training material is interesting and geared to her/his age and level of intellectual functioning.

Rationale for Teaching Assertiveness to Child Victims of Incest

Victims of incestuous abuse usually are passive, frightened, withdrawn, untrusting and noncommunicative. They suffer from low self-esteem and often have a variety of psychosomatic complaints related to suppressed anger and anxiety. Feelings and concerns about incest, the future of the family, the complicated relationships that exist with both parents, and the possibility of court involvement need to be expressed by the victim who needs to learn communication skills. The home has provided very poor modeling in self-assertion.

Instruction in Assertiveness Training for Child Victims

Readily available adult material regarding assertive behaviors can be easily modified to meet the needs of teenagers. The following special considerations are necessary when instructing pre-teenagers in this skill, however.

1. *Cognitive material should be kept to a minimum.* When used, it should be simplified and followed by examples and role plays related to the child's life. The child should learn only what she needs to know to become more communicative. Extraneous material of interest to the adult should be eliminated from the instruction.

2. *All material should be repeated in different forms,* to facilitate comprehension and to insure the fact that learned skills will be incorporated into the child's life. Practice is essential both in therapy and in the outside world. To sustain interest, charts and visual aids are useful.

3. To keep interest level high, *only a portion of each session should be devoted to learning assertiveness.*

4. In accordance with learning theory, *reinforcement is an important aspect of instruction.* Tangible rewards and social reinforcers should be used liberally as warranted by observable efforts on the part of the child.

Introducing and Teaching Assertiveness to the Client

Basic information regarding assertive behaviors should be imparted to the child. This material includes the following features.

1. *Rationale for Learning the Skill.* Briefly, the child should understand that she will get along better and feel better about herself if she learns to make her needs and feelings known to others in an open and honest manner.

2. *Definition of Assertive Behavior.* The therapist should model assertive behavior both verbally and nonverbally for the child, explaining the various elements demonstrated. Use a situation to model the behavior. For example, the therapist might say, "I am going to ask my boss for a raise, using assertive behavior. Try to pay attention to the things I say and do as I ask for the raise." The modeling then proceeds as follows:

"Mr. X, I have been working here for three years and my record is very good." (Notice, I am describing the facts—the situation—and I am standing very straight and looking Mr. X directly in the eye.) "I feel a little unhappy and upset because I have not had a raise." (See, I am telling my boss exactly how I feel.) "I think that I deserve a raise." (Now, I clearly tell him what I want and that my request really is reasonable—nothing ridiculous. That's important—to ask for something reasonable.) "If I get a raise, I'll feel really good about working for you." (Now I'm even telling him what will happen if he is fair and gives me a raise!)

Whatever the form of modeling used, it is important for the child to be made aware of both the verbal and nonverbal behaviors involved: the content of what is said (especially speaking to the issue and expressing feelings), how the voice is used (conversational but firm tone), facial expression (especially eye contact), and body expression (erect posture, hands at sides).

3. *Understanding Assertive Behavior.* The child should understand the three ways that people communicate with one another. The passive person timidly withdraws from confrontation and so elicits feelings of pity, confusion, or lack of respect from others. The aggressive person takes an offensive stance, displaying intolerance or hostility which antagonize others. A person who uses balanced assertiveness speaks objectively, logically and frankly from a position of calm self-confidence.

Role plays with the use of a cassette recorder are invaluable in imparting this information to a child. Choose situations related directly to the child's life and model each of the three types of behavior. Then, have the child model the behaviors. Finally use role play situations beginning with non-threatening ones such as, "Asking Mom to stay up an extra hour before I go to bed." Proceed to more difficult and emotionally-laden situations such as, "Telling Mom how I feel about testifying in court or pressing charges."

Ask the child to report how she feels—both as the sender and as the receiver—when role-playing the three types of behaviors. Some children respond to visual aids and enjoy making charts listing the three behaviors, their characteristics and the feelings associated with them. Others enjoy drawing figures to represent the passive, aggressive and assertive person. One victim named her three figures, Mrs. Meek, Mrs. Mad, and Mrs. Moderate.

4. *The Script.* Bower and Bower (1976) reduced the stages involved in assertive behavior to four steps, symbolized by the initial DESC for describing the situation, expressing feelings, specifying a change of behavior and expressing the consequences. An even simpler script for use with children is symbolized by the word **WIN:**

W = *What happened*/is happening, the situation as it existed/exists;

I = *Inside feelings* the child has about the situation;

N = *Needs and wants* related to requests and changes of behavior.

   Children learn this simple model easily and, in doing so, retain the most important elements of assertiveness.

5. *Put-downs.* The child should understand that even if she makes her needs know, she may not receive the response that she hopes for or have her needs met. Here, it is important to help the victim realize that her responsibility is not to change others to suit herself but rather to express herself—for herself. Examples of put-downs, described in Bower and Bower (1976) as "Downer Detours," should be modeled and role-played with appropriate assertive responses. Typical put-downs include the following:

"I don't care how you feel or what you want right now."

"I'll talk to you later."

"I'm too busy to hear what you have to say."

"You always need to make a fuss."

"You're completely wrong!"

The child learns to identify the put-down, to ignore it, and to proceed with her issues. She learns also that in some situations she will remain frustrated. Finally, it is important for her to realize that she herself may be in error in making unreasonable requests or in refusing to compromise. One of the hardest concepts for some children to accept is the art of compromise. Children do make unrealistic demands and often they are aware only of their feelings and not those of others. These notions are important to impart to the over-zealous victim who may erroneously view her newly learned skill as a method of getting her own way.

As noted earlier, success in teaching any skill depends upon practice. Each of the above-listed elements should be practiced, rehearsed and repeated formally and informally to insure absorption, integration and assimilation into the child's life.

Sometimes practice can have a confronting aspect. One case in my experience involved a seductive youngster, the victim of incest and multiple stranger-molestation. This child, verbally and nonverbally, could not say no to any male who approached her for any reason. After the basics of assertiveness had been imparted, I enlisted the aid of a male therapist to approach and annoy this child in order to elicit appropriate responses from her.

In the first session, following introductions, the male therapist simply placed his hand on the child's wrist for several minutes. The youngster was visibly upset, as demonstrated by the sudden onset of thumb sucking. However, she refused to say anything or to remove her arm. Confrontation followed as I made repeated remarks such as, "Do you like what he is doing?", and, "What are you going to do about this?" Finally, the child reacted aggressively by shouting, "Get away!" and quickly removing her arm. It was obvious that in the face of renewed emotional conflict, all learned skills temporarily were lost. Several practice sessions involving confrontation and emotionally-laden issues related to male aggression were necessary before the victim was able to deal with the male therapist assertively.

Contracts (see sample at end of chapter) specifying practice situations are useful with both children and adults. The child chooses a situation, often from a list prepared by the therapist, to practice assertiveness at home or at school. She then writes her script. The contract is returned the following week and the child (or her parent) reports on her progress. A gold star can be glued on the contract if success has been achieved. Contracts can be kept in a folder and when a certain number of stars are earned, the child receives a reward (ice cream, free time, games during therapy, or a small toy).

Situations to Practice Assertiveness (for Role Plays and Contract Use)

Non-threatening

1. The client asks for something tangible—gifts, money, rewards, extra time to play, fewer chores, more time with friends.

2. The client asks for something intangible—attention, under-
    standing, time with parent or friend, fewer arguments at home, af-
    fection.

Threatening

1. The client asks for something tangible—seeing Dad less often, not
    having to press charges, moving away, appearing or not appearing
    in court.
2. The client asks for something intangible—feedback from Mom re-
    garding her feelings and why/how she did not know that incest had
    occurred; understanding from friends, siblings and relatives re-
    garding incest; reaction to and response from Dad regarding in-
    cest.

A Sample WIN Contract for Use with Children

CONTRACT

I will be assertive in this situation:

_____

_____

_____

I will say: (use your WIN script)

_____

_____

_____

_____

When I was assertive, the other person said:

_____

_____

And the I felt:

_____

Agreement:	*Result:*
Signed: _____	Completed: _____
Witness: _____	Not Completed: _____
Date: _____	Date: _____

(Reason for non-completion): _____

_____

SECTION B:
The Wife

9
STRATEGIC THERAPY FOR SILENT PARTNERS IN INCEST FAMILIES

A treatment model is presented here for short-term intervention with noninterfering wives of sexual assaulters of daughters or stepdaughters. The women to whom this model applies are characterized by an all-pervasive use of the defense mechanism of denial—denial that continues even after the disclosure of incestuous assault, preventing effective therapeutic intervention on behalf of their daughters. Denial on the mother's part further complicates the treatment process as her reaction is a major determinant of subsequent psychological damage for the child.

The focus is directed toward wives since they and their daughters are the family members initially seen by therapists in the majority of cases of incestuous assault. The wives are referred to as silent partners since they are characterized by many leading authorities as consciously or unconsciously promoting the sexual activity between their spouses and daughters.

Rationale for the Model

The rationale used for a short-term directive model is based on the fact that the initial phase of sexual assault counseling requires crisis intervention because of the trauma posed by incest and, equally, because of the trauma posed by disclosure. The strategic approach is one that actively involves the therapist in directly influencing the client.

Direct intervention is necessary as a catalyst to help energize the wives of offenders who are usually immobilized by depression, low self-esteem, strong dependency needs and concern over the threat to the family that the disclosure of incest poses. A major therapeutic goal with such women is to create movement from denial to more productive modes of functioning.

Assumptions

The model assumes the validity of Kubler-Ross' stages (1969) of transition in the process of dying and further assumes that these stages apply with equal validity to other severe crises in the life process. When faced with severe trauma, individuals pass through five stages which begin with denial, then move through anger, bargaining and depression, to culminate in acceptance.

The model further assumes that passage through these five stages is therapeutic in itself. Equally important are the consequences of moving from the impasses created by denial to more action-reaction oriented affective states.

Utilizing the Model

The therapist actively engages in helping the client move from the denial phase by clarifying the value of that defense mechanism for maintenance of homeostasis. The majority of incest cases are of long-term duration and usually come to the attention of authorities only through some external or life-stage crisis such as a daughter's pregnancy, the onset of puberty with expanded social interests, or feelings of rejection by a daughter replaced as a love object by a younger sibling. Thus, denial has operated pervasively in these families, often for years, serving as a self-protective device to preserve the most basic of human needs—safety and security.

In many instances, to help a client move fully from denial to anger or to bargaining is a formidable task as total family disruption is threatened. Even when a woman consciously acknowledges the facts of incestuous assault, she may deny the full extent of it, project responsibility from the offender to the victim, or engage in an internal battle of approach-avoidance regarding the situation.

The task of the therapist is to find a competing value, a value more strongly cherished than those values invested in the denial mechanism. The competing value that the therapist attempts to elicit and use to advantage is a painful affective state from which the client will seek relief.

Denial operates in the client in part because it produces a state more pleasurable than that which would be elicited by the suppressed affects of guilt and fear. With denial operating so strongly, there is no motivation for change or growth. The motivation for therapeutic change derives from a state of pain. Hence, an effective way to motivate the denying client and mobilize her toward movement is to expose painful affective states that are blocked and suppressed.

In practice, the therapist attempts to intensify the guilt and fear underlying and perpetuating the operation of denial. Once the painful state is aroused, the client will seek relief and be effectively guided toward anger as the second stage in the progression through the five crisis stages outlined by Kubler-Ross.

The difficult part in the process is to find the appropriate intervention strategy that will guide the client from pleasure to pain without alienating her or causing a flight reaction. Least effective for crisis clients heavily invested in their defenses are any of the approaches that rely heavily on confrontation. The client can move with surprising rapidity with more patient and time-consuming therapeutic techniques based on the principles of learning theory where the therapist labels and interprets underlying affects and then verbally rewards the client for appropriate responses.

Once the deeply-entrenched denial impasse is broken, the remaining four crisis stages can proceed in natural progression, aided by patient guidance from effective therapeutic interventions.

Case Illustration

Thirty-four year old Mary voluntarily made an appointment to be seen at my counseling agency concerning treatment of her ten-year-old daughter, Annie. During the initial telephone intake, Mary stated, "Annie says my husband touched her three or four times where he wasn't supposed to." In actuality, Annie had been forced to engage in sexual intercourse and fellatio with her natural father for three years, two to three times weekly, facts freely admitted by the child during initial private sessions.

As the case unfolded, there emerged evidence of additional sexual activity on the part of the offender during the duration of his twelve-year marriage to Mary. Three years earlier, an eleven year old female neighbor had told Mary that her husband had forced her to have sexual intercourse when he was drunk. In addition, Annie claimed that her mother had come home on one occasion and surprised her father "zipping up" after forced fellatio. Hence, there was ample evidence of denial on Mary's part, denial which protected her from facing the anger and sense of betrayal that she felt toward her husband and toward herself for her inability to act decisively on her daughter's behalf. Guilt operated strongly in this woman, who had unconsciously decided to sacrifice her child's emotional health in order to maintain a precarious status quo involving protection and financial security.

It is neither within the scope of this discussion to discuss in detail unconscious motivations operating within the complicated dynamics of this family, nor to elaborate on subsequent legal and court proceedings. Present focus is on the therapeutic impasse that might have occurred during treatment due to the mother's denial of her husband's offenses even after their disclosure. Therapeutically, the first goal was to avoid that impasse and to activate underlying affects in order to mobilize Mary toward active support for her daughter, self-growth, and the responsible participation in the inevitable court proceedings that were to follow.

Work on eliciting and clarifying guilt and fear was considered a major therapeutic goal—one that required diligence and persistence on my part. The basic approach, initiated during the first contact and continuing for several weeks, involved clarification of affect followed by reinforcement for insights and self-labeling. In sessions with both mother and daughter, each time Annie recounted some aspect of the incestuous relationship which Mary had blocked or denied, I deliberately would interject such phrases as, "You must be feeling guilty hearing that. It is frightening to face the truth and begin to put two and two together" or, "It seemed easier to deny these incidents at the time than to deal with the guilt." Initially, Mary's response was verbal or silent assent but after several sessions she began to label her own underlying affect with open admission of guilt, fear and finally anger. It was at this stage of intervention that growth and change became possible.

10

SURROGATE MOTHERING AS AN INITIAL CATALYST FOR CHANGE FOR THE WIVES OF OFFENDERS

This discussion focuses on a therapeutic approach with one type of silent partner whose overall level of emotional and social functioning is regressed and/or fixated at an immature level, where coping mechanisms often are characteristic of those of a young child. Common characteristics of these women are:

1. strong dependency needs;
2. passivity and/or passive-aggressive behavior;
3. lack of assertiveness;
4. isolation and few outlets for varied forms of reality testing;
5. insecurity, both emotionally and socially;
6. feelings of inadequacy and low self-image;
7. use of denial as a primary defense mechanism, partly due to an inability to cope with reality;
8. inability to cope with reality due to poor problem-solving skills and/or poor frustration tolerance and/or fear of being overwhelmed by anxiety;
9. affective problems such as: anger, guilt and depression;
10. lack of trust and communication; and
11. inability to achieve normal mature genital sexual satisfaction.

Many of these characteristics are typical of and possessed by young children. Behaviorally, a woman with these immature qualities may actually contribute to setting up the incest situation, in which the daughter is forced into a position of role-reversal, where she becomes wife and mother in place of her female parent.

Compounding this state of regression is the crisis situation caused by the disclosure of incest. The crisis further exacerbates regressed behavior and often forces the wives of offenders into a condition where, initially, the primary therapeutic needs are for unconditional acceptance, understanding, protection and direction.

Dynamically, this condition results in large part from the poor parenting and poor parent models these wives have experienced in childhood. Often, their own histories reveal intergenerational problems with incestuous and other abuses. Denial pervaded their early lives and precluded the possibility of the development of mature coping skills, both behaviorally and emotionally.

Hence, the diagnostic picture that emerges clearly sets one possible direction for therapy. In the early stages of intervention, the therapist often is effective by assuming a parent role with this type of silent partner.

This situation is summarized in the following diagram.

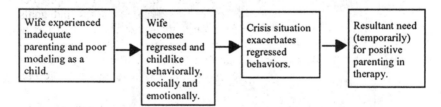

Parenting Needs of Silent Partners

Referring back to the original list of the characteristics of silent partners, therapeutic goals can be formulated as follows.

1. *Strong Dependency Needs:* Initially the client needs to transfer dependency needs to the therapist. Without a solid relationship based on consistency and borrowed ego strength, the client under stress will terminate therapy quickly. The approach is directive and nurturing.

2. *Passivity; Passive Aggressive Behavior; Lack of Assertiveness:* Insight therapy, modeling and instruction in assertive behaviors, again directively, are effective very early in the therapeutic process. Instruction, often on an elementary level, can begin early partly because of the pressing need for the client to resolve a number of situational problems, including a possible move from the home, initiation of the court process, confrontation with the offender, or open communication with, and support of, the daughter. Hence, it becomes a practical necessity for the client to master assertive behavior for crisis resolution.

3. *Isolation and Few Outlets for Varied Forms of Reality Testing:* A two-fold need for "reaching out" often exists for the socially and emotionally isolated silent partner. First, there is the need for her to confront the system via a wide variety of needed resources including public assistance, legal aid, medical care and housing opportunities. The therapist again assumes a nurturing parent role in which directive guidance facilitates growth. Here, the therapist should be sufficiently knowledgeable to make direct referrals, give concrete guidance as to the best resources, and serve both as liaison and buffer for the client as she faces a frightening and complicated array of bureaucratically-confusing services.

   Second, early in therapy, the isolated client needs to extend her social horizons in an effort to expand an often inadequate or faltering support system. Here again, the informed therapist begins by working with the client in structured values and goals clarification, as well as decision-making exercises, to arrive at concrete avenues for her to investigate. Career exploration (through community college courses or a battery of personality and personal preference inventories) is helpful along with referrals to church or singles groups.

4. *Emotional and Social Insecurity; Feelings of Inadequacy; Low Self-Image:* The therapist facilitates self-image building through insight work and through her own unconditional acceptance of the client. Friendly support helps to counteract feelings of inadequacy. In some cases it may be necessary for the therapist to "walk the client through the system" by setting up appointments at agencies such as Legal Aid and then accompanying her initially to these meetings. A balance needs to be maintained between fostering excessive dependency, thus increasing low self-esteem, and providing sufficient support to enable the client to experience success in the real world. Once the silent partner achieves any of her

desired goals (even one as simple as meeting with her daughter's lawyer for an interview) her self-esteem and confidence level are increased immeasurably.

5. *Use of Denial as a Primary Defense Mechanism Partly Due to Inability to Cope with Reality:* The typical (or usual) use of denial by wives of incestuous offenders poses special problems for the therapist. The preceding chapter refers to one treatment model that is recommended to facilitate breaking through the impasse of denial. The important point is that the client must learn new coping strategies if she is to become better adjusted.

The client uses denial because she has learned in her childhood to use this defense as a coping mechanism. It serves the same function for her as it does for the young child, i.e., it enables her to avoid painful reality and to maintain the status quo. In a very real sense, denial of reality is a way to avoid mature coping strategies for meeting inevitable life changes that both the child and wife of the offender feel unable to bear.

Educating the client regarding the all-pervasiveness of denial in her life can be an important aspect of therapy. Focusing on the use of this defense mechanism as it affects all aspects of her life provides a less threatening approach than dealing directly with the denial of incest. Areas on which to focus attention include choice of marital partner, alcoholism, social outlets, sexual relations and financial strain. A silent partner wife may say, for example, "I knew when I met him that he drank a lot but I never dreamed it was a serious problem." She also may deny the importance of social outlets or of a compatible sexual relationship with her husband, or she may claim total ignorance regarding the family's financial situation.

Slowly and patiently, the therapist begins to focus on those areas where denial clearly has operated. The wife needs help to understand that the use of denial, unconsciously aimed at protecting the self, creates intense guilt and anxiety and exacerbates low self-image. By contrast, the ability to deal openly with situations and to face reality is part of mature behavior and thus enhances self-image, gives the client a sense of control over her life and leads to the development of problem-solving skills.

6. *Affective Problems:* Guilt; Depression; Anger: In the early stages of therapy, it may be necessary for the clinician to identify and label affect for the client whose insights and ability to understand underlying feelings are limited. Mislabeling is a common occur-

rence with these women who often mistake sadness for anger or anger for guilt.

Focusing on feelings in the here-and-now is effective in explaining the dynamics of emotional states. For example, the client needs to learn that depression often is related to suppressed guilt and anger and that hurt frequently underlies the feelings we label as anger.

Well-known Rogerian techniques — paraphrasing, reflecting, clarifying — are effective in working with emotionally-blocked clients. Mild confrontation also can be useful, but only after trust is established (since, like hurt children, these women are vulnerable and expect rejection). Even the mildest confrontation, initiated too early in the therapeutic relationship, can elicit defensiveness and projection.

7. *Lack of Trust and Communication:* Communication is enhanced in the therapeutic relationship in obvious ways including modeling by the therapist, structured exercises related to assertiveness, and open encouragement of the client to verbalize her concerns.

Trust-building often is more difficult to accomplish because the client has learned since childhood to question the motivations of those people closest to her. Trust is enhanced by the therapist's early unconditional acceptance of the client, the clear establishment of the therapist's role, and her adherence to the guidelines of confidentiality. Any action that the therapist takes (report to Child Protective Services or telephone contact with the police, lawyers or other agencies) should be explained fully to the client, preferably before-the-fact.

Trust-building also increases when the dynamics of the therapist-client relationship are processed and dealt with openly and honestly. Self-disclosure on the therapist's part can be useful when it relates to therapeutic issues or enhances trust-building. A therapist who has suffered sexual abuse might share her own feelings about the experience and its aftermath.

The more authentic and genuine the therapist is, the more easily trust can be established. Hence, negative feelings should be shared as well as positive ones. For example, the therapist may feel anger regarding certain aspects of the incestuous abuse and can freely share her feelings provided that she is obviously sincere and does not judge nor criticize the client.

8. *Inability to Achieve Mature Genital Satisfaction:* The area of sexual functioning usually is not explored in depth initially in the therapeutic process, although questions do arise early and require some preliminary exploration. A question often posed by the victim is, "Why me? Why not Mom? When he needed someone, why didn't he turn to her?" In addition, the offender often rationalizes father-daughter incest by claiming that his wife was unavailable or frigid.

To help the client respond to anticipated questions and to become more comfortable with self-disclosure regarding her sexuality, the therapist should take a sexual history, either informally or formally (see Chapter on Sexual Enrichment). The history helps to desensitize the client and provides the therapist with useful information regarding areas of dysfunction to be explored in the later phases of therapy.

Conclusion

Surrogate mothering — in the form of fostering temporary dependency and providing unconditional acceptance, nurturance and direction — is an important aspect of therapy with the wives of offenders. However, two final issues must be emphasized. The therapeutic model presented here applies only to one type of silent partner. She should be identified clearly in accordance with the characteristics listed in the foregoing before any treatment plan is devised. Finally, surrogate mothering can be potentially dangerous in that it might foster rapid transference with which the therapist might not be prepared to deal. In addition, dysfunctional dependencies can result if the therapist is not careful to monitor her own behavior as well as the client's. For these reasons, it is wisest to use surrogate mothering only in the initial phases of crisis work, then gradually to wean the client as soon as it is deemed feasible.

11
RE-STRUCTURING CLIENTS' SELF-IMAGE THROUGH RETAPING

The wives of offenders in incestuous abuse cases are characterized by low self-esteem and guilt, often so severe that they become immobilized and unable to perform the necessary supportive functions for their victimized daughters. Such women tend to blame themselves, often unconsciously. Their feelings of guilt are exacerbated by professional attitudes that traditionally reinforce the notion of the wife as a silent partner who has either abandoned her daughter to the father's lust or colluded in the incestuous abuse.

Therapeutically, low self-esteem can be treated with a variety of modalities and techniques. One relatively simple and often quite effective method involves the dual approach of first identifying negative tapes, scripts or thoughts in the client's mind, then replacing these thoughts with more positive action-oriented ones, using auto-suggestion in the form of self-affirmations.

For affirmations to be effective the client must understand and give credence to the power of auto-suggestion and also must be committed to allocating a small amount of time daily to relaxation practice. Hence, this method is not effective with everyone. It is most suitable for two types: highly motivated wives who have much invested in maintaining family unity and reestablishing the status quo in the home, and wives whose feelings of guilt and low self-esteem with resultant anxiety are severe enough to interfere with daily functioning.

Negative Tapes

The tapes that run through the mind of an offender's wife often are verbalized in therapy. A common thread pervades these thoughts, a thread linked to the characteristic defenses of projection and denial and related most often to fear, low self-esteem, guilt, anger, and, less frequently to revenge and jealousy toward their victim daughters.

The first task of the therapist is to help the client identify these tapes. Usually, this process can be accomplished fairly rapidly, but in some instances it is useful to help the client label her own thoughts using a checklist for clarification. Following is a list of the most common negative tapes or thoughts of wives of offenders, along with affects and defenses associated with them.

1. I did not know incest occurred. (Denial)
2. I should have known this was happening. (Guilt, Self-blame)
3. Where was I while this was going on? (Guilt, Self-blame)
4. I should have been there. (Guilt, Self-blame)
5. It happened to me so what can we do about it? (Resignation, Revenge)
6. I cannot believe it happened. (Denial)
7. My daughter is lying. (Fear, Anger, Denial, Revenge)
8. My husband is a bastard. (Anger)
9. I cannot break up the home. I need financial and emotional support. (Fear)
10. There is nothing I can do about this. (Fear, Denial)
11. He'll kill (hurt) me if I take any action. (Fear)
12. It just didn't happen. (Denial)
13. I can't face this. (Denial, Fear)
14. It happened to me. It can happen to her! What's the big deal? (Revenge, Jealousy)
15. I know I should help but I don't want this exposed. (Guilt, Revenge, Fear, Denial)
16. What will people think of me? (Fear)
17. I cannot bear the court hassles. (Fear)
18. I don't want to put my daughter through the court process. (Fear)
19. My daughter hates me. (Projection)
20. She brought it on anyway. (Revenge, Jealousy, Denial)

21. I really wanted this to happen. (Revenge, Jealousy)
22. It's my fault. I wasn't there and/or never gave him sex. (Guilt, Self-blame)
23. He should get all that's coming to him. (Anger)

Most of these thoughts, associated with strong emotions and defenses, are non-productive in that they lead to increased immobility, fear, anger, depression and low self-esteem. Hence, once the thoughts or tapes are identified, it becomes the task of the therapist to educate the client in ways to transform them into ones that are positive, action-oriented and geared to enhance the self-image.

Auto-Suggestion/Auto-Conditioning

The first step is to educate the client in the process of auto-suggestion or auto-conditioning. The following information should be included in the instruction process.

1. We make suggestions to our subconscious every day. These suggestions involve our feelings, thoughts and behaviors.
2. Negative suggestions about ourselves cause us to feel useless and unworthy. The result is that we behave in self-destructive and non-productive ways.
3. Changing our thoughts changes the way we see ourselves and behave. Positive thoughts result in healthy emotions and productive actions.

Relaxation

Because auto-suggestion is effective in the relaxed state, the client next should be briefed in simple relaxation techniques, followed by practice in the therapeutic setting. The client should be advised that if the basic components of relaxation are used, the same physiological response results regardless of the specific technique used. Benson (1975) outlines some simple components necessary for the state of relaxation:

1. a quiet environment;
2. a mental device such as a word or a phrase which should be repeated in a specific fashion over and over again;
3. the adoption of a passive attitude, which is perhaps the most important of the elements; and

4. a comfortable position. Appropriate practice of these four ele-
    ments for ten to twenty minutes once or twice daily should mark-
    edly enhance well-being.*

Self-affirmations

The final step in this program involves the conversion of negative thoughts to positive thoughts or affirmations which are to be repeated in a relaxed state. The client should be assigned the task of taking her own negative thoughts and converting them into affirmations to be reviewed with the therapist. A General Instruction Sheet on the use of affirmations for clients, taken from the work of Sondra Ray (1976), is provided at the end of this chapter.

Bower and Bower (1976) provide a helpful list of positive Coping Self-statements similar to affirmations but more action-oriented. They give four classes of statements, described as follows: 1) Preparing for a Stressful Situation/Confrontation, such as court involvement or interviews with the police; 2) Confronting and Handling a Stressful Situation; 3) Coping with the Feeling of Being Overwhelmed (during the stressful situation); and 4) Reinforcing Self-Statements (to be used as rewards following situations where clients have coped successfully).** A client can easily devise a set of statements to fit her own style. For example, she might arrive at the following list of affirmations.

1. Fear will not help now but careful planning will.
2. I am able to get through this.
3. I will breathe deeply and relax as tension mounts.
4. I did it! I got through it!

The final tool provided in this chapter for use with clients is a list of common negative thoughts/tapes of wives of offenders along with their corresponding positive affirmations.

---

*Benson, H., M.D. with Klipper, M.Z. *The Relaxation Response.* New York: Avon Books, 1975, 27, reprinted by permission of the author and publisher.
**Bower, S.A. and Bower, G.H. *Asserting Yourself: A Practical Guide for Positive Change.* Reading, MA: Addison-Wesley Publishing Company, 1976, 60, reprinted by permission of the authors and publisher.

AFFIRMATIONS:
GENERAL INSTRUCTION SHEET*

1. Work with one or more positive statement every day. The best time is just before sleeping, before starting the day and especially whenever you feel "bummed out."

2. Write each affirmation ten or twenty times.

3. Say and write each affirmation to yourself in the first, second and third persons as follows:

    "I, _____, feel free to discuss *all* aspects of my sex life with my partner."

    "You, _____, feel free to discuss *all* aspects of your sex life with your partner."

    "She,_____, feels free to discuss *all* aspects of her sex life with her partner."

    Always remember to put your name in the affirmation. Writing in the second and third person is also very important since your conditioning from others came to you in this manner.

4. Continue working with the affirmations daily until they become totally integrated in your consciousness. You will know this when your mind responds positively, and when you begin to experience mastery over your goals. You will be using your mind to serve you.

5. Record your affirmations on cassette tapes and play them back when you can. I very often play them while driving in the car on the freeway or when I go to bed. If I fall asleep while the earphone is still in my ear and the tape is going, the autosuggestion is still working as I sleep.

6. It is effective to look into the mirror and say the affirmations to yourself out loud. Keep saying them until you are able to see yourself with a relaxed, happy expression. Keep saying them until you eliminate all facial tension and grimaces.

---

*Ray, S. *I Deserve Love: How Affirmations Can Guide You to Personal Fulfillment.* Mulbrae, California: Les Femmes Publishing, 1976, 27-29, reprinted by permission of the author and publisher.

7. Another method is to sit across from a partner, each of you in a straightback chair with your hands on your thighs and knees barely touching each other. Say the affirmation to your partner until you are comfortable doing it. Your partner can observe your body language carefully; if you squirm, fidget, or are unclear, you do not pass. He or she should not allow you to go on to another one until you say it clearly without contrary body reactions and upsets. When he or she does pass you, go on to the next affirmation. He or she can also say them back to you, using the second person and your name. He or she should continue to say them to you until you can receive them well without embarrassment. This is harder than it sounds.

COMMON NEGATIVE THOUGHTS OF WIVES OF OFFENDERS AND THEIR CORRESPONDING AFFIRMATIONS

Negative	**Positive**
1. I did no know incest had occurred.	Incest did happen and I know I can face the issue and forgive myself.
2. I should have known this was happening.	The past is over. There are problems in the present with which I can and will deal.
3. Where was I while this was going on?	The fact that I was not there does not make me a bad person. I am here now and that is what counts.
4. I should have been there.	It is O.K. that I was not there. I am now and I can act.
5. It happened to me so what can we do about it?	Because this happened to me and nothing was done, does not mean that I can't help now. I can do something.
6. I can't believe it happened.	Although this is hard to face, I can and will deal with it.
7. My daughter is lying.	I am angry and afraid and that is O.K. Still, I will not let my emotions twist my thinking. My daughter needs help and I am here to do what needs to be done.
8. My husband is a bastard.	Although I have right to my feelings, I will not let them interfere with sensible planning.
9. I can't break up the home. I need financial and emotional support.	The fact that I need support will not stop me from taking the right action for my family.
10. There is nothing I can do about this.	I can and will do what needs to be done.

Negative	Positive
11. He'll kill (hurt me) if I take any action.	The fact that I am afraid will help me seek needed protection while I carry through with required activities.
12. It just didn't happen.	I may have denied this in the past but I will not deny it now.
13. I can't face this.	I can and will deal with this. I can get through it.
14. It happened to me. It can happen to her! What's the big deal?	It *is* a big deal! My daughter needs me and I am here.
15. I know I should help but I don't want this exposed.	I can face the fact that this may have to be exposed.
16. What will people think of me?	I do not care what others think. I care what I think of me.
17. I can't bear the court hassles.	I am strong and can bear whatever happens now.
18. I don't want to put my daughter through the court process.	I am strong and able to support my daughter if court is the appropriate action to take.
19. My daughter hates me.	It's O.K. to admit my daughter and I have a complicated relationship. This has nothing to do with what needs to be done now.
20. She brought it on anyway.	I know I needed excuses for what happened. I don't anymore.
21. I really wanted this to happen.	I can admit to my having been mixed up and spiteful.
22. It's my fault. I wasn't around and/or never gave him sex.	I can forgive myself for what I may or may not have done. I am O.K.
23. He should get all that is coming to him.	It is O.K. to have these thoughts and feelings. I still can act sensibly.

SECTION C
THE OFFENDER

12
TREATING THE OFFENDER: EVALUATION OF MOTIVES AND POTENTIAL FOR CHANGE

Despite the proliferation of therapy programs for sex offenders, there are no long-term studies regarding treatability. With our current humanistic and optimistic orientation to the behavioral health sciences, we are left with both the fact of incest and the fact that attempts will continue to be made to find effective therapy for offenders. In addition, there are legal implications to consider as clinicians often are called upon to provide expert testimony regarding prognoses for offenders in custody. Hence, it is useful for the therapist to establish some criteria to evaluate motivation and potential for change among offenders seen in practice.

Because of the complexities of personality dynamics involved in incestuous abuse, it is imperative that careful evaluations and judgements be made. Therapists involved in incest cases should possess a high degree of expertise in psychopathology and diagnostic procedures.

In the best circumstances it is difficult to formulate accurate prognoses. In the case of incestuous abuse, the situation is still more complicated. First, there is the possibility of negative transference and strong emotional reactions on the part of the therapist in whom violation of the "last taboo" may elicit powerful and often punitive emotions. Second, many families beginning therapy are in a state of crisis, a situation which creates additional problems for the therapist attempting to evaluate individual members. Individuals in crisis respond atypically, often with a "fight or flight" reaction to immediate stress. Finally, incestuous abuse cases often involve legal ramifications that place the clinician in a stressful situation, attempting to formulate predictions aimed at safeguarding minors from future abuse. Judgement may be negatively affected by stresses and pressures over which the therapist has little or no control.

With some offenders all efforts to prevent recidivism are fruitless and costly. A therapy modality has not yet been devised to effectively treat the antisocial personality on a long-term basis. Certain characteristics summarized in a chart at the end of this chapter describe the antisocial personality. In addition, one of the ten clinical scales on the Minnesota Multiphasic Personality Inventory measures psychopathic deviance (The Psychological Corporation, New York, 1948). It has been found useful to administer this instrument prior to the commencement of therapy.

Groth (1978) notes that when assessing the offender, it is very important to distinguish between two patterns of pedophilic behavior, i.e., behavior described as sexual involvement of an adult with children or adolescents. He makes a clear differentiation between the fixated pedophile (a persistent pattern) and the regressed pedophile (a new activity). The fixated pedophile has a persistent and chronic compulsion. The regressed pedophile has a primary sexual orientation toward people of equivalent adult age but, due to precipitating stresses, displaces his sexual impulses onto children. Clearly, prognosis for rehabilitation for the regressed pedophile is more favorable than that for the fixated pedophile. The dynamics of pedophilia are different from those of incest. Nonetheless, Groth's characterizations of fixed versus regressed behavior are applicable to incest offenders.

Other general dimensions and indices useful in determining prognosis for deviant acts are:

1. Age of onset

2. Duration

3. Intensity and/or severity

4. Frequency of occurrence

If the age at onset is young and the duration long-term with considerable intensity and frequency of occurrence, the prognosis for rehabilitation is guarded.

Several assessment tools included at the end of this chapter will aid the clinician in formulating decisions regarding both the direction for therapy and the nature of prognoses to be formulated. First presented is the Case History Outline, a general assessment instrument for use in all therapeutic situations, which places particular emphasis on long-standing emotional, vocational, social, educational and sexual problems that are seen to indicate both the degree of motivation for change and the presence of multiple dysfunction. Second is a Therapist's Checklist of personality traits, characteristics and defenses. This tool is useful in forming a composite personality profile. The offender whose behavior indicates assaultive tendencies, defensiveness, denial, hostility, low frustration tolerance and antagonism is typically less amenable to treatment than the offender who presents a profile of apathy, fearfulness, inability to relate and low self-esteem. Finally, there is a Client's Checklist, again highlighting emotional difficulties.

As Groth (1978) notes, the clinician's overall evaluation of the offender will be based on a number of factors. Motivation for incestuous abuse varies and, in the end, the therapist must have sufficient data to respond to the following:

1. Is the offender an antisocial personality type? (If so, the prognosis is poor.)

2. Is the offender regressed or fixed in his behavior? (If he is regressed in behavior, the prognosis may be favorable.)

3. From the offender's view, do the gains from being healthy outweigh the gains derived from remaining sick? This question demands consideration of the consequences of not changing (loss of status, loss of family, imprisonment). It is important, however, to evaluate the degree of concern felt regarding the act itself and not simply the consequences.

4. Was the motivation for the act(s) a need for physical contact and affection or for aggression via force and threat? The prognosis may be more favorable in the former instance.

5. What strengths are there for the offender in his environment, family situation and personality make-up to counter current stresses?

PSYCHO-SOCIOPATHIC or ANTISOCIAL PERSONALITY

Description: This personality is characterized by lifelong ingrained maladaptive patterns.

Prognosis for Effective Therapeutic Interventions: Poor

Sample scale to be used for detection or corroboration of antisocial personality type on the following page.

Personality and Affective Realm
- Impulsiveness
- Absence of guilt and remorse
- Low tolerance for frustration
- Inability to tolerate criticism or confrontation
- Selfishness and egocentricity

Predominant Defenses
- Rationalization (plausible) for behaviors
- Denial (of actions, affects)
- Projection of blame outwardly

Characteristic Overt Responses to Environment
- Action-orientation
- Manipulation
- Expedience
- Selfishness

Behaviors in the Interpersonal Realm
- Manifestation of outward charm towards others
- Inability to learn from experience or punishment
- Repetition of conflicts with others and society
- Irresponsible behavior towards others
- Impairment in ability to relate: shallow, object relationships characterized by use of others for own ends

---

MORAL-AMORAL SELF-RATING SCALE

Directions: Place a check mark by one or more of the responses that apply to you.

1. When I make a mistake, I
   - ❏ go back and try again
   - ❏ admit it
   - ❏ try to cover it up
   - ❏ pass the blame on to others
   - ❏ lose my temper
   - ❏ figure that I really did not make a mistake at all
   - ❏ usually realize that it was someone's and not my fault.

   (Reveals: rationalization, denial, projection)

2. When I tell a lie, I
   - ❏ get physically or emotionally ill
   - ❏ realize that it is okay and that I had a good reason to lie
   - ❏ immediately regret it
   - ❏ feel guilty and/or sorry
   - ❏ don't even think about it
   - ❏ dislike myself

   (Reveals: remorse, guilt, rationalization)

3. If my boss tells me I am performing poorly on the job, I
   - ❏ feel angry and disgusted
   - ❏ try to do a better job
   - ❏ want to get back at him
   - ❏ feel downcast, hurt or upset
   - ❏ lose my temper
   - ❏ hope something terrible happens to him
   - ❏ brood for days
   - ❏ quit the job
   - ❏ lie to cover up the work I have been doing
   - ❏ explain why my work is not as good as usual
   - ❏ invite him to dinner or for a drink, hoping to change his mind

   (Reveals: manipulation, expedience, impulsivity, action-orientation, low frustration-tolerance, inability to tolerate criticism or confrontation, inability to learn from experience)

4. When my spouse (girl/boyfriend) asks me to do something I dislike but which needs to be done, I

❑   do it anyway to please her/him
❑   get angry and "lose my cool"
❑   tell her/him to do it her/himself
❑   do it but feel angry and hope her (his) day goes wrong
    (Reveals: selfishness, irresponsibility)

5. When I have done something wrong to someone or hurt another person, I
    ❑   apologize and genuinely regret it
    ❑   really do not care one way or another
    ❑   feel basically that the person deserved it
    ❑   hide what I did or deny what I said
    ❑   worry alot that the person will not like me
    ❑   feel that I learned something and will try not to repeat the error again
    ❑   make believe that it did not happen
        (Reveals: inability to relate, manipulation, denial, projection, rationalization)

6. Stealing is
    ❑   wrong or immoral
    ❑   okay if the thief is not caught
    ❑   scary
    ❑   likely to cause the thief much guilt and worry
    ❑   okay because society is a "rip-off" anyway
    ❑   only wrong because laws are set up to punish thieves
        (Reveals: guilt, remorse, expedience)

7. The best way to handle people is to
    ❑   do whatever is necessary to get what you need from them
    ❑   be charming so they will like you and do what you want them to
    ❑   be honest and genuine
    ❑   hide your true feelings because people cannot be trusted
        (Reveals: manipulation, inability to relate, expedience)

8. Basically, people are
    ❑   out to get you
    ❑   friendly and genuine
    ❑   interested only in themselves
    ❑   not to be trusted

❑ willing to help and do what they can for others
❑ just human, with qualities and faults
(Reveals: inability to relate, selfishness)

9. If I were having serious marital problems, I would
❑ talk it over with friends, family, minister or counselor
❑ take a good look at myself and my spouse to see which areas in our life need attention
❑ punish my spouse
❑ send my spouse to a counselor
❑ realize that marriage never works anyway
❑ try to make my spouse understand where he/she went wrong
❑ realize that she/he won't change anyway and it is best to seek a quick divorce and get on with my life
❑ try to communicate with my wife/husband about our problems and then seek outside help if necessary
(Reveals: inability to relate, action-orientation, projection, rationalization, denial)

10. The best way to handle problems is to
❑ leave the scene as fast as possible
❑ realize that I am not to blame anyway
❑ take action immediately
❑ stop, think and try to figure out solutions
(Reveals: action-orientation, impulsivity, projection)

11. Under pressure, I feel
❑ at my best, performing at high level
❑ much anxiety and need to act fast for relief
❑ tense and unable to handle the situation
❑ tense but able to perform
❑ capable of doing what is required
❑ unable to perform
(Reveals: action-orientation, low frustration tolerance)

12. The adage, a bird in the hand is worth two in the bush, is best explained by the following:
❑ get what you can out of life no matter what it takes or whom it hurts
❑ be careful taking risks as you may have something worthwhile to lose

☐   guard what you have at all costs
☐   dreamers are fools
(Reveals: expedience or self-interest)

13. When criticized, I
☐   immediately feel angry and defensive
☐   want revenge against the person criticizing me
☐   feel hurt and disliked
☐   am downcast and depressed
☐   often realize I need to change
☐   know that criticism is meant only to hurt others
(Reveals: inability to tolerate criticism, confrontation)

14. The use of alcohol is
☐   a sin
☐   fine in moderation
☐   an excellent way to relieve stress and relax
☐   a way to escape from troubles
☐   a personal matter and people can drink as much or as little as they like
☐   basically dangerous to health and to the safety of other people
☐   one of the best ways to get rid of frustration and anger.
(Reveals: expedience, absence of guilt and remorse)

15. The best way to discipline a child is to
☐   hit and spank
☐   lock the child in his/her room
☐   act immediately and naturally, even if the action is explosive
☐   take the strongest measures possible because children act badly to hurt their parents
☐   reason with the child
☐   use a variety of consequences including withdrawing special rewards
(Reveals: inpulsivity,   projection,   action-orientation, selfishness)

CASE HISTORY OUTLINE

A.   Identifying Data

Includes name, age, sex, date of report

B.   Presenting Problems

Includes reason and source of referral

C.   Background

1.   Health

Includes physical limitations, illnesses, psychosomatics, and physical trauma

2.   Education

Includes trends in grades, acceleration or retardation, learning disabilities, emotional handicaps, level of intellectual functioning.

3.   Employment-Vocation

Includes reasons for dismissals and job changes

4.   Sexuality

Includes complete sexual history, evidence of sexual abuse sustained, sexual trauma, preferences, orientation and dysfunction

5.   Criminality/Law

Includes violations, dates and court dispositions

6.   Military

Includes length of service, type and nature of discharge, court martials

7.   Drug and Alcohol Use

Includes specific chemicals used and frequency of use

D.   Current Situation

1.   Family Dynamics

Includes attitudes towards one another, stresses, marital adjustment, children's adjustment, cultural and ethnic implications, socio-economic status

2.   Social Situation

Includes isolation, recreational outlets, habits, neighborhood, hobbies, interests, affiliations

3. *Antisocial Acts*

Includes assaultive tendencies, acts of violence, sexual deviance, and a history of the sociopathic triad (enuresis, arson and cruelty to animals)

4. *Emotional Balance*

Includes degree of evenness in temperament, suspiciousness, impulsivity, excitability, mood swings, aggression, withdrawal, self-deprecation, self-concept, apathy, degree of integration, fantasy life, defensiveness, degree of reality contact

E.   Presentation of Self

1. *Appearance*

Includes manner, neatness and clothing

2. *Motor Behavior*

Includes mannerisms, peculiarities of gait and speech, repetitious acts such as involuntary twitching or fingertapping

3. *Speech Patterns*

Includes rate of speech, deliberation, breadth of vocabulary, coherence, repeated themes and motor gestures associated with speech

4. *Tension and Anxiety Level*

Includes expressions of worry and concern, hyperactivity, excessive perspiration, restlessness.

THERAPIST'S CHECKLIST

(Check the characteristics that apply to the client.)

- ❏ Extremely Nervous
- ❏ Fearful
- ❏ Nervous tics
- ❏ Inhibited
- ❏ Despondent
- ❏ Uncooperative
- ❏ Inattentive
- ❏ Evasive
- ❏ Shy
- ❏ Self-conscious
- ❏ Antagonistic
- ❏ Insecure
- ❏ Tense
- ❏ Irritable
- ❏ Defensive
- ❏ Denying
- ❏ Low Degree Frustration Tolerance

- ❏ Inaccessible
- ❏ Apathetic
- ❏ Evasive
- ❏ Low Self-Esteem
- ❏ Lack of Initiative
- ❏ Projecting
- ❏ Tendency to Physical Violence
- ❏ Self-defeating
- ❏ Inability to Relate
- ❏ Hostile
- ❏ Cynical
- ❏ Sexually Promiscuous
- ❏ Assaultive
- ❏ Depressed
- ❏ Rebellious
- ❏ Withdrawn

CLIENT'S CHECKLIST

Directions: Check any of the following that apply to you.

- ❑   Fainting, convulsions, seizures

- ❑   Weakness, paralysis, tremors

- ❑   Numbness, tinglings, "pins and needles" feelings

- ❑   Trouble walking, limping, balance or coordination

- ❑   Worried, upset, tense

- ❑   Always angry, bad temper

- ❑   Poor sleeping, bad or weird dreams

- ❑   Lonely, afraid

- ❑   Feeling "blue," depressed

- ❑   Thinking of suicide

- ❑   Trouble thinking

- ❑   Sexual problems (problems with erection, ejaculation, loss of desire)

- ❑   Memory problems

- ❑   Drinking problems

- ❑   Drug problems

- ❑   Always tired, fatigue

_____ Other

13
WORKING AROUND DENIAL TO FACILITATE CHANGE:
Contingency Management As A Behavioral Control For The Offender

The following discussion does not apply to the male offender who readily admits to his offenses, who demonstrates overt guilt and remorse, and who is desirous of immediate treatment to facilitate relief from neurotic misery caused by incestuous abuse. (This type of offender appears to be rare.)

Usually offenders do not voluntarily enter treatment.* They are pressured into it by the legal system or by wives threatening to disrupt the home if changes are not forthcoming. Hence, it is unrealistic for therapists to expect an open, self-confessional approach from men coerced into treatment, men whose lives have been permeated by denial and projection of responsibility. Clinicians find themselves expected to treat a client population composed of hostile, frightened, denying men who are anxious and angry because their lives have been disrupted and because they fear incarceration. Projection and denial are exacerbated in the face of accusations. The situation created is unusual in that, in their training,

---

*Recent research has raised serious doubts regarding the advisability of treating sex offenders still entrenched in denial. In reality, however, especially in situations where victim credibility is questioned, offenders often remain at home, forcing practitioners to deal pragmatically with less-than-ideal family constellations.

clinicians have been imbued with a mind-set that neurotic suffering is a motivating and necessary ingredient for successful therapy and that the presenting problem as stated by the client is the expected introduction to the therapeutic process.

Flexibility and some degree of innovation are required on the part of the therapist treating an unwilling client. The therapist may be asked temporarily to disown his/her own value system and genuinely begin where the client is, even if the client consciously and verbally denies the importance (or existence) of incestuous abuse. To confront such a client prematurely regarding ego-alien behaviors on his part is to frighten, alienate and possibly exacerbate such behaviors in the face of iatrogenic stress. The advocated approach is a three-fold one involving:

1. evaluation of potentiality for effective therapy;
2. zeroing in on workable, client-determined issues for behavior change; and
3. (despite possible denial) establishing the behavioral controls both mandated and necessary for the protection of minors involved.

Evaluating the Potential for Effective Therapeutic Outcomes

This evaluation process is essential for three reasons. First, the therapist has an ethical responsibility to treat the treatable. Second, because incestuous abuse is illegal, professionals are mandated to report all forms of it; hence, the likelihood of recidivism is of major concern both therapeutically and legally. Finally, caseworkers in state agencies are notoriously known to be overworked, with burgeoning client populations. Often social service workers do not have the time to evaluate offenders as carefully as required before referring for on-going therapy.

The previous section provides an evaluation procedure to assess client accountability for growth in the therapeutic situation. The main issue is that identification of character disorder must be followed by caution and realism when attempting to treat the personality type recognized as pedophilic. The evaluation should be approached tactfully but very thoroughly. If change is not likely, the clinician may terminate therapeutic intervention and find it necessary to refer the offender back to the state monitoring agency for possible restraining action.

Zeroing in on Issues: Determining the Degree of Covert Neurotic Misery and Issues Around Which This Misery Focuses

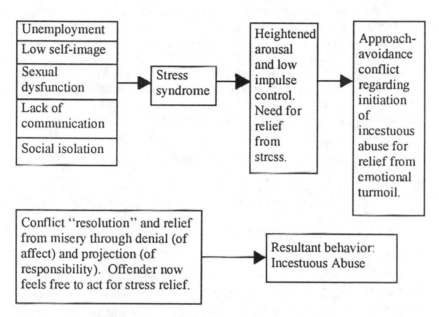

It already has been established that it is the uncommon offender who openly acknowledges he is suffering because of his involvement in incestuous abuse. However, incestuous abuse often is symptomatic of any number of underlying stresses that have precipitated the abuse and caused a degree of neurotic suffering sufficient to motivate the desire for change. It is around these issues, some of which are identified below, that therapeutic goals center:

Awareness of the characteristics of typical offenders and their families facilitates focusing on key issues. Awareness and knowledge alone, however, are not sufficient. The therapist must determine the value the offender has invested in changing problem areas of his life. The process of determining the relative weight of the offender's values is, in itself, therapeutic, for the client begins to focus on his desire to claim his own needs and to commit himself to change. A series of open-ended inquiries in the form of either a written or verbal questionnaire, or informal interjections throughout initial therapy contacts, serves to clarify values for the client. Some general questions to ask include the following.

1. What does the client want most in life?
2. Where does he see himself in five years? Ten years?
3. What career aspirations does he have?
4. Which is more important to him, family life or economic security?
5. How does he like to spend Saturday nights?
6. What is the worst/best thing his son or daughter could do?
7. At what time was he happiest? What was occurring in his life at the time?
8. How important does he feel sex is in married life?
9. What is a friend? What does he value in friendship?
10. How does he manage money?
11. How would he react if his wife had an affair?
12. What quality is most important to him in a spouse?
13. How does he define "crime?"
14. What is the best/poorest decision he has made and why?
15. What does he want his obituary to say about him?
16. Who in his life has influenced him the most? How?
17. What expectations (of himself, of others) has he met or failed to meet?
18. What major crises or turning points has he experienced?
19. What reaction does he have to alcohol or drug abuse?
20. How does he describe a successful person?
21. How does he describe himself?

Once the process of values clarification is completed, the therapist can begin to help the offender focus on concrete behavioral change in key areas.

Often at this stage it is helpful to formulate therapeutic goals in a contractual form to enhance both client accountability and sense of responsibility (the by-product of which is increased self-esteem) and to give added assurance to the therapist of a commitment on the client's part. A simple behavioral contract contains the following elements.

1. Client's name (first person).
2. Task or change to accomplish.
3. Reason for task or change.
4. Date change is to be effected.

A sample contract would read as follows:

I, John Doe, will attend Dr. X's on-going workshop on Sexual Dysfunction to facilitate an understanding of my relationship with my wife. I will begin attendance on the first day, August 5, and will complete the full sequence, ending October 10.

Signed _____
(Client's signature)

Clearly, the therapist's approach is orientated toward behavior change and growth. Of utmost importance, however, is the alliance formed between the therapist and client, which must be based on trust, warmth, support and empathy. Acceptance, conveyed by the therapist through clarification of affect and reflection, is essential to a process that is non-confronting and aims at validation of the client as a unique and worthwhile human being.

The Rogerian model is advocated for use with the client who denies incestuous abuse (but who is not deemed to be an antisocial personality) largely because of the negative feelings such a client harbors about himself. For such an offender admission would constitute an unbearable disclosure of his safely-guarded ego-alien core. Only with an understanding and accepting therapeutic approach that leads to self-validation will the client begin to improve his self-image, experience hope, and derive the required strength and courage to make changes.

Establishing Behavioral Controls

During the time that the therapeutic process unfolds, it is important to establish behavioral controls for the offender. The therapist is responsible for helping to ensure the safety of any minors involved. When denial continues to operate and the crime of incest is not dealt with directly by the therapist, dissonance and stress involving the possibility of further criminal behavior will persevere.

Behavioral controls can be instituted directly or covertly. Because denial is so deeply entrenched in this type of client, it is sometimes possible for the therapist to prevent negative reactions by avoiding direct use of the word incest while instituting behavioral controls with positive directions, such as "You are not to touch the daughter at any time," and to receive no negative reaction as long as incest is not labeled directly.

A contractual commitment to weekly or semi-weekly therapy can contribute to additional control. Also, it is usually possible to form an agreement that the wife, victim-daughter or other siblings in the home will inform the therapist of (potential) incestuous abuse. The client can be informed that his family will contact the agency if difficulties arise. Finally, the offender should be informed that therapy is available to help him and his family, but that in the event that changes are not forthcoming, the authorities will be notified.

Case History

Jane, 30, called in tears to state that she just had learned that her husband of two years, Bill, 29, had engaged in digital penetration of her 12-year-old daughter, Christie, the night before. She stated that Christie told her about the incident after school and Jane was calling "as soon as possible to get help for Bill."

A. Background Information and Family History

During the initial intake, Jane and Christie were seen alone and together. The history I obtained from Jane revealed the following relevant background data:

1. A product of a broken marriage, Jane wed her first husband at 16 "to escape" from the multiple dysfunction present in her natural home. The marriage lasted nine years during which time her husband physically abused both Christie and Russ, now 13.

2. Shortly after Jane's divorce, she met Bill who also came from a broken home. He had a lengthy juvenile record involving numerous misdemeanors. Bill had been diagnosed as hyperactive as a youngster and had seen numerous counselors and probation officers over the years.

3. Jane and Bill lived together for three years during which time they experienced financial stresses but were compatible sexually and emotionally. Christie never liked Bill, always hoping that her natural parents would reunite, but Russ idolized his stepfather, an expert in karate.

4. Following their marriage two years ago, Jane began to experience a declining sexual interest. The change for her began after Bill returned home one day with semen on his crotch, convincing Jane that he had committed adultery although he denied any extramarital involvements.

5. Jane stated that the first indication of any "trouble" between Bill and Christie occurred two months before when she saw her husband fondle the girl's buttocks. Christie confirmed the fact that she, too, first felt uneasy with Bill at that time and that he since had fondled her breasts twice. The trend had culminated in Bill's current criminal offense.

B. Evaluation and Treatment

The first session resulted in data gathering, rapport building and clarification of the necessity to notify Child Protective Services of the occurrence of child molest. The family chose not to press changes but agreed to have Christie spend her nights at a friend's home until Bill could be seen for an assessment two days later.

The information I obtained from Bill corroborated that given by his wife and stepdaughter, with one glaring exception. Bill claimed that he "never touched Christie." He was sensitive about the issue and seemed less concerned about legal repercussions than about the act itself. When asked what it would mean if he had, in his own words, "touched Christie," he replied, "It would mean I was a filthy pervert."

A complete history was obtained and an informal battery of assessment instruments was used to facilitate the evaluation. Bill was given the Moral-Amoral Self-Rating Scale, the Client's Checklist and the Draw-A-Person Test, and he was rated on the Therapist's Checklist. (See end of chapter for results.)

I formulated a composite personality profile of this young man, on the basis of information elicited by various instruments used and from personal interviews with him and his family. The Moral-Amoral Rating Scale revealed low impulse control, anger, rationalization, projection, denial, inability to tolerate criticism or confrontation, and action orientation. Still, there were indications that Bill experienced some degree of guilt and remorse regarding his actions (see responses to questions #2, #6, and #7). The Client's Checklist indicated a high level of depression and anxiety. The Therapist's Checklist and the Draw-A-Person (see interpretation following the drawing) corroborated these impressions.

Even though denial of incestuous abuse appeared to be a deeply entrenched defense, Bill was deemed suitable for the therapeutic setting. Positive factors indicated in the profile included motivation to change, i.e., the desire for help and the willingness to commit himself to therapy; the presence of guilt regarding actions he nonetheless refused openly to admit, and the emergence of key issues around which the therapeutic process could focus. Among the most pressing issues for Bill were the following: desire to maintain family unity and strengthen marital ties through improved communication; need for improved sexual relations with his wife; presence of low self-image exacerbating anxiety and depression; and the fact that the entire family was socially isolated.

The first and second issues were approached initially through joint communication sessions with Bill and Jane. "I-messages" and assertiveness training were used to help Jane and Bill clarify their needs and request changes from each other. Of prime concern was the fact that Jane described Bill's sexual approach to her in the last year as rape. He, in turn, found his wife cold and rejecting. It was clarified for the couple that they had set up a no-win situation where Bill's approach alienated Jane and this, in turn, increased Bill's frustration, sense of impotence, and need to force his attention on her. The result was total withdrawal on Jane's part.

Improvements in the couple's sexual relationship was evident within weeks, with the use of autogenic relaxation techniques (Jane), sensate focus, and bibliotherapy. Of particular value to this couple were: The Joy of Sex: A Gourmet Guide to Love Making (Comfort, A., New York: Simon and Schuster, 1972); How to Stay Married (Lobsenz, N.M. and Blackburn, C. Greenwich, CT: Fawcett Publications, Inc., 1972); and Intimate Feedback: A Lover's Guide to Getting In Touch with Each Other (Hobson, B. and Hobson, C. New York: Simon and Schuster, 1975). Hobson and Hobson's exercises were especially helpful in diffusing anxiety by providing structure for at-home hours at times of stress while enhancing both physical and emotional intimacy.

Bill's low self-image and the couple's social isolation were the next areas of concern. Bill agreed to register for one course at a local community college and he became a black belt karate instructor three nights per week at a small school in town. Jane found part-time employment.

It should be emphasized that these changes were possible not only because Bill and Jane invested heavily in maintaining their marriage but because of the tacit, implicit threat of involvement of the authorities if changes were not forthcoming. During the months of therapy, Bill was seen at least once weekly alone or with a family member, as per a contractual arrangement with me. Additional behavioral controls were established by the formation of my alliance with Christie who, with Bill's knowledge, was advised to contact me at any time she felt discomfort in her stepfather's presence. Finally, for the first four weeks of therapy, Christie was not left alone with Bill for any length of time and especially not during the evening hours when previous incidents of molesting had occurred. At no time, however, was Bill confronted regarding his actions. The therapeutic approach, following that of Carl Rogers, was warm, empathic and supportive.

C. Follow-up

Six months following the occurrence of incestuous abuse the problem had not recurred. The prognosis seemed favorable and if difficulties again arose, it was likely that the family would seek outside intervention since they already had one successful therapeutic experience. Therapeutic interventions were judged effective in this case despite continuing denial of illegal, incestuous actions on the part of the offender.

On the following pages, Bill's evaluation process through use of the Moral-Amoral Self-Rating Scale checklists and Draw-A-Person test are reproduced with his responses recorded.

MORAL-AMORAL SELF-RATING SCALE

Directions: Place a check mark by one or more of the responses that apply to you.

1. When I make a mistake, I
   - _____ go back and try again
   - _____ admit it
   - _√_ try to cover it up
   - _____ pass the blame on to others
   - _√_ lose my temper
   - _____ figure that I really did not make a mistake at all
   - _____ usually realize that it was someone's and not my fault.

2. When I tell a lie, I
   - _____ get physically or emotionally ill
   - _____ realize that it is okay and that I had a good reason to lie
   - _√_ immediately regret it
   - _√_ feel guilty and/or sorry
   - _____ don't even think about it
   - _____ dislike myself

3.   If my boss tells me I am performing poorly on the job, I
___√___   feel angry and disgusted
_____   try to do a better job
_____   want to get back at him
_____   feel downcast, hurt or upset
_____   lose my temper
_____   hope something terrible happens to him
_____   brood for days
_____   quit the job
___√___   lie to cover up the work I have been doing
_____   explain why my work is not as good as usual
_____   invite him to dinner or for a drink, hoping to change his mind

4.   When my spouse (girl/boyfriend) asks me to do something I dislike but which needs to be done, I
_____   do it anyway to please her/him
___√___   get angry and "lose my cool"
_____   tell her/him to do it her/himself
_____   do it but feel angry and hope her (his) day goes wrong

5.   When I have done something wrong to someone or hurt another person, I
_____   apologize and genuinely regret it
_____   really do not care one way or another
_____   feel basically that the person deserved it
___√___   hide what I did or deny what I said
_____   worry a lot that the person will not like me
_____   feel that I learned something and will try not to repeat the error again
___√___   make believe that it did not happen

6.   Stealing is
___√___   wrong or immoral
_____   okay if the thief is not caught
___√___   scary
_____   likely to cause the thief much guilt and worry
_____   okay because society is a "rip-off" anyway
_____   only wrong because laws are set up to punish thieves

7.   The best way to handle people is to
_____   do whatever is necessary to get what you need from them
_____   be charming so they will like you and do what you want them to

_____ be honest and genuine
__√__ hide your true feelings because people cannot be trusted

8. Basically, people are

_____ out to get you
_____ friendly and genuine
__√__ interested only in themselves
__√__ not to be trusted
_____ willing to help and do what they can for others
_____ just human, with qualities and faults

9. If I were having serious marital problems, I would

_____ talk it over with friends, family, minister or counselor
_____ take a good look at myself and my spouse to see which areas in our life need attention
__√__ punish my spouse
_____ send my spouse to a counselor
_____ realize that marriage never works anyway
_____ try to make my spouse understand where he/she went wrong
_____ realize that she/he won't change anyway and it is best to seek a quick divorce and get on with my life
_____ try to communicate with my wife/husband about our problems and then seek outside help if necessary

10. The best way to handle problems is to

?

_____ leave the scene as fast as possible
_____ realize that I am not to blame anyway
_____ take action immediately
_____ stop, think and try to figure out solutions

11. Under pressure, I feel

_____ at my best, performing at high level
__√__ much anxiety and need to act fast for relief
__√__ tense and unable to handle the situation
_____ tense but able to perform
_____ capable of doing what is required
_____ unable to perform

12. The adage, a bird in the hand is worth two in the bush, is best explained by the following:

?

_____ get what you can out of life no matter what it takes or whom it hurts

_____ be careful taking risks as you may have something worthwhile to lose

_____ guard what you have at all costs

_____ dreamers are fools

13. When criticized, I

√ immediately feel angry and defensive

_____ want revenge against the person criticizing me

√ feel hurt and disliked

_____ am downcast and depressed

_____ often realize I need to change

_____ know that criticism is meant only to hurt others

14. The use of alcohol is

_____ a sin

_____ fine in moderation

√ an excellent way to relieve stress and relax

√ a way to escape from troubles

_____ a personal matter and people can drink as much or as little as they like

_____ basically dangerous to health and to the safety of other people

_____ one of the best ways to get rid of frustration and anger.

15. The best way to discipline a child is to

_____ hit and spank

_____ lock the child in his/her room

√ act immediately and naturally, even if the action is explosive

_____ take the strongest measures possible because children act badly to hurt their parents

_____ reason with the child

_____ use a variety of consequences including withdrawing special rewards

CLIENT'S CHECKLIST

Directions: Check any of the following that apply to you.

_____	Fainting, convulsions, seizures
_____	Weakness, paralysis, tremors
_____	Numbness, tinglings, "pins and needles" feelings
_____	Trouble walking, limping, balance or coordination
__√__	Worried, upset, tense
_____	Always angry, bad temper
_____	Poor sleeping, bad or weird dreams
__√__	Lonely, afraid
__√__	Feeling "blue," depressed
_____	Thinking of suicide
__√__	Trouble thinking
_____	Sexual problems (problems with erection, ejaculation, loss of desire)
_____	Memory problems
__?__	Drinking problems
_____	Drug problems
_____	Always tired, fatigue

_____ Other

THERAPIST'S CHECKLIST

(Check characteristics that apply to client.)

Extreme Nervousness	Inaccessible
√ Fearful	Apathetic
Nervous tics	√ Evasive
Inhibited	√ Low Self-Esteem
Despondent	√ Lack of Initiative
Uncooperative	√ Projecting
Inattentive	Tendency to Physical Violence
Evasive	√ Self-defeating
√ Shy	Inability to Relate
Self-conscious	√ Hostile
Antagonistic	Cynical
√ Insecure	Sexually Promiscuous
√ Tense	Assaultive
Irritable	√ Depressed
Defensive	Rebellious
√ Denying	Withdrawn
√ Low Degree Frustration Tolerance	

CLIENT'S DRAW-A-PERSON RESPONSE

Description:

There is a floating male figure with fairly heavy shading and arms akimbo. Hands are hidden behind the back. Face is three-quarters profile. Eyes are poorly delineated. Upper torso and head are more shaded than lower part of the body.

Interpretation:

There are several indicators of strong and severe feelings of insecurity, dependency needs and inadequacy, along with signs of inadequate adjustment. The placement is off center and the hands are hidden. The legs are floating and the stance is slanting. Compensatory defenses are evident in the placement while anxiety is seen in the stroking and shading. Hostility and guilt are revealed by the closed eyes. Virility strivings are seen in the emphasis of the hair. Impulsivity is evident by the omitted neck, and compensatory feelings of weakness and possible social inadequacy are revealed by the emphasis on the chin.

14
BREAKING DOWN THE COMPONENTS OF AFFECTIVE REACTIONS: ALTERNATE STRESS MANAGEMENT TECHNIQUES

The treatment model proposed here is designed for a specific but common type of incestuous offender — the regressed male with identifiable precipitating stresses and identifiable affective reactions resulting from stress. According to Groth (1978) adult sexual offenders against the young can be categorized according to whether or not their sexual involvement with children is preferred (fixed) or only resorted to under stress (regressed).

Since this model is based on learning theory and contains a number of cognitive elements, the study is further limited to the treatment of offenders whose reality contact is fairly intact and whose capacity for insight and self-awareness is fairly adequate.

The rationale for focusing attention on precipitating stresses with resultant emotional reactions is based on the importance of identifying the motivation behind incestuous abuse. The treatment process will reach an impasse if a diagnostic assessment of motivation is not completed. Such an assessment can be achieved once it is understood that the motivation for sexual abuse results from a combination of precipitating intrapsychic and situational stresses with resultant affective and behavioral manifestations.

Assessment Data

The model proposes a three-stage educational and experiential program for bringing about an understanding of stress, breaking down or compartmentalizing affective reactions, and finally instituting behavioral change. Before the process can begin, however, the therapist must understand the psychological and personality adjustment problems of the offenders, the current stresses, and finally the predictable results both affectively and behaviorally.

A typical regressed offender may have a variety of personality adjustment problems including poor impulse control, immaturity, low frustration tolerance, poor self-esteem, limited adaptive capacities and interpersonal difficulties. Stresses compounding life-coping skills may include an irregular employment history, financial strain, marital difficulties, family overcrowding and social isolation. Psychologically, the offender has unresolved intrapsychic conflicts that customarily have been repressed or displaced. Given this background of personality adjustment, psychological and situational difficulties, it is easy to understand how any increase in intrapsychic or situational stress can result in an erosion of the defense structure, with resultant emotional turmoil and deviant acting out to relieve internal pressures.

The Model

The model is derived from learning theorists, primarily Donald Meichenbaum and Dennis Turk (1976). It is proposed because of its simplicity, its easy comprehensibility for the offender, and its focus on behavioral change for problem areas in the client's customary mode of functioning. The basic approach is to treat cognitions along with behaviors through a three-phase program of stress inoculation.

The first phase is educational. The client is provided with a conceptual framework to understand the nature of stress and resultant reactions. Stress produces physiological arousal and is exacerbated by self-defeating thoughts. Once the offender fully comprehends the nature of his physiological reactions, he is instructed in methods for the control of stress reactions, alternate ways to perceive and respond to stress and the substitution of positive self-coping phrases and affirmations for self-defeating thoughts that may cause, contribute to, and exacerbate stress.

The second phase involves rehearsal of behaviors and cognitive coping skills. The offender practices appraising reality and controlling negative thoughts through substitution. He acknowledges and relabels arousal and practices alternate modes of stress management.

The final or third phase allows the offender to test and practice new learned skills in real-life situations.

Case Illustration

Nineteen-year-old Frank was treated following a single incident of forced fellatio with his four-year-old brother. An abbreviated analysis of the situation revealed the following diagnostic data:

1. *Personality Adjustment Problems:* Frank had a lengthy history of weak impulse control and low frustration tolerance, as evidenced by a number of factors including a violent temper, poor school adjustment and several minor infringements with the law — notably truancy, violation of curfew and shoplifting. He dropped out of high school during his senior year and held five different jobs between his seventeenth and nineteenth year. Frank lived with his parents and siblings in a home characterized by massive family dysfunction related to his father's alcoholism and chronic unemployment and also to his parent's continual fighting. Three of Frank's five siblings were experiencing difficulties in school and two had been adjudicated incorrigible by the courts. In this strife-ridden environment Frank had a very poor self-image exacerbated by his own chronic history of personal failure.

2. *Psychological Factors:* At the age of five, Frank had been sexually assaulted by an uncle who forced him to perform fellatio. Two subsequent episodes of forced fellatio with older adolescent boys occurred when Frank was eleven and thirteen. Frank remembered these incidents in considerable detail although he avoided recall because of the feelings of anger and guilt that remembering aroused in him. Sexually, Frank described himself as "all male" with a strong heterosexual

orientation.   In reality, he had experienced considerable frustration and rejection by female companions.

3. *Precipitating Situational Stress:*   Just prior to the incestuous assault of his brother, Frank had been fired from his fifth job for poor performance.   At the same time, his sister, recently separated from her husband, joined the household with her two young daughters.   Frank was forced to share a room with his two teenage brothers which entailed a disturbing loss of privacy.

The diagnostic data revealed considerable chronic and precipitating stress for this emotionally unstable young man whose reaction to crisis was characterized by a reactivation of conflicts related to the trauma of early sexual assault.   Under stress, Frank re-experienced early trauma, partly by protecting himself against imagined threats through identification with the aggressor.   The act against his brother was an aggressive, forced assault precipitated by anger.

Frank's reality contact and capacity for insight were deemed adequate although his intellectual and educational limitations necessitated a reality-based, concrete orientation to therapy.   The first step in the treatment process was to outline in easily comprehensible terms the various stresses in Frank's life.   The process was educational, relying heavily on concrete, simplified explanations of the arousal mechanism and the fight-flight reaction and their relationship to stress.   Physiological reactions were related to life crisis using the Holmes-Rath Triggering Events Rating Scale to tabulate Frank's stress points over the previous year with the resultant prediction of emotional and/or physical distress.

Frank was shown how a stress overload for him resulted in a particular affective reaction which he, himself, labelled "anger."   Anger precipitated the incestuous assault of his brother, anger so intense that Frank barely remembered the incident, which had followed a minor family dispute.   Frank was able to break down his anger into the following stages, which I helped him outline and label.

1. A painful, disturbing event (job loss, loss of privacy) leading to the onset of conscious projection and generalization characterized by thoughts of failure and "casting blame outward."

2. A general state of malaise and free-floating anxiety.

3. A strong desire to seek revenge.

4. A state of heightened stress resulting in a need to seek relief through action.

Once the anger reaction was compartmentalized, Frank understood that at any point on the continuum prior to the final stage, he could stop the progress of arousal by cognitively and behaviorally assuming control of his affective state through altering both activities and thought patterns.

After Frank had integrated a solid conceptual framework of the arousal mechanism and the resultant anger he experienced, he was able to work on a program of rechanneling thoughts and activities and of practicing alternate stress management through simplified relaxation techniques. He was shown how his inner tapes consisted of negative, depressing and self-defeating thoughts related to his sense of inadequacy and personal failure. Frank listed as many of these thoughts and phrases that ran through (his) head during a typical day as he could recall, along with their opposites in the form of positive affirmations. Phrases such as, "I goofed again," and, "That guy is a jerk," were transformed into positive words denoting hope and change such as, "I think I can do better next time," and, "I can handle him differently."

The second and third phases of the treatment model involved rehearsals and application in the environment. These phases followed in rapid succession. Considerable progress was noted in life-coping skills and reduced anxiety. The model was particularly appropriate for this offender because situational factors were not likely to change drastically and hence the acquisition of new coping skills was deemed a necessity.

SECTION D
THE FAMILY

15
A BEHAVIORAL RE-ENGINEERING APPROACH TO FAMILY DYSFUNCTION AND SOCIAL ISOLATION

The behavioral re-engineering approach provides a useful model to therapists of family disruption. The model involves preliminary insight work for the family followed by systematic behavioral therapy for each member. Monitoring is necessary for a period of time (six months to one year) to insure maintenance of change patterns. The use of this model does not preclude the possibility of, and need to, work on other therapeutic issues concomitantly.

Three almost universal problems among incest families are misplaced needs for nurturance, role confusion and social isolation. These issues will be the focus of behavioral re-engineering here.

Preliminary Insight Therapy

A system of behavioral re-engineering should not be instituted in the home until the motivation to change has been explored. Factors involved in motivation for change include (a) external pressure from legal ramifications, (b) internal pressure (need to maintain status quo) and (c) the client's degree of insight into intrafamily relationships. Families who gain insights into their mutually destructive ways of relating to one another are more apt to alter patterns for an increased sense of emotional well-being and healthy functioning.

Insight work into misplaced needs for nurturance and role confusion requires understanding of how need satisfaction has operated in the home. An example of this follows.

Mother's needs have not been met. Unable or unwilling to be assertive, she chose to meet her needs through the defenses of sublimation, suppression and denial. Father's needs, also unmet, were expressed passive-aggressively and displaced onto his daughter. The victim's needs were ignored and exploited. Thus, in general, each member's needs were thwarted and family patterns of behavior were regressed, resulting in child-to-child interactions. Mother reacted to Father with the primitive childlike defense of denial both of incest and of his needs. Father reacted to Mother in an equally regressed manner, with revengeful passive-aggressive behavior. In a sense, Mother played the role of "hurt little girl" and Father played "nasty little boy" while the child was the victim of both, forced into the dual role of family protector and spouse.

The important issue to stress in insight work involving misplaced needs for nurturance and role confusion is that the family's pattern of interaction was dysfunctional. In the end, no member's needs were met in a satisfying, healthy or productive way.

Insight work regarding social isolation as a contributing factor is relatively simple. The enmeshed triad is isolated from the start. Later, the existence of antisocial behavior within the family quickly leads to shame, feelings of alienation and fear of disclosure. In order to cope with these feelings and in order to perpetuate the enmeshment that exists within the family, members become even more isolated and socially withdrawn. Social activities are curtailed and friendships dissipate.

Once insight work is completed regarding the dysfunctional aspects of the three target behaviors (misplaced needs for nurturance, role confusion and social isolation), the therapist is ready to help family members begin to effect healthy behavioral changes. The three behaviors can be dealt with simultaneously with a systematic approach of re-engineering, summarized below.

Outline for Behavioral Change for Target Behaviors

A.   *Problems:* Target problems are misplaced needs for nurturance, role confusion and social isolation.

B.   *Goals:* Alternate behaviors are taught to help the family meet needs in healthy and productive ways and to alter dysfunctional behavioral patterns.

C.   *Steps for meeting goals:*
   1.   Therapy for family members is instituted, involving sexual dysfunction counseling for parents and effective communication skills training (assertiveness training) for the entire family.
   2.   The social-emotional support system is expanded in order to diffuse needs and allow for gratification of needs in alternate, socially acceptable ways.
   3.   Stress management techniques are taught.

D.   *Methods:*
   1.   A sexual history highlights areas of dysfunction that require intervention.
   2.   Therapy includes family and individual work on a weekly or semi-weekly basis with objectives clearly elaborated.
   3.   Assertiveness training is taught systematically, with in-session and at-home practice required.
   4.   Behavioral changes designed to enhance and expand the social life of family members are specified. The victim might join the girl scouts or a skating or drama club. The mother might choose to re-activate specific friendships or make one new friend a month through her job, the church or P.T.A. The father can set similar goals. Either or both parents might become involved in job training or re-entry academic programs.
   5.   Stress management is taught through the use of educational materials, bibliotherapy and tapes. The family is instructed in systematic deep muscle relaxation, autogenic relaxation techniques or similar methods for in-session and at-home practice.

The Contract Approach

For each behavioral change specified, a contract is devised to insure implementation and measure progress. Since the three target behaviors overlap, they can be worked on simultaneously. However, no more than two or three behaviors should be focused on at the same time. For example, a couple might contract to work on one aspect of their social life while simultaneously working on a single area of sexual dysfunction.

The contract can be verbal or written, but it must be as specific as possible. Each contract should be stated or written in the form of "I-messages" to stress the client's ownership of the problem and to emphasize accountability for change. The contract should include the problem, the goal, the method toward reaching that goal, and the time allotted or estimated for evidence of measurable change. Below is a contract devised by the author for working with one couple in therapy:

Contract for Behavioral Change

1. *The Problem*

   I, _____ (the silent partner) am non-responsive sexually to _____ (offender). I, _____ (offender)   have   been   insensitive   to _____'s (silent partner's) sexual needs and wants.

2. *The Goals*

   I, _____ (the silent partner) want to become more sexually responsive. I, _____ (offender) want to become more sensitive to my wife's sexual needs and wants.

3. *The Method*

   I, _____ (silent partner) and I, _____ (offender) will practice the method of sensate focus as instructed in therapy.

4. *Time estimated for evidence of measurable change*

   We, _____ and, _____ (both partners) will practice sensate focus three to four times weekly at night for two weeks and will report briefly during each therapy session regarding progress and/or problems encountered.

The contract provides incentive and specifies problems, goals and methods. The approach may appear to be complicated, since the family is working to improve three major areas of functioning via several contracts for behavioral change for each area. In actuality, it is a simple, progressive and systematic method with built-in provisions for accountability and measurable change.

16
CONFRONTATION ON HIDDEN AGENDAS IN THE FAMILY

Hidden agendas abound in families whose members have been involved in the abnormal expression and gratification of sexual needs. In therapy for such families, confrontation regarding the hidden agendas is crucial to resolution of underlying issues and implementation of long-term behavioral changes.

Some therapists refuse to confront clients because of the risks involved. Improperly timed or moderated confrontation can result in resistance, severe agitation or withdrawal for the poorly integrated client. In addition, some clients, especially those who characteristically use projection as a defense mechanism, may react with hostility to confrontation and terminate the therapeutic process.

Also, some clinicians are reluctant to confront because of their own unresolved psychological pitfalls such as 1) sadistic tendencies and impulses which are (unconsciously) guarded against by the use of reaction formation in therapeutic encounters; 2) need for ego gratification to be derived from the client's approval and acceptance; and 3) emotional blocking that impairs ability to act affectively or tolerate affective reactions from others. Since confrontation can be a vital aspect of individual, group and family therapy, these difficulties must be resolved before the therapist can be effective with victims, offenders and silent partners.

Confrontation may be used in family therapy when certain conditions are present. Each member should be assessed as having sufficient ego strength to bear confrontation, coupled with a capacity for insight. A high level of trust should have been established with the therapist. Finally, family members must be supportive of one another and ready to face underlying issues.

Issues Requiring Confrontation

Each family in therapy presents its own set of hidden agendas. As the therapist gains knowledge of family dynamics she/he will uncover the issues that the family systematically avoids. Typical incestuous families, however, share common hidden agendas known (subconsciously) to each member but neither faced directly nor verbalized. Some typical patterns found in hidden agendas are identified and discussed below.

1. *Mother Really Knew.* Victims generally suspect that their mothers were aware of the incestuous relationship that they shared with their fathers. If asked directly, a victim will admit to suspicions that the mother was a covert participant in the triad, citing innumerable instances in which suspicion regarding parental conspiracy was present.

On the extreme end of the continuum are situations where mothers witnessed sexual intercourse between their daughters and husbands and subsequently denied it. One ten-year-old wondered what her mother was doing when her father entered her (the child's) bedroom for 20 to 30 minutes each night. Another young victim recalled her mother entering the room as her father was zipping up following forced fellatio.

It is important for victims to confront silent partners regarding their persistent and deep denial. Such confrontation is quite effective in family work because the father-daughter alliance provides a strong catalyst to force the mother to deal with past realities that she effectively has blocked for years. Victims begin to perceive family relationships in clearer perspective as the father no longer totally assumes a "bad guy" role.

Victims who are unable to confront their mothers regarding the denial of incest can suffer very serious emotional consequences. A double-bind situation results when the victim perceives an unexplained paradox: Mother, the protector, acted indifferently when the victim needed her most and then denied all knowledge of what she openly witnessed or surely suspected. The anger that the victim feels toward her mother is deep and unresolved. One client, an 18-year-old victim of long-term incest, was hospitalized for severe depression with (transient) psychotic features. The significant element that emerged in follow-up therapy in a sexual assault group was not the fact that she had sexual relations with her father, but, rather, the anger that she harbored toward her mother for repeatedly witnessing incest and subsequently denying all knowledge of the father-daughter relationship during court hearings.

2. *Why Me?* A second issue concerning the victim relates to what she perceives as parental exploitation. The victim knows that her father has sexual needs which should be met by her mother. Instead, he chose to use her for sexual gratification. Mother allowed her to be used. Mother did not meet the father's needs and he did not seek to have those needs met by a surrogate adult partner.

The victim has a strong need to confront both parents regarding the issue of child exploitation. With the help of the therapist, she needs to face her father regarding her underlying self doubts. Victims question what they did to precipitate the abuse. Were they seductive? Was something intrinsically different about, or wrong with, them? Were they "bad?"

Here it is essential that confrontation be monitored and guided carefully by a skilled therapist. Confrontation must result in the father's acknowledgement of responsibility for his actions and in reassuring the victim that incest was not a result of anything that she said, did, felt or thought at any time. The victim should not be subjected to confrontation unless the therapist is confident that it will be resolved honestly, with full admission of guilt and responsibility on the father's part.

3. *Victim Enjoyment.* Some incest victims abhor the entire experience; others respond physically at times; and still others feel ambivalent regarding the emotional component involved in a close relationship with their fathers. Victims who have worked through the trauma often admit that the most difficult aspect of therapy for them was reaching a level of honesty where they could admit to themselves that there were enjoyable aspects in the incestuous relationship.

It is important to "clear the air" and establish a deep level of honesty on all levels. Hence, confrontation by the therapist

regarding victim enjoyment is effective in family therapy. However, confrontation on this issue should be mild and carefully
timed. Careful resolution is imperative to extinguish guilt for
the victim. The victim, offender and "silent partner" all must
realize that physical enjoyment of sexual contact relates to anatomy and to physiological response. On an emotional level, the
physical contact between the father and daughter may have been
the only manifestation of affection and demonstration of caring
that the victim ever experienced.

   If this issue is not dealt with openly, the mother will continue to doubt and question the nature of her daughter's involvement with her father. Also the father will remain in doubt since
he may have been aware of a positive response from his child
which could have provided him with an additional excuse to
continue his actions and subsequently to rationalize them.

4. *Father's Revenge.* There are a number of motivating factors for
    incestuous involvement. One of them is revenge by a husband
    against an emotionally and physically indifferent spouse. The
    withdrawn and cold wife becomes a catalyst for the offender's
    actions. When revenge is deemed as a (partial) motive for
    incest, both partners (though primarily the offender) need
    confrontation in therapy.

      The offender must be confronted by the therapist and the
    wife on several issues simultaneously. He must realize the depth
    of his anger and how this anger was passive-aggressively dis-
    placed onto his daughter, an innocent family member. At the
    same time, he needs to understand that he bears full responsibil-
    ity for the manner in which he chose to cope with his wife's sex-
    ual indifference. What efforts did he make to help his wife
    overcome her indifference? Did he suggest that they seek pro-
    fessional help? In the face of rejection, did he turn to female
    adult companionship for sexual gratification, or to his own
    child?
      The mother needs to be confronted also by her spouse and
    therapist on the manner in which she chose to handle sexual dys-
    function. Did she communicate her emotional and physical
    needs to her husband? Did she seek counseling? On some level,
    did she suspect that the offender might turn his attention to their
    daughter when rejected by her?

5. *Father's Rationalizations.* Characteristically, offenders deny incestuous involvement. When they are forced to admit their actions, they continue to allow denial to operate in the form of minimization and rationalization. Therapists who work primarily with incest families are known to list, sometimes in stunned horror, the endless rationalizations that they hear from the offenders—rationalizations calculated to justify the incestuous behavior in which they were involved. Below is one such list.

"I wanted my daughter's first sexual experience to be good."

"The Bible said to go forth and procreate and I didn't want to be unfaithful."

"It was the alcohol. I didn't know what I was doing."

"She asked for it."

"It was her flimsy nighty."

"She said she wanted to wrestle with me all the time."

"It was dark and I thought she was my wife."

"I had a vasectomy so I knew she couldn't get pregnant."

"I wanted to protect her from all those perverts."

"I was only checking for breast cancer."

"My wife is frigid."

"I wanted to keep it in the family and not play around."

"I never went all the way and she loved it."

The variety of excuses verbalized by offenders is endless and each rationalization is designed to project blame and remove the onus of responsibility from the offender. Individual, group and family therapy involving the offender all require that he be confronted, often harshly, by each family member and by his therapist, on his denial and his resultant rationalizations.

The offender literally must be forced to realize that he bears full and complete responsibility for his actions. His wife and daughter need to hear him acknowledge that sense of responsibility. Hard confrontation often is necessary. One therapist turned to the offender and said, "You may not be able to control what it (the penis) does but you damn well can control where you put it!" Another therapist, equally firm in confronting the offender, told him that she didn't care if his daughter sat on his face naked. He still was responsible for initiating sex with a minor child.

6. *Playing Mom.*   Silent partners tend to abdicate the responsibilities of wife, mother, homemaker and sexual partner. It is not uncommon to find the silent partner working evenings or nights. She does not cook, clean nor care for the younger children. She is unavailable to her husband for private, intimate times or for sex. She is unavailable to her family to perform the responsibilities of homemaker and mother. The silent partner often subtly forces her daughter into those roles. The result is that the victim performs all of the chores, cares for the younger children and gradually begins to meet her father's emotional and physical needs.

In these cases, the mother rationalizes her behavior. She will claim that her marriage was failing and that she did not have the financial resources to be on her own; hence, she withdrew. Or she may claim that she only could find a night job and had "no idea" that her daughter was assuming her responsibilities.

The silent partner who rationalizes her behavior in this manner requires confrontation by both her daughter and her husband. She, like the offender, must reach a level of honesty where she is able to assume her share of responsibility for exploiting her daughter and for the incestuous abuse that occurred in the home.

Conclusion

The problems in incest families are interrelated. The relationships are enmeshed and complicated. Because of the all-pervasiveness of defenses such as rationalization and denial, and because of the complex family dynamics that have become solidified and that have met numerous secondary gains, resistance to change and insight is strong. Hence, confrontation often proves to be an effective therapeutic method to use when working with the triad.

SECTION E
THERAPY GROUPS

17
THE VICTIM GROUP

The victim group can be one of the most powerful and emotionally cathartic methods for treating incest. It is an invaluable method to help victims achieve two primary goals—goals that must be reached if they are to gain some semblance of emotional and sexual adjustment in their future lives. These goals for participants are: 1) to share their common experience with incest and thereby receive validation, understanding and support, and 2) to vent often deeply suppressed feelings surrounding that common experience.

Because members share a defined common experience and because goals are delineated clearly from the onset, there can be some flexibility in the manner of setting up a victim group, in the establishment of norms (whether the group is to be open or closed, length of the meetings, etcetera), and the composition of members. However, certain guidelines are necessary and will be the focus of this chapter.

Format and Group Composition

Due to the intensity of emotion in sexual assault groups, it is wise to adhere to a comfortable time limit for each of the meetings. For small groups, one and one-half to two hours is suggested. For larger groups, two to two and one-half hours is optimal, although variations are possible and sometimes necessary. Some therapists prefer to maintain closed groups where new members are not admitted. In closed groups, trust and confidentiality are easy to maintain and a level of intensity and closeness can occur in a relatively short length of time. However small, closed groups do not offer a great diversity of experience and can become quite ingrown. The emotional climate of the open, ongoing group often helps to diffuse some of the intensity and provide members with an opportunity to hear and empathize with a variety of experiences. On the other hand, members of open groups often are not screened carefully and repeated catharsis for each entering member can result in a constant atmosphere of emotional tension that precludes the possibility of in-depth work. Confidentiality is more difficult to guard in open groups and re-introductions of long-time members become tedious.

Regardless of whether the group is open or closed, it is preferable to conduct a group composed of members all of whom have experienced one form or another of sexual assault of else have been involved peripherally in sexual abuse. Mixed groups (containing some members who were getting divorced, others who were experiencing difficulties with sexual relationships, and others who were victims of incest) have proved to be successful. However, cohesion is established much more quickly and defenses are more easily by-passed, when all participants share similar problems. Rapport can be almost immediate. While self-disclosure is possible among relatives, it is wiser to include members who are strangers to one another and for whom the issue of maintaining confidentiality poses no problem. Ages can be mixed although pre-teenagers should not be included in an adult-teen group where insights come rapidly, catharsis often is powerful, and cognitive material is easily comprehensible.

One successful group in the author's experience consisted of the following membership: a fourteen-year-old who had been brutally assaulted by a stranger at age seven; a seventeen-year-old who had been sexually abused by her stepfather from ages eleven to thirteen; a thirteen-year-old who had experienced multiple stranger rape; a forty-two-year-old victim of father-daughter incest whose husband was a convicted child molester; and a thirty-five-year-old counselor who had been a victim of incest with her uncles from ages seven to fifteen. (Excluded from the group were two adults, victims of childhood incest, who showed paranoid tendencies and hysterical traits, respectively.) Members were chosen in part on the basis of their current level of functioning, the favorable prognosis for change for each one, and the over-all degree of emotional stability they demonstrated in behavioral and affective areas. The group was co-facilitated by two other leaders, a female therapist and a paraprofessional who had been involved in father-daughter incest between ages six and sixteen and who had worked through much of the trauma.

Confidentiality

In victim groups, confidentiality assumes great importance and needs frequent reinforcement. There is both a real and imaginary issue to consider here. For victims, the possibility of violation of confidentiality relates both to the trust issue and to the often real danger that any violation can pose.

Some victims are involved in the court process or have been threatened by the offender or believe that it is incumbent upon them to protect the offender. Hence, violations of confidentiality can endanger their lives, sense of security or future plans.

In an imaginary sense, victims often feel that they are betraying the offender by self-disclosure. Many victims never have told anyone about the offense, maintaining their secret for sometimes 20 to 30 years. Even though the father with whom she had experienced childhood incest was dead, one teenage victim, following disclosure in group, feared that the offender was lurking around every corner. So intensely do some victims relive the experience that, upon disclosure, they become like children, frightened of the dark, of all sudden gestures, and of male strangers. Feelings of insecurity are relieved and renewed trauma diminishes when victims find the group to be a confined safe place in which to self-disclose.

Facilitation

Most victims feel more comfortable with female therapists. The more unlike the offender the facilitator is, the more comfortable the victim feels. A male clinician can be introduced into the therapeutic process at specific times after a certain trust level has been established, especially to help work through specific issues such as those involving role plays between victim-offender or resolution of problems involving male-female sexuality.

Co-facilitation usually is necessary for several reasons. Victim groups often are powerful and unpredictable. Hence, backup support may be needed following particularly emotionally-charged sessions. In addition, co-therapists are needed for role plays and modeling. Finally, victims often are blocked and sometimes require hard confrontation to help break through their defenses. The process of confrontation is safer and more effective if one therapist assumes the role of "bad guy" (the confronter) while the other assumes a nurturing role following confrontation (the supporter).

Whenever possible, it is helpful to have group members who are at various stages of working through trauma. Members who have resolved initial stages of trauma are empathic in helping blocked victims and often can serve as paraprofessionals in facilitating therapy through modeling, self-disclosure and role plays.

In general, facilitation involves imagination, sensitivity and courage. The emotionally-charged atmosphere requires an experienced therapist who is aware of all interactions and who is facilitating and supporting each member toward beneficial growth. The therapist must be aware of the delicate choice between confronting the silent, withdrawn victim or allowing her to remain passive in group until she can gradually arrive at a state of readiness to deal with her underlying issues. Whenever confrontation is used, sufficient time should be allotted to process feelings afterwards. If confrontation has been particularly heavy, the victim should be assured of the therapist's availability for further processing during the interval between group meetings.

In one on-going group, a fourteen-year-old member had been silent for the first three weeks. Finally, members began to confront her regarding her feelings about her father with whom she had been involved in long-term incest from ages seven to twelve. The youngster's first response, which was "I feel sorry for him...I'm not angry," prompted the group to confront her more heavily, repeatedly asking her what she would do or say to her father if he came into the room at that very moment. I enlisted the aid of a male therapist who, following a briefing, entered the room and began to laugh at the girl, taunting her and telling her that she had enjoyed the sexual experiences with her father. Almost immediately, the victim lashed out at the male therapist, calling him a "fucking bastard" and screaming that she "hated his fuckin' cock." The male therapist continued his taunting while the girl began to strike him with a pillow provided by one of the group members. Her physical and emotional release lasted for ten minutes, ending with 45 minutes of processing her feelings with the support of both therapists and group members, several of whom cried as they identified with her intense reaction.

For several days thereafter, the youngster felt shaky, tense and irritable. She barely slept at night and feared that her father was following her everywhere even though he no longer lived in the same state. She was seen individually for support during this time. In the next group session, she spoke of sensing relief that "felt like a ton had been lifted from my back." Her overall demeanor was more assertive and she stated that she never had realized the intensity of the anger she felt toward her father.

There were repeated sessions involving role plays, letter writing and the like, all designed to allow this youngster to ventilate and to re-experience the original trauma. Once deeply suppressed feelings were released (anger, guilt, feelings of rejection, feelings of worthlessness) she was ready to deal with cognitive insights, many of which related to her impaired (promiscuous) relationships with a number of older boys.

Activities

The content of therapy in sexual abuse victim groups will vary depending on the readiness of members to deal either cognitively or experientially. The ideal group should afford members with an opportunity for experiential work followed by the assimilation of cognitive insights. Almost all of the exercises and techniques contained in this book are suitable for group work. Hence, only a few techniques, particularly appropriate for victim groups, will be highlighted.

Role plays are used extensively in group. They often occur spontaneously and usually involve situations with victims' offenders or with victims' mothers. Sometimes a level of resolution can be reached when the victim role-plays confrontation with the "real" parent. The gestalt empty-chair technique also is effective along with the "unsent letter" read before the group (described in detail earlier in this book).

Art therapy also is helpful, tapping the unconscious rapidly and creating cohesion among members. Particularly effective are exercises directly related to the assault, such as drawing the offender or drawing the setting in which the offense occurred. Clay is a very powerful medium to use in group along with dream depiction, either through collage, modeling or drawing. The mandala, likewise powerful, is less threatening because it involves a basically cognitive process.

Cognitive material should be presented in an on-going manner rather than in lecture form and should include bibliotherapy. Members can be encouraged to share learnings and experiences from their readings. Some successful groups have included the participation of speakers from Parents Anonymous, rape crisis centers and the police department.

Conclusion

Without expert leadership and careful screening, groups can be dangerous for some members, creating intense anxiety that remains unresolved or breaking defenses without follow-up in the form of reintegration. For these reasons, it is incumbent upon therapists to receive proper training and background experience in sexual assault therapy, both in individual and group work, before establishing a victim group.

18

THE WIVES GROUP

The wives group can be extremely instrumental in helping to improve family and individual functioning for silent partners and their loved ones. The basic purposes and format of the group are similar to those of women's support groups being facilitated in agencies throughout the country. Hence, the focus here will be limited to highlighting some special considerations that relate to specific needs and issues of silent partners.

Issues that Merit Attention in Group

Typical silent partners feel alone, guilty and frightened. They have low self-esteem and have been isolated from society at large. Thus, their world views are narrow. They are shy and ill-at-ease with others. Because denial has operated so all-pervasively throughout their lives, they are not in touch with genuine affect. Feelings have been blocked or suppressed to the degree that they no longer are easy to identify and label.

The following goals, based on needs and concerns of silent partners, have been formulated.

1. *Self-image building.* Self-image building will come through support, shared experiences, acceptance and assertiveness training. Generally, silent partners respond best to warmth, reflection and clarification of affect. Usually, they do not respond to hard confrontation. Since their self-esteem is so low, they perceive confrontation as a form of judgement and rejection. These women are guilty which increases their

sensitivity to the reactions of those around them. Even "therapeutic silence" can result in undue anxiety, feelings of rejection and withdrawal on the part of silent partners.

Assertiveness training is useful for self-image building. The basic guidelines for assertiveness should be presented and practiced in group and with at-home assignments.

2. *Insight.* Generally, insights come slowly for silent partners because of the operation of denial. However, insights can come fairly rapidly in a group setting where identification is strong among members. It is not unusual in group for a member to be recounting, in a rational and controlled manner, incidents of incest in the home while other members silently are crying as they identify with what is being told. Because identification can be so powerful, the therapist or facilitator should be sensitive to, and aware of, the reactions of all members. The women whose behavior requires special monitoring are the ones who are consistently silent in group and/or display nonverbal involvement through attentiveness, eye contact and empathic crying.

Extreme anxiety can be generated among members due to the open self-disclosures made in group by other women. Such disclosures can trigger extreme guilt or fear in others who are not yet ready to face underlying affects. In such instances, it may be necessary for the therapist to arrange individual sessions for the support of any woman who is reacting strongly to the self-disclosures of others.

3. *Release and the opportunity to ventilate.* The group affords members an ideal opportunity for ventilation and release of suppressed affect. Ventilation and release may occur spontaneously, but the therapist should be prepared to use necessary techniques to stimulate catharsis (gestalt empty-chair, role plays, letter writing).

It is important for the therapist not to have stereotyped notions regarding what constitutes client issues. In one group, several sessions were spent attempting to facilitate release for a client who appeared angry at her husband for numerous convictions on charges of child soliciting, child molestation and exhibitionism. When this women finally was permitted to "write an angry letter about anything you wish" she surprised the entire group by writing an imaginary letter to her dead mother. The content of the letter related her rage against her mother for silently punishing her at age five for innocent acts of child sex play that had occurred some thirty years earlier with a four-year-old male neighbor.

Once her issue became clear, she could focus on anger toward her mother. In future group meetings, it became clear that the original incident recounted (child sex play) masked even deeper anger harbored toward her mother for allowing her father to be subtly seductive with her for ten years. The father hugged her "too tightly," wore an open bathrobe in her presence, asked her to take showers with him during the latency period, and always kissed her on the lips.

The woman had become confused and angry about his behavior, which she felt did not quite constitute molestation. She had displaced this anger onto her mother, whom she perceived as the all-knowing protector who neither clarified the father's confusing behavior nor stopped it from occurring. Insights into these complicated and pathological family dynamics could occur only following "release" and ventilation of formerly suppressed material which helped to clarify underlying issues.

4. *Education through providing information.* Wives of offenders need education, partly for support and to help them feel comfortable about self-disclosure and partly because of the reality of widespread sexual assault of children in the United States.

It is very helpful to gather local statistics on sexual assault and incest and to invite local speakers to give presentations to the group. Sexual assault centers and rape crisis centers usually are willing to send speakers without a fee to talk before interested groups. The police department can provide basic data on sexual assault, criminal proceedings and self-defense. Inquiries by group members regarding specific issues related to court proceedings can be answered by local authorities.

Self-image is greatly enhanced by information that validates the surprising prevalence of the incest experience and by teaching women that they and their offspring do not need to submit sexually to anyone against their will. The theory of learned helpfulness, i.e., where the victim internalizes blame and becomes a helpless, willing pawn for the aggressor, should be elaborated. The common experience of all victims — alcohol abuse, sexual assault, battering — should be highlighted to stress the universality of oppression and the need to react with assertiveness and a sense of self-worth.

5. *Goals and values clarification leading to decision-making.* Silent partners often need goals and values clarification. The disclosure of incest in the family has constituted a major life crisis for these women who suddenly grapple with decisions regarding the possibility of divorce, the necessity of becoming a wage earner, often for the first time in their lives, and the prospect of changing residence and becoming head of household.

   The group can incorporate values and goals clarification within its format and/or use written and verbal structured exercises specifically designed for self-growth and change. The exercises can be simple, brief and easy to complete in group or at home for sharing later in group. The following goals clarification exercise is helpful in group work.

Sample Goals Clarification Exercise

1. Number each item below from 1 to 10 to represent your goals. Let #1 represent your strongest goal, #2 a slightly less important goal, and so forth.

   What I want most from my life is

   _____ financial security

   _____ a good job/career advancement

   _____ spiritual growth

   _____ a comfortable home

   _____ to see my husband punished

   _____ to see my husband receive help

   _____ to live alone

_____ to live with my husband and children

_____ close friendships

_____ time to pursue my hobbies and interests

_____ a better education

_____ to live near/with relatives

_____ other (specify) _____

2. Referring to your top 3 responses, jot down procedures (ways that you can reach your goals), problems you will encounter in attempting to reach those goals, and methods to overcome those obstacles. Work with each goal at a time.

Goal #1 _____

Procedures	*Problems*	*Overcoming Problems*
_____	_____	_____
_____	_____	_____
_____	_____	_____

Goal #2 _____

Procedures	*Problems*	*Overcoming Problems*
_____	_____	_____
_____	_____	_____
_____	_____	_____

Goal #3 _____

Procedures	*Problems*	*Overcoming Problems*
_____	_____	_____
_____	_____	_____
_____	_____	_____

3. Pair up with another group member so that each of you can discuss your goals, procedures, problems you expect to encounter and ways to overcome those problems.

Whatever technique or exercise is used, goals and values clarification should be positively oriented, supportive and yet realistic. The basic steps toward sound decision making should be clarified and presented sequentially, i.e., values clarification, goals and procedures toward reaching those goals.

Conclusion

The wives group basically is supportive. The women share a common bond and are ready to grow and form new friendships. The group can be a positive experience for facilitators and members alike and it represents one of the least threatening and most hopeful aspects in the treatment of incestuous families.

19
THE SEXUAL
ENRICHMENT GROUP

In a manual such as this, inclusion of material on sexual dysfunction and sexual enrichment is essential. Sexual dysfunction characterizes the family where incest has occurred. The typical offender has sought gratification in pedophilic responses or he derives primary satisfaction from pregenital acts. In many cases, the wife has been unresponsive to her spouse and unavailable for sexual activities. The daughter almost always is destined to suffer from long-term repercussions in terms of her own sexuality and her fear of, or aversion to, mature genital gratification. She may express her feelings by non-responsiveness, homosexuality, promiscuity or abstinence.

The material presented here can be adapted for individual therapy, or can be used both in couple or same-sex groups. Same-sex groups may be composed of offenders, adult victims or wives of offenders. The focus is on education through the use of bibliotherapy, mini-lectures and handouts. However, as in all group work, sharing is essential for cohesiveness, support and the effect of the contagion factor to operate positively among members. Hence, time always should be allotted for shared experiences in the form of self-disclosure, feedback from group members and progress noted among couples or individuals.

The clinician or facilitator is not expected to be a sex therapist. The material presented is introductory and designed to stimulate sharing, insights and awareness as well as to highlight areas that might require deeper intervention from a qualified sex therapist.

Choosing Prospective Group Members

Any motivated victim, offender or wife, can benefit from the material presented here. However, the therapist might wish to evaluate potential for change among prospective participants and to discriminate among categories of offenders, victims and wives by classifying them into suitable groupings.

One method to evaluate potential for change takes into consideration three factors: types of sexual offense, duration, and age of onset for the victim. If the victim were very young at the age of onset and if the offense has been long-term involving more than fondling or petting, the prognosis for all family members is not very favorable.

Another consideration involves assessment of antisocial characteristics among offenders (see Chapter 12). A Sexual History highlighting pregenital fixations and fixed pedophilia appears at the end of this chapter. The potential for change among offenders who are fixated at a pregenital level is poor. Temporary regressed behavior which occurs during periods of anger, depression or stress, is more amenable to change.

A workable group should include members who are at a similar place psychologically and behaviorally. Hence, it would be unwise and unprofitable to include several fixed offenders with antisocial personalities in a group composed also of offenders whose psychosexual functioning has been essentially normal except for regressed behavior during periods of stress. Equally, the adult victim who has experienced a single episode of fondling by her father during her adolescence may be experiencing different problems from the adult victim of long-term father-daughter incest involving sexual intercourse.

Didactic Material to be Included in Therapy

The Sexual History which follows is a valuable tool for group therapy. In addition to serving as a method for screening prospective group members, it can be used to help the therapist focus on specific client issues. In addition, responses can be used as a basis for sharing between partners or among couples.

While specific client concerns deserve prime attention and form the basis for therapy, general educational material on human sexuality should be included in group work.   Two useful books that provide basic information are: *Man's Body: An Owner's Manual* and, *Woman's Body: An Owner's Manual,* both by the Diagram Group, Paddington Press Ltd., New York (1976 and 1977, respectively).   The manuals, which detail bodily functions and changes across generations and provide an overview of sexuality and health problems, can be assigned as textbooks or used by the therapist to insure that relevant material has been covered.   Whatever text is assigned, the therapist should discuss the following issues.

- The male and female sex organs
- The mechanism of sexual arousal for both males and females
- The "anatomy" of sexual intercourse
- Positions for sexual intercourse
- Oral sexuality
- Masturbation
- Menstruation
- Hormonal changes
- Homosexuality
- Pregnancy
- Female menopause
- Hysterectomy
- Male climacteric
- Venereal disease and its effects on health
- The effect of stress, alcohol, depressants and stimulants on sexual arousal

Sexual dysfunction is a particularly relevant topic to include in the education of the group.   Even the therapist who does not specialize in sexual counseling should be knowledgeable concerning the common sexual dysfunctions listed below.

Male dysfunctions

1. Premature ejaculation: absence of voluntary control over ejaculation
2. Impotence: erectile failure at all times throughout life (primary dysfunction); transient erectile failure (secondary dysfunction)
3. Retarded ejaculation: failure to ejaculate intravaginally (primary or secondary dysfunction)

Female dysfunctions

1. General sexual dysfunction: psychologically, lack of erotic feel-
    ing; physically, inability to lubricate and lack of physiological
    change in the genital area, (i.e., the vagina does not expand and
    there is no formation of the orgasmic platform)
2. Orgasmic dysfunction: inability to reach orgasm (primary or sec-
    ondary dysfunction)
3. Vaginismus: tightening of the vaginal walls so that penetration is
    impossible (primary or secondary dysfunction)
4. Dyspareunia: painful intercourse

Sexual dysfunction should be discussed in relation to therapeutic
modalities available to clients.   These are described in *The New Sex
Therapy* by Helen Singer Kaplan, Brunner-Mazel Inc., 1974, and *The
Behavioral Treatment of Sexual Problems* by Jack S. Annon, Mercantile
Printing Company, Ltd., 1975.

There are a number of valuable books that can be recommended for
group members.   A bibliography of more than 50 books on human
sexuality is available from: Information Service, Institute for Sex
Research, 416 Morrison Hall, Indiana University, Bloomington, IN, 47401.

It is useful for the therapist to become familiar with a number of
books so that he or she can direct clients to appropriate, usable materials
regarding such diverse aspects of sexuality as emotional response,
communication skills, pleasuring, self-therapy, statistical data and couples'
exercises. A few helpful books are recommended below for specific client
concerns:

Altman, C. *Lovemaking: You Can Be Your Own Sex Therapist.* New
York: Berkley Publishing Corp., 1977.

Includes techniques for self-therapy using desensitization, relaxation
and a number of programmed exercises for practice.   Illustrated and
designed for the lay population.

Barbach, L. *For Yourself. The Fulfillment of Female Sexuality.* New
York: Doubleday and Co., 1975.

Focuses on self-pleasuring for the non-orgasmic female.

Comfort, A. *The Joy of Sex.* New York: Simon and Schuster, 1972.

Includes material to stimulate the senses. Tasteful illustrations of various sexual postures.

Hopson, B. & Hopson, C. *Intimate Feedback: A Lover's Guide to Getting in Touch with Each Other.* New York: Simon and Schuster, 1975.

Includes guidelines to physical, psychological and spiritual communication. Numerous exercises.

Powell, J., S.J. *The Secret of Staying in Love.* Niles, Illinois: Argus Communications, 1974.

Includes exercises in dialogue to enhance communication and emotional involvement.

Walker, G., with Smith, A.P. *Me and You and Us.* New York: Peter H. Wyden, Inc., 1971.

Includes over 40 couples' experiences, verbal and non-verbal, including fantasizing, pleasuring, trusting, letting go, enhancing intimacy, and deepening communication. Illustrated.

Conclusion

Even in groups oriented toward education and the growth of cognitive insights, didactic material should be interspersed sensitively, with sharing and self-disclosure among members as well as discussion of the material presented. If homework assignments are given, feedback should be shared the following week. Hence, it is important to maintain a balance to insure a high interest level. Finally, sexual fulfillment is linked to every other aspect of interpersonal relating. Thus, it is important for the therapist to focus on sexual enrichment — but not to the exclusion of communication skills, honesty and trust-building.

SEXUAL HISTORY: BACKGROUND DATA

1. Did you engage in sex play as a child?

2. If so, how did you feel at the time?

3. How did your parents feel about sex play among children?

4. Thinking back now, how do you feel about having engaged in sex play as a child?

5. What do you remember about your parents' sex life? Were they affectionate with one another? Did you ever witness sexual intercourse between your parents?

6. How do/did you feel about your parents' sex life?

7. When did you first learn about sex? What did you learn? From whom?

8. What did your friends tell you about sex?

9. How did you feel about your physical development and changes in your body? If female, menstruation, pubic hair, breast development? If male, pubic hair, growth of genitals, first erection?

10. When was your first sexual experience? How old were you? With whom did you have sex? How did you feel about it?

11. Describe subsequent sexual experiences and your feelings then and now about them.

12. Did you ever have a homosexual experience? How did/do you feel about the experience.

13. Did you/do you engage in masturbation? How do you feel about masturbating?

Body Image

1. If female, how do you feel about the male body? If male, how do you feel about the female body? How do you feel about your/the opposite sex's genitals?

2. What part of your body do you like the best? What part of the opposite sex's body do you like the best?

3. What part of your body do you dislike the most? What part of the opposite sex's body do you dislike the most?

4. Are you embarrassed by/ashamed of any part of your body? Which part?

5. How do you feel about being seen naked?

Responsiveness

1. Is sex satisfying for you? If not, why not?
2. What do you describe as a satisfying sex life?
3. Are sex and love the same thing for you?
4. Have you ever been/felt rejected sexually? If so, how, when and in what way?
5. Do you describe yourself as inhibited or free sexually?
6. If you felt free sexually, what would you do?
7. What type of foreplay do you enjoy?
8. How long would you like to engage in foreplay?
9. How often (many times per week) do you want/need sex?
10. Do you prefer sex in the morning, afternoon, or at night? In the dark? Only in the bedroom? With total privacy?
11. Do you prefer sex to be pre-planned or spontaneous?
12. What excites you sexually? Makes you anxious? "Turns you off?"
13. Do you always reach orgasm? Is it easy for you to climax?
14. Do you usually initiate sex? If so, do you prefer it that way?
15. If male, do you have erections with little stimulation?
16. If male, do you ejaculate always? Quickly? Delayed? At the same time as your partner climaxes?
17. If female, do you want/need direct clitoral stimulation during sexual intercourse? Do you ever reach orgasm through sexual intercourse without direct stimulation?
18. How do you feel about oral sex? Anal sex? Varied positions during intercourse?
19. React to the following: group sex, switching couples, pornography, homosexuality, sex with minors.
20. Do you fantasize during, before, or after sex? Describe your fantasies.
21. Can you tell your partner what you want/need sexually? Can you share your responses to this questionnaire with your partner? If not, why not?

20
THE COUPLES
COMMUNICATION GROUP

As with any group, success of an incest couples group will depend largely on the composition of the group and the congruence of leadership style to membership, group expectations, goals, objectives toward reaching those goals, and the norms established. In addition, basic guidelines for establishing any successful group include: 1) careful interviews of prospective members before acceptance for group work, with due consideration given to readiness for the experience, and 2) firm establishment of norms and guidelines including the length of sessions, the anticipated length of time that the group is expected to continue working together, and an agreement regarding norms (particularly confidentiality and whether or not the group is to be open or closed).

The therapist whose major goal is improving communication and intimacy is wise to adhere to certain principles that will facilitate group process:

1. Male-female co-therapists form a valuable leadership team, both in terms of their ability to model roles and interactions and in terms of same-sex identification.

2. The focus of the communication group is skills training and not therapy. Therefore, the group should be short-term (approximately six sessions) and goal-oriented.

3. The objectives toward reaching the goal of improved communication should be carefully delineated by the therapist. For example, objectives should include improved listening and attending skills, assertiveness training, increased understanding as demonstrated through practice in reflection, paraphrasing and clarifying, and improved observation skills.

4. A model is useful since it eliminates extraneous, non-goal oriented content and since it helps the therapists achieve a planned balance between didactic content and experiential growth.

5. The distinguishing feature between the incest couples group and other communications groups is the variable of long-term anti-social and illegal behavior in the home which must be dealt with openly and honestly through discussion.

The model presented here specifically is designed for three to four couples who have had previous individual counseling, who have worked through the initial trauma and crisis of incest, who choose to remain united in their marriage, who are deemed prepared for the group experience, and for whom a major therapeutic issue is impaired communication. This six session model is open to modification and is intended as a guide only. Sessions run one and one-half to two hours, though timing is not considered a crucial factor. In general, one hour is allowed for planned activities; fifteen minutes for processing the session; and fifteen minutes for the presentation of cognitive material, which is usually accompanied by handouts or homework assignments.

A summary outline of the six sessions will be followed by detailed instructions and handouts for conducting each session.

SUMMARY OUTLINE

1. Session I: Introductory
    A. Introductions
    B. Establishment of goals, norms and expectations
    C. Establishment of rapport and cohesion among members
    D. Introduction to Communication Time-Line and "I-messages"

2. Session II: Assertiveness Training and Deepening Communication

A. Establishment of relationship between stress and communication problems

B. Practice in use of attending skills and "I-messages"

C. Introduction to assertiveness training via DESC script and assigned text

3. Session III: Assertiveness Training

A. Coverage of key aspects of assertiveness—DESC script, Downer Detours, Contracts

B. Practice of assertiveness via role plays

C. Deepening communication through the use of Marital Satisfaction Inventory and journal-keeping

4. Session IV: Incest

A. Shared experience regarding Marital Satisfaction Inventory and journal-keeping

B. Coverage of didactic material regarding incest

C. Shared in-depth experience regarding incest

5. Session V: Enhancing Greater Intimacy

A. Guidelines for giving/receiving feedback and for observing nonverbal behaviors

B. Modeling by leaders and practice among members on giving/receiving feedback and observing nonverbal behaviors

C. Review of basic learnings from sessions 1-5

6. Session VI: Closure

A. Summary and evaluation of workshop

B. Personal self-evaluations and sharing perceptions, insights and future goals

C. A closing, intimate experience for members: the Mandala

SESSION I: INTRODUCTORY

A. *Objectives*

    1. To introduce leaders and participants

    2. To establish group goals, norms and expectations

    3. To begin to establish rapport and cohesion

B. *Activities are presented in progressive order*

    1. Material is introduced by leaders.

        a. Information is geared to establish an informal, intimate atmosphere (self-disclosure regarding marital status, children, interests).

        b. Leaders establish their own authenticity and credibility (qualifications, experience, style of leadership).

    2. Leaders briefly elaborate on group goals and norms.

        a. The importance of honesty and openness regarding shared experiences of incest is discussed.

        b. The need for confidentiality is emphasized.

    3. Group members introduce themselves round-robin fashion.

        a. Members give first names and basic informational data including years married, occupation, and number, sexes and ages of children.

        b. Members tell what brought them to group.

        c. Members self-disclose regarding incest in each family.

    4. Group expectations are discussed.

        a. Norms are clarified.

        b. Members respond to the question, "What do I see as the central problem in communication in my marriage and how does this problem relate to incest in my home?"

    5. Exercises for self-awareness are introduced.

        a. Each couple prepares and then shares with group members a communication time-line.

        b. Handout sheet #1 is distributed.

6. Cognitive material is presented.

   a. Leaders briefly explain "I-messages" and active listening and their value in communication.

   b. Examples are provided.

   c. Copied sheets are given to each couple for self-study and practice.

   d. Handouts #2 and #3 are distributed.

   e. Couples are instructed to practice mutual "I-messages" and active listening at home, using the Communication Time-line as a guide. (For example, each partner is instructed to discuss his/her feelings regarding significant marital life events and highs and lows in communication, while the other partner practices attending skills by listening attentively and non-judgementally.

7. Session I ends with group processing.

   a. Members share feelings about group.

   b. Members process their interactions and give general feedback to one another.

HANDOUT #1 FOR SESSION 1

COMMUNICATION TIME-LINE

Instructions:

1. Draw a straight line across a blank sheet of paper. This line represents the length of time you expect to be married. Mark off segments as follows: courtship or engagement, early marriage, middle marriage, today's date, anticipated future.

2. Graph your communication level over the years until today's date. Then continue your graph marking off the degree of communication you expect to have with your spouse in the future.

3. Place an (X) identifying significant life events that occurred at peaks and lows of communication with your spouse. Label each (X) by identifying what occurred at that time.

4. Use your time-line to discuss: a) the relationship between life events and communication in your marriage; b) differences in your and your spouse's perception of communication patterns in your marriage, and c) your separate diagnoses and insights regarding your communication pattern along with your recommendations for helpful changes.

Sample Communication Time-line (for clarification)

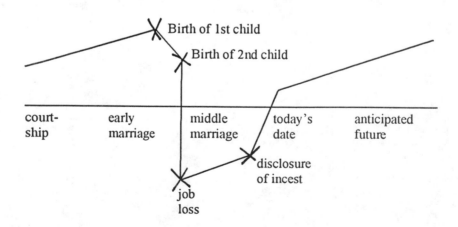

HANDOUT #2 FOR SESSION I

"I-MESSAGES"

The "I-message" helps us to communicate with other people honestly and openly. It allows us to say what we feel and think without hurting or attacking another person. One reason that the "I-message" is effective is that it focuses on behavior and not on the person. When you communicate with the "I-message," you describe your feelings and thoughts about the other person's behavior. You do not describe him/her.

The "you-message," on the other hand, focuses on the other person, not the behavior. The receiver feels defensive, "put-down," criticized, and judged. The "you-message" is not an effective way to communicate.

An example of an "I-message" is:

I AM NOT BEING GIVEN AN OPPORTUNITY TO SPEAK. (The action is described.) THAT MAKES ME FEEL VERY UPSET AND FRUSTRATED. (The feeling is described.)

An example of a "you-message" is:

YOU ARE VERY ANNOYING (No action is described and the focus is not on behavior. The other person feels attacked.)

HANDOUT #3 FOR SESSION I

ACTIVE LISTENING

Listening, like speaking, is a skill that requires certain attitudes and behaviors. Warmth, genuineness and empathy are three major prerequisites to skillful listening. You must be willing to take the time to listen and you must want to hear what the other person is saying to you. Your attitude is conveyed by both your verbal responses and non-verbal behaviors.

Attitudes Required for Active Listening

Active listening requires an attitude of acceptance of the other person's feelings and thoughts, no matter how different they may be from your own. Acceptance encourages sharing. Clarify, interpret, reflect and paraphrase but do not impose your feelings on the other person. Examples of accepting phrases include, "You really are upset with me;" "You sound blue;" "I understand that you are concerned about your job;" and, "It seems as if I hurt your feelings." Examples of non-accepting phrases include, "You think I am stupid;" "You shouldn't be blue;" "Your boss is just smarter than you are;" and, "You are too sensitive." Non-accepting phrases are judgemental and convey the message that you believe the other person should modify his/her thoughts to match your own.

Non-verbal Behaviors Required for Active Listening

Stand or sit near the other person. Maintain good eye contact and an erect yet comfortable posture. Do not fidget, check your watch or show other signs of boredom and tension. If you do not have time to listen, be honest and schedule a time when you can be available.

SESSION II: ASSERTIVENESS

TRAINING AND DEEPENING COMMUNICATION

A. *Objectives*

   1. To begin to deepen communication in the here-and-now

   2. To begin insight work regarding cause-effect patterns involved in communication difficulties

   3. To expand upon "I-messages" by incorporating them in assertiveness training

B. *Activities*

   1. Group discussion: The focus is on "I-messages," couples' progress in home practice and insights gained from the Communication Time-line. Participants are encouraged to use "I-messages" and attending skills during group discussion. Leaders verbally reinforce appropriate communication behaviors.

   2. Cognitive material: A mini-lecture by leaders demonstrates the cyclical relationship involved in the onset and perpetuation of a communication breakdown. Leaders include the concept that stress (external, internal) contributes to the problem of communication breakdown. Communication problems cause additional stress, which further exacerbates communication difficulties and finally can result in dysfunctional behavior (incest). Antisocial behavior, in turn, results in further isolation and alienation (intra- and extra-familial).

   3. Fishbowl exercise: Each couple takes turns in the center of the group. Spouses alternately practice "I-messages" and attending skills to discuss their individual perceptions of how stress has affected their behaviors over the years. The group provides feedback after each couple has taken a turn in the center of the fishbowl.

   4. Additional cognitive material: Leaders explain the relationship of "I-messages" to skills training in assertiveness. Handout #1 DESC script is reviewed and distributed for self-study. Handout sheet follows.

5. Assignments: Couples are assigned the task of completing a contract for practice and assertiveness (Handout sheet follows). The following book is recommended:

    Bower, S.A. and G.H. Bower. *Asserting Yourself: A Practical Guide for Positive Change.* Reading, MA: Addison-Wesley Publishing Company, 1976.

    Couples are given copies of Triggering Events Rating Scale to complete at home. (Handout sheets follow.) All material is to be discussed with spouses.

6. Group processing: The focus is on processing interactions.

HANDOUT #1 FOR SESSION II

DESC SCRIPT FOR ASSERTIVENESS TRAINING*

DESCRIBE	Use objective words. Avoid inflammatory labeling.
EXPRESS	Use "I-messages" to express feelings and thoughts: Say "I feel," not, "You make me feel..." Say "I think," not, "You make me think.."
SPECIFY	Ask for one observable, REASONABLE behavior change. Seek agreement. Negotiate this change if necessary.
CONSEQUENCES	
POSITIVE:	Offer "reward" (consequence) that is valuable to other and you can give.
NEGATIVE:	(Think of reasonable "punishment" that fits the "crime." Caution: SAY this ONLY when all else fails and you are WILLING and CAPABLE of implementing it.)

---

*Bower, S.A. and Bower, G.H. Asserting Yourself: A Practical Guide for Positive Change. Reading, Massachesetts: Addison-Wesley Publishing Company, 1976, p. 60. Reprinted by permission of the authors and publisher.

HANDOUT #2 FOR SESSION II

ASSERTIVE TRAINING CONTRACT

_____
Name
_____
Date

Describe the situation in which you will be assertive:

Describe what you will say, using the DESC script:

_____

Date of completion:

Describe how you felt before, during and after the interaction:

Describe how the other person responded to your assertiveness:

HANDOUT #3 FOR SESSION II

TRIGGERING EVENTS RATING SCALE*

To change the situation, we must become aware of the specific events that are influencing our behavior; we must understand the source of our tension. Listed below are 43 "triggering events" or "life events" which stimulate you to experience varying amounts of tension or stress. Check the specific events you have experienced in the past two years. If they've happened twice, put that number of points down twice. Then add points together to get your score.

150-199:   Mild
200-299:   Moderate
Over 300:   Severe life crisis

Life Event	Stress Level	My Points
1. Death of spouse	100	
2. Divorce	73	
3. Marital separation	65	
4. Jail term	63	
5. Death of close family member	63	
6. Personal injury or illness	53	
7. Marriage	50	
8. Fired at work	47	
9. Marital reconciliation	45	
10. Retirement	45	
11. Change of health of family member	44	
12. Pregnancy	40	
13. Sex difficulties	39	
14. Gain of new family member	39	
15. Business readjustment	39	
16. Change in financial state	38	
17. Death of a close friend	37	

Life Event	Stress Level	My Points
18. Change to different line of work	36	
19. Change in number of arguments with spouse	35	
20. Mortgage over $10,000	31	
21. Foreclosure of mortgage or loan	30	
22. Change in responsibilities at work	29	
23. Son or daughter leaving home	29	
24. Trouble with in-laws	29	
25. Outstanding personal achievement	28	
26. Spouse beginning or stopping work	26	
27. Beginning or end of school	26	
28. Change in living conditions	25	
29. Revision of personal habits	24	
30. Trouble with boss	23	
31. Change in work hours or conditions	20	
32. Change in residence	20	
33. Change in schools	20	
34. Change in recreation	19	
35. Change in church activities	19	
36. Change in social activities	18	
37. Mortgage or loan less than $10,000	17	
38. Change in sleeping habits	16	
39. Change in number of family get-togethers	15	
40. Change in eating habits	15	
41. Vacation	13	
42. Christmas, Chanuka	12	
43. Minor violations of the law	11	

My Total Points:

*Developed by T.H. Holmes and R.J. Rake. "The Social Readjustment Scale," *Journal of Psychosomatic Medicine* 2 (1967): 213. Reprinted by permission of Pergamon Press, Inc.

SESSION III: ASSERTIVENESS TRAINING

A. *Objectives*

1. To provide expanded knowledge of assertiveness training

2. To practice assertive skills, especially as related to family dysfunction

B. *Activities*

1. Cognitive: The leaders present a brief overview of assertiveness, stressing the difference between passive, aggressive and assertive behaviors, the importance of the DESC script in successful communication, and the need to be aware of Downer Detours as presented by Bower and Bower. The relationship between assertiveness and mental health is highlighted. Members are encouraged to continue with self-study, practice at home, reading Bower and Bower, and enrolling in assertiveness training courses or workshops at local community colleges or mental health clinics.

2. Experiential: Contracts for use of assertive behaviors are reviewed. Additionally, role-play situations are distributed. (Handout sheets follow.) The couples alternately role-play the situations specific on their contracts, along with situations devised by leaders. Feedback from all group members is encouraged.

3. Homework: Marital Satisfaction Inventory and Sentence Completion forms are distributed for completion at home. Members of each couple are encouraged to read each other's responses. Couples are assigned the task of beginning Communication Journals using written "I-messages" frequently and focusing on affect. Initial focus of journal writing is: major life crises and highs and lows in marital life, as well as reactions to the way each situation was handled. Journals are to be shared each evening with spouse following ten minutes of writing by each partner. (Handout sheets follow.)

4. Group processing: The focus is on a brief processing of interactions.

HANDOUT #1 FOR SESSION III

DOWNER DETOURS

The Downer Detour is a put-down used by the receiver to evade an issue.* Downer Deteours include the following.

"We'll discuss this later."

"You are so pretty when you get angry."

"You are complaining all the time."

"I have a headache and cannot be bothered now."

"You really do have problems."

"We talked about that last week."

"It's really your problem."

Do not be put off or put down by evasive tactics. Acknowledge the receiver's thoughts or feelings and then continue with your assertive script, focusing on the issue in question. For example, you might reply to a Downer Detour in the following ways.

"We may have talked about this last week, but I need clarification now ..."

"You want to discuss this later so let's set a time — one hour from now."

"I may have a problem but that is not the issue ..."

---

*Bower, S.A. and G.H. Bower. *Asserting Yourself: A Practical Guide for Positive Change.* Reading, MA: Addison-Wesley Publishing Company, 1976, p. 143. Reprinted by permission of the authors and publisher.

HANDOUT #2 FOR SESSION III

ROLE PLAYS FOR ASSERTIVE TRAINING

Situation 1:

Your husband or wife tells you he or she does not want to discuss your feelings regarding the recent disclosure of incest in your home. You want to tell him or her how important it is for you to be able to communicate about the sexual abuse that has occurred in the family.

Situation 2:

Your husband or wife seeks evasion through alcohol, drug abuse, constant fatigue or constant activity. Hence, there are few intimate moments between you now. You are requesting a change in his or her behavior.

Situation 3:

Your wife or husband is overprotective of the children, allowing them few outlets or friends, especially since the disclosure of incest in your home. You feel that she or he is not acting in the children's best interests and want to tell him so.

Situation 4:

Your wife or husband isolates the family. Former pleasurable activities (dancing, eating out, visiting friends) gradually have been eliminated from your weekly routine. You feel that this change in your life is unhealthy for you and for your marriage and request a change.

Situation 5:

Your husband or wife's attitude has changed gradually over the months. He or she has become dominating (or mothering or passive) in specific ways that you can document. You are not happy with this change of attitude and want to tell him or her so.

HANDOUT #3 FOR SESSION III

MARITAL SATISFACTION INVENTORY

	Yes	No	Some-times
1. My spouse understands me.	___	___	___
2. My spouse shows affection and tenderness to me.	___	___	___
3. My spouse is sensitive to my moods and feelings.	___	___	___
4. Our sex life is a good one.	___	___	___
5. We share many intimate moments.	___	___	___
6. My spouse trusts me.	___	___	___
7. I trust my spouse.	___	___	___
8. We show our feelings to one another.	___	___	___
9. I can be honest and open with my spouse.	___	___	___
10. Our communication is effective.	___	___	___
11. I am satisfied with my marriage.	___	___	___
12. My spouse encourages me to grow and change in ways that are good for me.	___	___	___
13. We share the same values, hopes and dreams.	___	___	___
14. My spouse and I agree about child-rearing practices.	___	___	___
15. We argue about finances.	___	___	___
16. My spouse does not understand the importance of my daily activities/job.	___	___	___
17. We are attracted to one another.	___	___	___
18. My spouse loves me.	___	___	___
19. We do not discuss our emotional problems and inadequacies.	___	___	___
20. Our social life is satisfactory.	___	___	___
21. We have few, if any, political or religious differences.	___	___	___
22. I feel a sense of emotional stability and security in my marriage.	___	___	___
23. My spouse approves of and values me.	___	___	___
24. We are friends as well as lovers.	___	___	___
25. I would marry my spouse again.	___	___	___

HANDOUT #4 FOR SESSION III

SENTENCE COMPLETION
(FOR HUSBAND OR WIFE)

1. What I admire the most about my spouse is _____
    _____

2. What I admire the least about my spouse is _____
    _____

3. My spouse currently is concerned about _____
    _____

4. More than anything, my spouse wants the following from his or her
    life _____
    _____

5. If I could change one thing about my spouse it would be _____
    _____

6. My spouse's greatest fear is _____
    _____

7. My spouse's happiest moment was _____
    _____

8. In his or her relationships with other people, my spouse _____
    _____

9. Together, my spouse and I _____
    _____

HANDOUT #5 FOR SESSION III

GUIDELINES FOR KEEPING PERSONAL JOURNALS

The journal is an excellent way to help you focus on issues and feelings related to your past and present marital life. Write in your journal for 15 minutes each day. Then, exchange journals with your partner. Finally spend ten to fifteen minutes sharing your feelings and perceptions about what you have written and read.

Suggested topics for your journal:

1. Major life crises (highs and lows) in our marital life and how we have handled them.

2. Who am I? Who are you?

3. My greatest needs and wants.

4. My most painful experience.

5. How I felt about you before the disclosure of incest and how I feel now.

6. My understanding of how we became an incestuous family.

7. What I hope for us in the future.

8. Me as a sexual being.

9. The hardest emotion for me to share and why.

10. Goals I have for my future.

SESSION IV: INCEST

A.   *Objectives*

    1.   To desensitize group members to their common experience of incest.

    2.   To provide cognitive material regarding incest in order to deepen insights and self-awareness.

    3.   To encourage in-depth discussion of incest among couples and group members.

B.   *Activities*

    1.   Review of homework assignment. Couples are encouraged to share their experiences in and feelings about journal-keeping as well as insights gained from maintaining and sharing journals.

    2.   Cognitive material. Leaders review basic knowledge regarding incest. Incest questionnaires are distributed for completion and discussion. (Handout sheets follow.) Note: For information only, the most common responses elicited from a random sample of 25 psychiatrists, psychologists, social workers and counselors in the Phoenix, Arizona metropolitan area during 1979-1980 are noted on the sample questionnaire provided.

    3.   Experiential. Dyads among non-couples are formed to discuss cognitive insights gained from questionnaires. Couples then are paired to process their feelings about the incestuous experience. Leaders rotate among pairs to reinforce in-depth communication via expression of affect, "I-messages" and assertiveness. Leaders model appropriate communication behaviors when necessary.

    4.   Group processing. Interactions are processed. Feedback is given by group members to leaders and to one another.

HANDOUT #1 FOR SESSION IV

INCEST QUESTIONNAIRE

Below are ten statements pertaining to incest patterns which professional workers, parents, children and others have discussed in relation to this problem. Please indicate whether you believe these statements to be true, "Never," "Rarely," "Sometimes," "Frequently," or "Always."

	Never	Rarely	Some-times	Fre-quently	Always
1. Incest offenders and their wives have been victims of sexual abuse in the past.	—	—	√	—	—
2. Families in which incest occurs tend to be socially isolated.	—	—	—	√	—
3. Incest is more common in multi-problem families, i.e., families experiencing financial, emotional, etc. stresses.	—	—	—	√	—
4. Incest is more prevalent in families troubled by alcohol and drug problems.	—	—	√	—	—
5. A primary family defense in incest families is denial.	—	—	—	—	√
6. Male offenders, i.e., fathers and step-fathers, outnumber female offenders in incest cases.	—	—	—	—	√
7. Female victims outnumber male victims.	—	—	—	—	√
8. The victim children in incest families tend to be seductive with adults.	—	—	√	—	—
9. Special expertise and training is needed to treat cases involving incest.	—	—	—	—	√
10. Incest is a family problem where each member is equally responsible for its occurrence.	—	—	√	—	—

Please check the following statements, "Yes" or "No:"

		Yes	No
1.	Incest is equally common to all social classes.	√	___
2.	Incest is much more prevalent now than in the past.	___	√
3.	In the majority of incest cases, the offender's behavior with the victim is physically brutal.	___	√
4.	Cases involving stepparent-stepchild incest are as psychologically damaging to the victim as cases involving natural parents.	√	___
5.	Offenders ultimately must bear responsibility for incest.	√	___

Please circle one or more of the following:

1. Child victims of incest are characterized by:

    (guilt)   (fear)   (anger)   need for attention/affection

    unusual attractiveness   inability to communicate

    (role reversal with same-sex parent)

2. Adult offenders in incest families are characterized by:

    (guilt)   (anger)   fear   (strong dependency needs)

    (hostility)   (immaturity)   sexual dysfunction

    seductiveness   (inability to communicate)

3. The non-offending parent in incest cases is characterized by:

    (unconscious awareness of the problem)   (guilt)   anger

    (fear)   (strong dependency needs)   hostility

    sexual dysfunction   immaturity   seductiveness

    passive-aggressive behavior   (inability to communicate)

    subtle encouragement for incest to occur

4. Most incest families are:

    (urban)   (rural)

5. The majority of incestuous relationships result in:

    (fondling/petting)   (sexual intercourse)   fellatio

    cunnilingus   anal sex

6. The most common age group in which incest occurs is:

    0-5   (5-10)   (10-15)   15-20

7. In terms of long-range psychological repercussions, the most
    damaging age for incest to occur is:

    0-5   (5-10)   (10-15)   15-20

8. Short-term effects for incest victims include:

    (nightmares) tics (fears) enuresis (phobias) (anger)

    (guilt) (anxiety)   vague aches & pains   headaches

                    digestive problems

9. Long-term effects for incest victims include:

    (promiscuity)   (truancy)   learning disabilities

    (runaway)   (sexual dysfunction)

            breaking the law (theft, curfew violations, etc.)

10. The most desirable treatment for families involved in incest is:

    Incarceration of the offender

    (Outpatient psychiatric/psychological care for the offender)

    Inpatient psychiatric/psychological care for the offender

    (Family therapy)

    Removal of child from the home

    Removal of offender from the home

SESSION V: ENHANCING INTIMACY

A.   *Objectives*

1.   To provide guidelines for giving and receiving appropriate feedback and for observing non-verbal behaviors.

2.   To review basic learnings covered in previous meetings.

B.   *Activities*

1.   Cognitive material: Leaders give mini-lecture on "Giving and Receiving Feedback" and "Non-verbal Behaviors." (Handout sheets follow.)

2.   Modeling: Leaders role-play situations involving giving and receiving feedback.

3.   Experiential: Members list marital situations, past or present, related to the need to give feedback and pair off as couples to practice.   Each partner then provides feedback to the other regarding his or her style of communicating both verbally and non-verbally.

4.   Review of communication skills: Leaders provide a review of "I-messages," assertive behaviors, active listening guidelines for giving and receiving feedback.   Members are encouraged to maintain journals and to use assertiveness contracts when needed.

5.   Group processing: Feedback is shared regarding the session.

HANDOUT #1 FOR SESSION V

GUIDELINES FOR GIVING AND RECEIVING FEEDBACK

Through feedback we see ourselves as others see us. Giving feedback positively is a skill we all can learn. It involves a verbal and non-verbal process that lets another person know our feelings and perceptions about her or his behavior. Receiving feedback also is a learned skill, involving attentive listening followed by an open exploration and response to what has been stated. The receiver should respond only after the feedback process has been completed.

Giving feedback in a helpful, caring manner involves the following guidelines:

1. Use "I-messages" so that feelings are expressed directly. For example, say "I appreciate your attentiveness."
2. Focus on behaviors and not motives underlying those behaviors, judgements or personality traits. For example, say, "You screamed at me three times tonight."
3. Be specific. Focus on definite actions and behaviors. For example, say, "When you scream at me, I become frightened."
4. Focus on the here-and-now whenever possible. Give feedback immediately after the event. For example, say, "When you just cried, I felt very sad."
5. Learn to give positive feedback. Negative feedback often causes defensiveness. Positive feedback encourages appropriate behaviors. When giving negative feedback, use the following format: "When you do _____ (specific, concrete behavior), I feel _____ (your reaction)."
   When feedback is not effective, it may be for one or more of the following reasons.
1. It has not been given according to effective guidelines.
2. It comes too often or not often enough.
3. It comes too late or too soon.
4. If focuses on behaviors that cannot be changed.
5. It focuses on behaviors where the incentive to change is weak.

HANDOUT #2 FOR SESSION V

NON-VERBAL BEHAVIORS

We communicate both verbally and non-verbally. Verbal behaviors include the content of our speech, tone of voice, quickness of response and speech flow. Non-verbal behaviors include posture, gestures and the eye contact.

For attentive listening and honest communication, eye contact should be direct. Avoid glancing to the side, downward or away. Be natural. Do not stare at the other person. If you are standing, maintain an erect posture on both feet. Do not slump, lean to one side or turn away. If you are sitting, maintain comfort but, again, do not slump or turn aside.

Gestures and movements should match the verbal content of your speech. Avoid fidgeting and playing with your hands, clothes or hair when you are communicating with or listening to another person. Do not lean forward or backward or show signs of boredom and tension.

Facial expressions should coincide with the verbal message you are conveying. Laughter, smiles and frowns can be appropriate. Constant grinning, smiling or frowning is disconcerting and shows that you are preoccupied with your own thoughts and not listening to the other person.

SESSION VI: CLOSURE

A. Objectives
1. To summarize and evaluate the workshop
2. To share perceptions, insights gained and goals for the future
3. To provide an intimate closing experience for group members

B. Activities
1. Summary and evaluation: Leaders summarize goals, methods (or plans) and activities of the past five weeks. Workshop evaluation forms are distributed among members and responses are discussed. Members share goals for future growth and plans for meeting those goals. (Handout sheets follow.)
2. Experiential: Members draw mandalas. (Handout sheet follows.) Round-robin: each member shares feelings and insights gained from this experience.
3. Members conduct a final processing of interactions.

HANDOUT #1 FOR SESSION VI

EVALUATION OF WORKSHOP

1.   Did you find this workshop helpful? If so, in what way? If not, explain.

2.   What did you find most helpful in this couples group? What was least helpful?

3.   If you could change the structure of this group in any way, what would you do?

4.   What would you have liked to see included that we did not cover?

5.   Comment on how you would lead a communications group for couples who have been involved in incest in the home.

HANDOUT #2 FOR SESSION VI

SELF-EVALUATION

Check the communication behaviors you can "own:"

1. Listening attentively to others. _____

2. Stating clearly what you think. _____

3. Expressing what you feel. _____

4. Interrupting others. _____

5. Encouraging others to communicate with you. _____

6. Being aware of another person's feelings. _____

7. Giving direct feedback. _____

8. Accepting feedback openly and honestly. _____

9. Accepting ideas or feelings that differ from yours. _____

10. Self-disclosing. _____

HANDOUT #3 FOR SESSION VI

THE MANDALA

Note to Leaders: The mandala drawing is a well-known technique used by art therapists. The mandala is a cognitive rendering of the self. Within an outlined circle, the participant draws marks, forms or shapes in various colors, starting in the center and working outward, to represent her or his core or inner self. For this exercise, you will need to provide a sheet of white paper, 8-1/2 x 11, along with flow-tip pens (preferably six available colors) for each participant. Use a round plate to trace a circle on each sheet of paper.

Instructions:

Mandala is an ancient word for circle. The circle represents the self. You are going to show your inner self or core by using different colors, shapes, forms or symbols to make your mandala. First, relax and get into a comfortable position. Take a few minutes to think about what you want to show in your mandala. Then, starting in the center, begin to work outward, using colors and strokes in any way that you choose. When you are done, turn the sheet over and write about what you did, what you revealed about yourself, and how you felt making your mandala.

PART IV:
INNOVATIVE AND
PRACTICAL
TREATMENT
TECHNIQUES

The final portion of this book consists first of general approaches, principles and techniques for use with children and adults. Much of the existing literature is repetitious, elaborating on every aspect of interviewing techniques with general client populations, but offering little in the way of concrete suggestions for work with incest families. Special knowledge and expertise is required to work with incestuous abuse cases but it is an insult to the clinician to assume that she or he lacks a solid foundation of training in therapeutic interventions.

Hence, the first section in this part has been kept deliberately brief, focusing only on useful material related specifically to interviewing techniques and on attitudes required for work with incest victims and their families. Such material can and should be incorporated into the therapeutic style of the practicing clinician.

The second section in this part consists of specific techniques for use with children and adolescents. Many of these techniques are subject to modification to suit the specific therapeutic modality (individuals, groups, dyads, triads) and the age(s) of the clients. Since no previous systematic work has been done in the area of evolving and setting forth techniques and tools for use with incestuous families, the material presented here should prove to be of value to the clinician. All of the techniques have been chosen because of their effectiveness and their relationship to specific therapeutic goals.

Some words of caution are in order. The philosophy of therapy on which this work is based in predicated on the two important assumptions given below.

1. The primary concern in any therapeutic situation is the therapist-client relationship. No technique or tool can replace that relationship. The therapist is not a technician and the patient is not a subject for experimental analysis. In other words, any technique merely is adjunctive, and as such is useful in facilitating a certain therapeutic end, but it is not an end in itself.

2. An eclectic therapeutic approach is the only one possible, based on individual differences in the client population. Briefly, whatever works within the framework of professional ethics and morality is usable in a therapeutic setting.

SECTION A:
GENERAL APPROACHES, PRINCIPLES AND TECHNIQUES FOR CHILDREN AND ADULTS

THERAPEUTIC GOALS FOR CHILDREN, ADULTS AND FAMILY

It is axiomatic that before a therapist formulates a treatment plan she or he must perform a case analysis or diagnosis. In incest cases, the situation is complicated because individual pathology exists in the context of pathology based on interactive patterns within the family. Each situation will vary; however, generalizations based on our knowledge of family dynamics in incest families do exist.

Certain dysfunctional affective and behavioral states characterize the incestuous triad. The first task of the therapist is to perceive clearly the areas of dysfunction, outlined in the chart below, and to link those areas to therapeutic goals:

Dad	*Mom*	*Daughter*
Lack of communication .... $\Rightarrow$	$\Leftarrow$.................. $\Rightarrow$	$\Leftarrow$..................
Low self-esteem .... $\Rightarrow$	$\Leftarrow$.................. $\Rightarrow$	$\Leftarrow$..................
Denial at some level .... $\Rightarrow$	$\Leftarrow$.................. $\Rightarrow$	$\Leftarrow$..................
Misplaced sense of responsibility .... $\Rightarrow$	$\Leftarrow$.................. $\Rightarrow$	$\Leftarrow$..................
Guilt .... $\Rightarrow$	$\Leftarrow$.................. $\Rightarrow$	$\Leftarrow$..................
Victim .... $\Rightarrow$	$\Leftarrow$.................. $\Rightarrow$	$\Leftarrow$..................

Sexual incompatibility .... $\Rightarrow$ $\Leftarrow$		
Betrayal of trust $\Leftarrow$ .... $\Rightarrow$ Lack of trust		
	Role reversal	Role reversal
	encouraged $\Leftarrow$ .... $\Rightarrow$ accepted	
Manipulation	Withdrawal from	
Low Impulse Control	family; passivity	Symptomatology

From the preceding, it is clear that certain family and individual issues emerge in the incestuous triad. All three of the family members are victims. All have low self-esteem and lack communication with one another. In some cases, each family member denies the impact of incest. To some extent, all suffer from anger and guilt and have a faulty or misplaced sense of responsibility. In addition, there are issues centering specifically around the marital relationship (sexual incompatibility), the mother-daughter relationship (role reversal) and the father-daughter relationship (betrayal of trust). These are the key issues on which therapy must focus, issues that should be dealt with forthrightly, with each member individually, in dyads and as a family unit (assuming that the family decides to work together toward reconciliation). The modalities used will vary with the individual family, their level of intellectual functioning, their capacity for insight, the age of the child, the cultural meaning incest assumes for each member and the time-crisis factor. Nonetheless, certain general principles will apply in treatment and these are outlined below.

Interview Techniques

Trust is lacking in incest families. Not only has the concept of trust been violated within the family by both parents as protectors of the child but the family has probably engaged in antisocial and illegal behavior for some time. Hence, the first rule of therapy is honesty and openness on the part of the therapist who must begin slowly and patiently to model trust and to establish trusting bonds with each member. The therapist should directly clarify his or her role, the goals that are being set forth for the family, and any legal ramifications. The family should be advised of all legal aspects and their consequences.

The second rule of therapy is to seek immediate resolution of any potential complications, based on a full assessment of the family's response to incest. For example, typically a family enters a therapy situation following disclosure by the daughter of long-term incest in the home. Issues requiring immediate resolution often involve the following:

1. Even if the father is willing to enter therapy, should he remain in the home? With the added stress created by disclosure, it is likely that, without outside coercion to enforce its cessation, incest will continue. It is wise for the offender to leave the home during the initial stages of therapy.

2. Are other children in the home involved in incest? In many cases, other children are or have been involved either directly or peripherally as witnesses to incest. Each child should be evaluated individually.

3. Does the victim want to press charges? The victim should be interviewed alone without family influence and given full information regarding all aspects of the court process — from the physical examination to the nature of anticipated questions from police and attorneys. (The therapist should be well informed about state laws governing incest and possible penalties. She will be required to notify the authorities of the existence of incest and should proceed according to state law.)

4. Is the victim in need of medical attention? Incest rarely is brutal but all victims of sexual assault should be checked medically for venereal disease. Teenage victims may require pregnancy tests. In addition, the victim may need medical attention for symptoms accompanying or resulting from severe anxiety.

5. Is the mother assuming a protective role for her children or is she angry and rejecting? In the presence of a hostile or rejecting mother, the child might feel additional victimization. Child Protective Services might be required to remove the victim from the home if the atmosphere is not supportive and if Dad does not leave.

6. If the father leaves the home, what immediate financial effect will his absence have on the family? The mother may require a referral for financial aid from the city or state, or she may need to rely on relatives for assistance.

7. What is the psychological impact of disclosure on the immediate and/or extended family? If the support structure for the family is not adequate, referrals to community agencies may be necessary.

Initially, a directive approach to families as well as individuals is advisable because a crisis situation usually exists at time of disclosure. Positive guidance, through information and answers to questions regarding the future of the family as a unit and the availability of needed help, is essential to families in crisis. Later, once the crisis has been resolved and the family members begin the second and third stages of therapy, a variety of therapeutic modalities can be used. Successful therapy usually involves three stages of intervention, stated below.

STAGE 1: CRISIS RESOLUTION
Involves a directive approach, focusing on issues and immediate situational and legal concerns. Involves each family member individually and may involve dyad or family sessions. Includes full assessment of family and of each family member. May include intervention by outside agencies, including legal authorities, the hospital or child protective services.

STAGE 2: BEGINNING RESOLUTION OF THERAPEUTIC ISSUES
Involves the use of various therapeutic modalities with each family member individually, in dyads and as a family unit. Involves the institution of behavioral change in the home and the exploration of affective states through confrontation, gestalt techniques, and insight and reality therapies. Includes examination of roles and relationships through communication work with and among the three primary individuals involved in incestuous abuse.

STAGE 3: FINAL RESOLUTION OF THERAPEUTIC ISSUES AND RECONCILIATION OF THE FAMILY UNIT
Involves continuing self-exploration, maintenance of behavioral change in the home and values clarification. Includes supportive group and family work. May include long-term participation in incest-victim, incest-wives, and incest-offender groups.

The wisest approach to use with incest families involves therapy mandated by court order, or, in the absence of legal pressure, therapy by contract. There are several reasons that a degree of coercion is useful for offending families in therapy. After the initial crisis has been resolved, the family often loses interest in continuing therapy. Their immediate suffering has been relieved and there is a strong tendency to return to the status quo, to avoid social ostracism by withdrawing from individuals perceived to be in positions of authority, and/or to revert to the same pattern of denial that formerly permeated their lives and allowed for the continuation of incest in the home over the years. In addition, offenders do not seek therapy voluntarily and often exert covert or overt pressure on the entire family to abandon the therapeutic process.

Therapy by contract can be informal or subtly coercive, depending on the perceived willingness of the family to engage in long-term work. The family should be informed that the plan will involve approximately three months of crisis resolution, followed by six months of resolution of underlying issues through individual and family therapy. Thereafter, members will be expected to participate in group work for an indeterminate length of time. It is within the ethical province of the therapist to advise the family that if they fail to participate in therapy with a reputable clinician or at a reputable mental health clinic, the authorities will be informed.

Attitudes and Approaches

The attitude of the clinician in working with incest families is a strong determinant of the success or failure of the therapeutic process. The therapist should have resolved her or his own feelings regarding incestuous abuse. The practice of therapy should not afford the therapist an opportunity to work through her or his own unresolved issues. A non-judgemental, non-punitive and unbiased attitude toward all family members is crucial. If the therapist has strong feelings about specific behaviors or attitudes in the home, these should be stated openly and honestly as personal values rather than as judgements or universal pronouncements of right and wrong.

A balance of sympathetic concern and professional calm is a prerequisite for rapport and trust-building. In a crisis situation, a non-directive, unresponsive or matter-of-fact attitude can convey indifference. In addition, one function of the therapist is to educate and to model appropriate objectivity for family members who flounder emotionally and behaviorally as social outcasts in the environment. At the same time that the therapist models concern, she must remain calm and capable since she often is the only objective person on whom the family in crisis can rely.

The approach used with family members will vary depending on individual client differences and the exact situation precipitating the need for intervention. In addition, it is most helpful to use different approaches (in general) with the offender, his wife, and the victim. These are discussed below.

The Offender

A rather firm, sometimes confronting, approach is required with the offender who usually tries to project responsibility for his actions and minimize their impact, or to use manipulation in order to avoid legal and other consequences for his actions. Both assertiveness and the ability to focus on issues are needed by the therapist, whose initial goal with the offender is to help him fully acknowledge and take responsibility for his own behavior. Without such acknowledgement, therapeutic ends often are thwarted. Early in the therapeutic process the clinician may require the offender to face the victim, thus allowing her to deal openly with her feelings about his actions. Such a joint confrontation helps to instill a sense of responsibility in the offender, as do the requirements that he leave the home and contract for "enforced" therapy.

The Silent Partner

A firm approach also may be required with the silent partner—especially if she continues to deny the existence of incest in the home or if she persists in blaming her daughter for its occurrence. More likely, however, the wife will appear guilty and confused. Initially, it is important for the clinician to avoid confronting attitudes that could increase her sense of guilt. Confrontation may alienate her and further impair her self-image. An attitude of active listening and reflection, tempered with tolerable doses of reality, builds rapport at a time when a mother's allegiance, both to her child and to the therapeutic process, is important. Once rapport is built, careful confrontation can be used to help the mother break through her impasse of denial. Even then, however, confrontation should be used with caution since some mothers unconsciously seek a punishing agent in the therapist for alleviation of their sense of guilt.

The Victim

The approach to the victim is complicated and requires a fair degree of both sensitivity and perceptiveness. The age of the child determines the attitude of the clinician. Young children respond best to a gradual, tentative approach involving befriending and slow trust building, which relies heavily on non-verbal methods. Older children and teenagers often manifest a desire to talk and to trust — while at the same time, on a deeper level, they may be quite guarded, constantly testing the authenticity of the therapist.

In general, the child should be interviewed privately at first and the therapist's role as helper and friend should be fully clarified. The child should be encouraged to talk about the events surrounding incest and her feelings associated with them. Ventilation is necessary even in the face of resistance or fear. Details regarding incest should be explicit and fully elaborated, always with the therapist using and appreciating the language of the child. A questionnaire on molesting sometimes facilitates the talking process, especially with teenagers. The questionnaire legitimatizes the inquiry process for the teenager and places a comfortable distance between her and the therapist. (A sample questionnaire is provided at the end of Chapter 6.) Finally, the teenager's or child's feelings always should be clarified, reflected upon and accepted rather than discounted or mollified.

An issue that often poses some difficulty for the therapist centers around the victim's request for answers. The child may ask directly if she should press charges against her father or how the therapist would feel if she were the incest victim. Again, honesty is the best approach. The therapist states, and takes ownership of, her own feelings and choices of behavior. She offers alternative choices and empathically verbalizes the various feelings incest victims experience. For example, filing charges against an offending father can result in both negative and positive consequences. In court, the child must openly state that her father abused her. She may fear the court process, the public declaration of incest, and the possible consequences of the entire process. Her fears are legitimate. On the other hand, the child may experience a therapeutic emotional release with an accompanying decrease in guilt through courtroom proceedings.

Female Versus Male Therapist

A female therapist is deemed to be the appropriate choice, at least initially, in situations involving male offenders and female victims. The child especially will relate most readily to a non-threatening figure who is totally unlike the offender in whom she has lost all trust and toward whom she has mixed and confused emotions. Later on in the therapeutic process, a male clinician can be introduced, often as a co-leader in group work or to deal with specific issues. Role plays with male therapists have particular impact and are effective in helping to work through identity and psychosexual issues for the victim.

SECTION B: SPECIFIC METHODS FOR USE WITH CHILDREN AND ADOLESCENTS

22
ART TECHNIQUES

The Draw-A-Person (D-A-P) with Modified Questionnaire and the Kinetic Family Drawing (K-F-D)

The Draw-A-Person technique described in detail by Hammer (1958), as a projective instrument, lacks experimental validation. It never should be used alone for the purpose of diagnosis or categorization. As part of a battery of clinical tests, however, it yields valuable information and insights regarding conflicts, pathology and personality structure. As with other nonverbal methods, the Draw-A-Person cuts through defenses and quickly taps the unconscious. Also, it is a very useful tool for stimulating dialogue with reluctant, shy and resistant children and adolescents.

Equipment and instructions for the D-A-P are simple. White paper, 8-1/2" x 11", and a pencil with eraser, are all that is needed. The instructions are, "Please draw a person." If the child draws a stick figure, cartoon or caricature, she or he is asked to draw a complete figure (head, body, arms, and legs). Some clinicians caution the child at the onset to draw the total figure. No other instructions are given. The reluctant, hesitant or self-conscious client might ask a number of questions such as, "Should I put clothes on it?" or, "What if I can't draw?" It is very important that the therapist reply neutrally to such questions with answers, such as, "Draw whatever you like," or, "I'm not concerned with how good an artist you are." After the first drawing is completed, request a second one that depicts a person of the opposite gender. Use the words: "I see that you drew a girl. Now please draw a boy," or, "I see that you drew a boy. Now please draw a girl."

Interpreting the D-A-P takes practice. The literature is replete with burdensome interpretive principals (Goodenough, 1926; Machover, 1949) where the rendering of each part of the body allegedly symbolizes specific conflicts or measure a degree of intellectual functioning. Hypothetical speculations abound and have created a general suspicion in the public mind as to the use of drawings for interpretive purposes. Careless speculation is unfortunate and merely heightens anxiety in clients who fear nonverbal techniques because of lack of familiarity with method and purpose and also because of awareness that some measure of control over defenses will be lost.

It is much more useful and much less damaging to the client for the therapist first to familiarize her or himself with drawings of both stable and unstable clients of all ages. This experience helps a therapist to begin to distinguish intuitively the standard from the deviant. It also is helpful in learning what typically can be expected from the renderings or various age groups and of individuals with varying intellectual and artistic capabilities. In addition, it is important for the clinician to become familiar with the renderings of brain-damaged individuals and of chronically ill clients whose organ-preoccupation may be highlighted in the drawings, thus reflecting excessive concern over bodily function or impairment.

When interpreting, describe the drawings first. Usually the description gives a clue to personality make-up, predominant concerns and possible pathology. For example, take note of the drawing on the following page which was rendered by a ten-year-old boy. Descriptively, we see a primitive figure with a large head. The figure is disoriented in space and demonstrates gross immaturity. There is a lack of detail and clothing and a poor integration of bodily parts. From this description alone the therapist would suspect regression and emotional problems in the youngster. Equally important was this boy's behavior as he drew. The child was anxious about the task, and fidgety and compulsive about finishing his drawing, all of which suggested insecurity and possible low self-concept.

The following basic factors should be considered by the clinician when interpreting the D-A-P.

1. *Behavior of the client during task accomplishment* (anxious, resistant, compulsive, defensive, other descriptive term).

2. *Size and placement of the drawing.* Is the drawing very small (an indication of insecurity or inadequacy) or large (a possible sign of aggression especially if much pressure is used)? Is the drawing centered, indicating an appropriate sense of self in relationship to the environment?

3. *Distortions, exaggerations and omissions.* If the client omits, distorts or exaggerates certain parts of the body, he or she may be revealing preoccupations or the presence of denial.

4. *Shading, scribbling and cross-hatching.* Immoderate use of these contours possibly points to anxiety, preoccupations or fixations.

5. *Comparisons and sequence of figures.* Males generally draw their own sex first; females draw females. Exceptions may indicate sexual confusion or conflict. Conflict also can be revealed if one figure is noticeably larger or smaller than the other.

6. *Excessive detail and addition of accessories.* Compulsivity and/or dependency needs often are seen in clients whose renderings show much detail. Accessories also may be signs of dependency or insecurity. Precision can show preoccupation with structure.

7. *Pencil pressure.* Heavy stroking may indicate aggression and acting-out tendencies while light pressure may signal depression.

Children who have been sexually abused often render nude figures with explicit genitalia or emphasis on secondary sex characteristics. (See drawings on the following pages.) It is not usual for children or adults of any age to draw nude figures unless they are specifically instructed to do so. Such renderings are an indication of conflict and pathology. When children do draw explicit sexual characteristics it often is useful to ask them to label all of the body parts and to discuss their function. As the children describe their drawings they begin to express many of their conflicts and concerns. Additionally, the therapist becomes familiar with the child's particular terminology. It should be noted that the drawings of sexually abused children often are admissible in court.

Standard questionnaires to accompany the D-A-P for children and adults have been devised. A typical questionnaire follows this discussion. In responding to the questions, most children intuitively realize that they have drawn themselves or a significant figure in their lives. However, because the questions are phrased in the third person they are less threatening to the defense structure and thus tend to elicit deeply honest responses.

It is important to keep these questions brief as children lose patience quickly. Questions can be modified to suit the particular child. In addition, instead of completing the whole questionnaire it often is fruitful to focus on

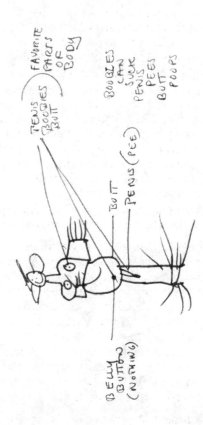

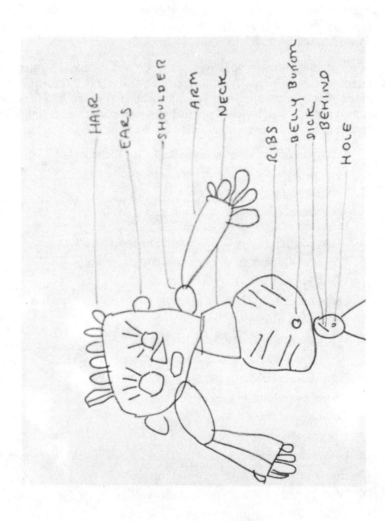

areas that elicit emotional responses. For example, if a child responds to the question, "What do you dream about at night?" by stating that she has nightmares, the questions that follow should be designed to help her elaborate on the content of her dreams, the times of occurrence, the emotions associated with them and her feelings about her dreams.

For children known to have been sexually abused, a modified questionnaire can be used. Typical questions that elicit information and associated affects regarding abuse are important, as they work to focus the interview on an area that the child resists but needs to explore. Examples of appropriate questions to use with children are listed below.

1. What part of you body do you like/dislike the most?
2. What is the worst thing that ever happened to you?
3. How do you feel about your body?
4. What person do you love the most/least? What do you love about that person?
5. Whom do you like to be alone with the most/least?
6. Why would someone threaten you? How?
7. What do you think about in bed at night?
8. Do you like to be alone? If not, why not?
9. Do you sleep alone?
10. When do you pretend to be asleep?
11. What would you do if a strange man came up to you?
12. How would you like to change your Mom/Dad?
13. Do your parents get along?
14. Do you prefer men or women?
15. Are you afraid of the dark?
16. Do you have stomachaches? Suffer from headaches? Wet the bed?
17. How many school days have you missed?
18. What part of your body hurts you?
19. What is the best/worst thing you have done?
20. What dreams do you have about your Mom/Dad?
21. What do you dislike about men/women?
22. If you had a secret, what would it be?
23. Whom would you like to tell about your secret?

Sensitivity and perceptiveness are necessary when using projective instruments. If a child is anxious and very resistant, it may be damaging to probe too quickly. Intersperse emotionally-laden questions with more neutral ones to diffuse anxiety. The modified D-A-P questionnaire is quite useful with the victim who has a good relationship with her therapist, has an intact ego structure, and is ready, though resistant, to deal openly with the incestuous abuse.

Static family drawings reveal the same valuable information as individual and self-drawings. Additionally, largely through placement and size of the figures, they point to roles in the family, significant figures in the child's life, patterns of intimacy, and conflicts among members. In the drawing on the following page we see Mom separated from the rest of the family members by an anonymous figure which was clearly placed to represent a barrier to family unity. The child, Tim, makes a clear statement about how he perceives his family or wishes them to be. Tim further protects himself from his mother by placing himself between his sister and father.

Kinetic Family Drawings (K-F-D), studied in detail by Burns and Kaufman (1970), are even more revealing than static ones for assessment, for eliciting affect, and for encouraging dialogue. The instructions are simple: "Draw everyone in you family, including you, doing something." Family dynamics and interactions are highlighted as evidenced in the drawings on the following pages. Robin, aged 12, had been sexually abused by her stepfather. She did not portray her figures in action but rather in a state of readiness. Especially in the second drawing, there is a sense of imminent danger. In the first drawing, she portrays her mother, her stepfather, and older sister Sally, 16. Kevin, rendered in red and black, is a devil with a pitchfork. He dominated the scene with large hands. (The form of sexual abuse had been fondling and digital penetration.) Sally is seductive, handing Kevin flowers. (Sally, too, had been sexually abused by Kevin, and, unlike her sister, refused to report her stepfather to the authorities.)

In describing her drawing, Robin said, "My mother is saying, 'What can I do?' I'm in the next room.'" (The mother denied knowledge of the abuse and was ambivalent about which course of action to take following disclosure.) In the second drawing, Robin portrayed herself alone with Kevin. Kevin clearly is separated from her by a box as he, a sad, clown-like figure, points a phallic instrument in her direction. Robin, sad, childlike and seductive, thinks, "HATE." Clearly these drawings revealed more about Robins's emotional state than could be elicited by the clinical interview alone.

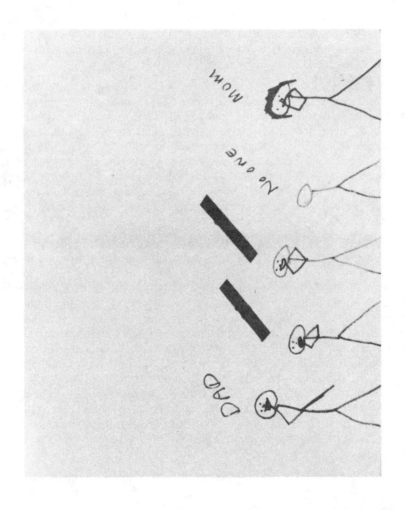

TYPICAL DRAW-A-PERSON
QUESTIONNAIRE FOR CHILDREN

1. How old are you?
2. Whom do you live with?
3. What would you like to do when you grow up?
4. In what ways are you smart?
5. What do you do best?
6. What three wishes do you have?
7. What makes you angry? happy? scared? nervous? worried?
8. What are some things you don't like about yourself?
9. What do you dream about at night?
10. What do people say about you?
11. What do you do when you are angry?
12. What does your mother do when you are bad? Your father?
13. How would you change your family if you could?
14. What pleases your mother about you? Your father?
15. How do you describe your friends? Your enemies?
16. How many friends do you have? Enemies?
17. What do you friends like about you?
18. What do you like to do best?
19. How do you feel about school? About your teacher?
20. Whom would you wish to be like?
21. How healthy are you?
22. When do you lose your temper?

The Self-Cartoon

Children involved in incestuous abuse suffer from low self-esteem resulting partly from guilt and a misplaced sense of responsibility. Their inner dialogue tends to reflect thoughts such as, "I must be bad or this would not be happening to me." Many clinicians simply assume that the victim suffers from a poor self-concept requiring supportive therapeutic measures. Before attempting to help the child build a new self-image, a graphic description of her or his current self-evaluation is effective because it furnishes both therapist and child with a visual and concrete image of the child's self-perception. Such an image not only carries much impact but also helps the therapist focus on specific areas of impairment.

One effective vehicle for evaluating self-image is the Self-Cartoon, a tool to help the child focus on the real verses the ideal self-image. The instructions ask the child to draw a well-known cartoon character "that reminds you of yourself." On the back of the sheet, the child is asked first to write a description of this character. Second, he or she is asked to write the reasons "why the character reminds you of yourself." A case illustration will demonstrate the effectiveness of this technique.

John, aged ten, had been involved in homosexual incest for a short time during his seventh year when his alcoholic father returned home briefly from prison. By his tenth year, John was in therapy for a variety of acting-out behaviors including showing pornographic literature and photographs to younger children. He presented himself as a fairly confident youngster whose D-A-P, seen on the following page, revealed nothing particularly unusual. His Self-Cartoon, however, portrays Porky Pig, whom John described as "both kind and nasty, lazy except when he's going to be killed, silly and fat, just a pig in the mud." John had a slight speech impediment which his mother reported had been exacerbated for several months following the incestuous relationship with his father. Hence, we see Porky portrayed as stuttering and described by John as "having trouble saying things." Unable to talk about the abuse he had sustained, John also "had trouble saying things" both in terms of speech and in terms of self-disclosure.

The Self-Cartoon graphically illustrates the degree of self-hatred John felt, self-hatred further highlighted when the boy was asked to draw the most unpleasant thing he could think of. John's drawing, labelled "Satan, ugly," resembles his Self-Cartoon. The noses, outlines of the heads and shapes of the mouths are identical. The eyes are similar with a blank, staring expression, and the hair and horns in the two drawings also resemble each other. What resulted from this exercise was an emotional release for the boy and valuable information to use in focusing on priority treatment issues.

Drawing the Assault and Reacting to the Offender

It is very important therapeutically that child victims of incest have an opportunity for release and catharsis in a warm, accepting and supportive setting. Various methods are used to encourage release. The effectiveness of all of these methods is totally dependent on the positive, trusting relationship established between child and therapist. Drawing assignments, carefully chosen to meet individual needs, are valuable tools in such a situation. They help the child by allowing for release; the therapist and child in building rapport; and the courts by providing additional evidence of incest.

One particularly useful two-part assignment involves asking the child to draw the assault, then asking for a reaction to the offender on paper. The assignment should be very specific and the language used in the instructions should be geared to the child's age and level of intellectual functioning. For example, the therapist might say the following to a young female victim of father-daughter incest: "Please draw what you described as 'Daddy touching' you. Pick one occasion that you remember clearly and draw what happened at that time. Next, draw a picture of how you felt when Daddy touched you. Put him in the picture, too. Show how he felt and let him know your feelings," Finally, ask the child to elaborate on the following on the back of each paper.

1.   What I drew.
2.   How I felt.
3.   How Daddy felt.
4.   How I feel now.

On the following page is a drawing by an eleven-year-old girl who was involved in a long-term incestuous relationship with her father. Seven painful attempts culminated in the small drawing on the lower right, which shows two figures merged together with explicit male genitalia depicted. The child says, "Get off me you stupid ediat (idiot)." The drawing clearly is labelled, identifying the act as rape. This particular child had difficulty disclosing to me the fact that fellatio-cunnilingus was forced upon her by her father and the drawing helped her to discuss these acts for the first time.

This same child completed a second drawing on the next page depicting a dream involving "Larry (Dad) beating Diana (herself)." The father had threatened to kill Diana if she ever revealed the nature of their relationship. Following disclosure, Larry was arrested. At the time Diana

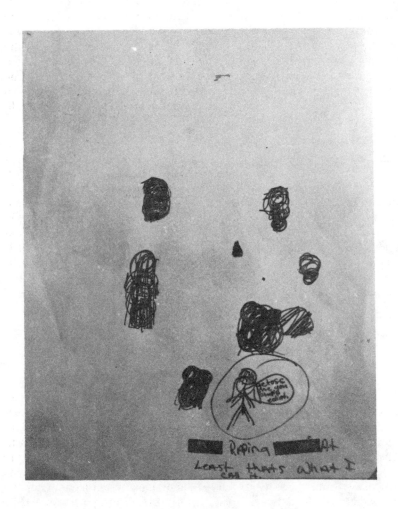

depicted her dream he was about to be released from jail on his own recognizance. This drawing, along with Diana's detailed account of her dream, proved to be very instrumental in convincing the judge that the offender should remain in jail pending the final hearing in Superior Court.

Diana's sister Sandy, aged nine, suffered from minimal brain damage (MBD), chronic migraine headaches and severe behavioral problems necessitating medication (30 mg. Elavil daily) to control violent and dangerous temper outbursts. Physical examination revealed an enlarged vagina and that the child masturbated destructively and continuously. She was terrified of her father. Still, Sandy denied incestuous involvement with her father.

Interviewing techniques were not effective in eliciting fruitful responses from this child. However, she did respond to play therapy, clay work and, to a lesser extent, drawing. On one occasion, she was asked to "Make believe Daddy did to you what he did to Diana." Previously, Sandy had stated she knew her Daddy "did something" to Diana but she did not know what. Sandy drew an assault (see following page) and labeled it "Daddy fooling with Sandy." Her identification of affect was appropriate, showing the offender smiling and the victim unhappy and angry. She provided the following, revealing responses to a modified D-A-P questionnaire.

1. How does Sandy feel?..."She's mad."
2. What else does she feel?..."She feels weird."
3. What does weird feel like?..."It feels bad and scared."
4. What is she going to do?..."She won't do anything about it."
5. Why?..."Because Daddy would get mad."
6. Suppose she told Mom?..."Mom would yell at Dad."
7. And then what would happen?..."They would fight."
8. And then what?..."Daddy would whip Sandy hard."
9. How does Daddy feel fooling with Sandy?..."He feels happy."
10. How does she know that?..."Because he's smiling."
11. Does he say anything?..."Yes, he says, 'does it feel good?'"
12. And what does Sandy say?..."She doesn't say anything because she is making believe she is asleep."
13. Did it happen more than one time?..."No."
14. When did it happen?..."In the wintertime."
15. Where was Mom?..."Home, in the living room."
16. How did it really feel?..."It hurt, like a headache."

Thus, in one drawing, we have the "full story" from a child too frightened and confused to verbalize her feelings. Additionally, we find a direct connection between the migraine headaches from which she suffers and the sexual abuse sustained by her father.

Shaping Via Directive Drawing

Many lay persons and clinicians alike attach a certain mystique to art and are reluctant to tamper with or be directive with the use of the media. Thus, one of the least emphasized aspects of art therapy relates to its educational value, which is referred to only peripherally in the literature. Teaching the successful manipulation of materials is viewed as a means to enhancing self-image and stimulating creativity. Art media, however, are tools subject to manipulation. Being harnessed to ideas and concepts, they have great educational value for behavior-shaping.

Two case illustrations demonstrate the value of art for shaping appropriate behaviors. The first involves a seductive seven-year-old girl who had been sexually molested by her father from her second year until his death by a self-inflicted gunshot wound when she was four. Between her fourth and seventh year, this child had a history of multiple stranger-molestations. Her mother initiated therapy following the most recent molestation by a man who offered the youngster an ice cream cone if she would "suck his dick." The child agreed compliantly with little evidence of fear or revulsion. Therapeutic needs were multiple, involving working through the early trauma of incest and of witnessing her father's death. One aspect of therapy, however, involved behavior-shaping with the nonverbal (art therapy) linked to the verbal (assertiveness training).

Inappropriate social responses and behaviors (in general, compliance, coyness, flirtatious laughter, seductive dress) were identified and specified. With the mother's cooperation, a system was instituted to extinguish these behaviors and responses gradually, by means of rewards (for appropriate actions and words). In therapy, part of the session was devoted to practice and rehearsal of appropriate, assertive responses to any adult who might approach this youngster for illicit purposes.

Art was used to integrate and reinforce new behaviors. Following verbal rehearsal of appropriate response, the child would illustrate, in strip cartoons with dialogue in balloons, the various situations she might encounter with a potentially threatening adult. In addition to helping to integrate newly learned verbal skills, art served other purposes for this youngster. For her, art was a pleasurable endeavor, one that diffused much of her anxiety and guilt and helped cement her relationship with the therapist. Art also allowed her to fantasize about potentially threatening situations and thus to manipulate and gain control over them. For example, as she became more skilled in assertiveness, she drew smaller male figures and her written, assertive dialogue became larger, almost dominating the various scenes.

The second illustration concerns a six-year-old male child who had been brutally incestuously assaulted by his father, a diagnosed paranoid schizophrenic, from the age of two to five years. In therapy, this youngster showed a persistent preoccupation with depicting nude figures with explicit, often grossly distorted genitalia.

Since I believed this boy needed to work through trauma, therapeutic goals initially involved allowing for free expression of affect, both verbally and non-verbally. As the months proceeded, however, the behaviors (including a preoccupation with sexuality and nudity) increased and it was deemed important to begin to extinguish inappropriate social behaviors before generalization could occur.

The method was simple. Appropriate (nonsexual) responses were rewarded and inappropriate (sexual) responses were ignored. This youngster entered therapy one day and was asked to draw his person with clothes on. The child, fully taken aback, replied, "I can't do that. I don't know what that looks like." I engaged in interactive drawing with him to provide literal instruction in appropriate figure depiction. The technique worked and thereafter the boy was rewarded for socially acceptable drawings. A new direction for verbal and nonverbal therapy was established and as a result there was a slight decline in his voyeuristic and masturbatory activities in the home, thus indicating the possibility for generalization of appropriate behaviors.

Depicting the Positive and Negative Aspects of Parents

Child victims of incestuous abuse have ambivalent feelings about both parents. Often they are angry at their mothers for not providing adequate protection for them in the home or for ignoring the incestuous acts. At the same time, many of these youngsters have been forced into the surrogate wife-mother role, since they feel a need to protect their mothers. Many of the girls feel betrayed by, angry at, and frightened of their fathers. For some, however, there is a sense of loyalty as well. The father may have been a major source of affection and pleasure (perhaps the only one) for them; furthermore, his presence in the home often signifies financial and emotional security for the entire family.

Part of the therapeutic process for ambivalent youngsters involves helping them sort through their mixed emotions while working toward acceptance and values clarification. Verbal methods can be quite effective, while nonverbal techniques can be used adjunctively to add impact and clarity to insights.

Listing Mom's and Dad's attributes, both positive and negative, can be followed by drawings of those attributes (for younger children, of "the Good and Bad Mom" and "the Good and Bad Dad"). Even quite young children are capable of establishing a dialogue between the various parts of their parents. Kinetic drawings of "Our Happy Family," "Our Sad/Upset Family at Home Doing Things," and "My Family the Way I Wish it Would Be," also are useful, as are collages where the child chooses magazine pictures to represent his/her parents or parts of them. Illustrations of feelings, whether through drawings, collage or clay work, stimulate focused discourse badly needed by these confused youngsters.

Clay

Clay models often express conflicts symbolically. As with drawings, defenses quickly are by-passed in an unfamiliar situation with an unfamiliar medium and insights can come rapidly from visual productions. In addition, clay is a valuable avenue for communication for victims who find verbalizing difficult.

Any modeling material is effective, although water-based clay is most commonly used and quite inexpensive. Either a directive or non-directive approach can be used. The victim may be asked directly to model the assailant or to show some aspect of the assault; or she simply may be advised that there are many ways to express herself and that she may manipulate the clay in any way she chooses in order to show something about herself. When the victim completes her work, the therapist says simply, "Tell me about it."

Clay is not an appropriate medium for all victims and the clinician should have at least a rudimentary knowledge of the handling of the material, the possible dangers of its use, and the typical and atypical reactions that may occur. Some points to be considered are listed below.

1. Very young or regressed children may not be ready for clay. If the child treats the medium as if it were two-dimensional by smearing

or consistently flattening it, it is not appropriate for her. Instead, she should be given drawing or painting materials.

2. Clay therapy sometimes elicits uncontrolled anger. To some degree this may aid in release of pent-up emotions; but rage that gets out of hand can be counterproductive. Also, care should be taken to guard against inconsistencies in the therapeutic approach. If the therapist is working with the child to instill social controls and appropriate social behaviors, she or he may find that clay elicits uncontrolled anger in a child not ready for such expression.

3. Repetition compulsion can occur with some victims. Adult victims generally do not model explicit genitalia unless they specifically are directed to do so or unless they are psychotic. However, young victims of sexual assault may repeatedly model the penis or breast. While such modeling may represent working through the trauma, equally it may signify an impasse, a compulsion or an exacerbation of the conflict through the use of the medium.

4. Very insecure or very rigid and/or conventional victims may not be appropriate candidates for clay therapy. The medium does elicit anxiety reactions that may be counterproductive to therapy. Equally, resistance from rigid or conventional personalities may present an insurmountable barrier.

5. Masking, blocking or screen modeling are common forms of resistance that occur with clay work. The victim may or may not be aware of the conflict but will defend against disclosure. Meares (1960) discusses three types of screen models: a) where the object modeled is nonspecific (a man instead of Dad). b) where a part of the environment is modeled (a table or chair), and c) where directions are misinterpreted so that conflict-free objects are modeled (ashtrays, dishes). Meares suggests that the therapist avoid confrontation in such situations. Instead, repeat the directions, provide reassurance and reeducate about the task at hand.

The Worst Concept Drawing

The Worst Concept Drawing is a tool the author devised that is based on the Most Unpleasant Concept Test, a projective method used by some psychotherapists and described by Hammer (1958). As with all projective instruments, interpretations are subjective and based on reactions to instructions as well as on content categories. The Most Unpleasant Concept Test provides material that can be adapted either to assessment or to elicit affect through free associations.

Instructions for the Worst Concept Drawing are as follows:

1. Ask the child to picture in her mind the worst thing that ever happened to her, the worst thing she can imagine happening to her, or the worst dream she ever had.
2. Ask the child to depict her image on paper.
3. On the reverse side of the paper, ask the child to describe in writing both her drawing and the feelings she has about it.
4. Finally, encourage verbal free association about her responses.

Combining the drawing technique with writing and finally verbalizing can be quite powerful. The technique is effective both with individuals and in groups. Group members can be asked to free associate about their various individual depictions, in round-robin style, either to set a climate for catharsis, or to focus on a single member's work. What follows are the free associations of a single teenaged group member about the drawing of a co-member, a victim of long-term incest.

"Someone got her guts cut out."

"Pain."

"Complete seclusion from reality."

"Going blind."

"Mugged and raped in the woods."

"Death."

"A big blast."

"A broken heart."

"Afraid."

"Pulled into Hell's creation."

"Burned for eternity."

The group was composed of 12 teenaged females, many of whom had been sexually assaulted or were victims of incest. In a single session where the focal point was drawing the worst concept, they discharged much anxiety, got in touch with underlying affect (fear, anger), and self-disclosed more openly than most of them had been able to do in individual therapy. The session helped to unite the group and to provide direction for future work both individually and in group. On the following pages are the drawings of nine of these group members, along with their own written descriptions of their depictions.

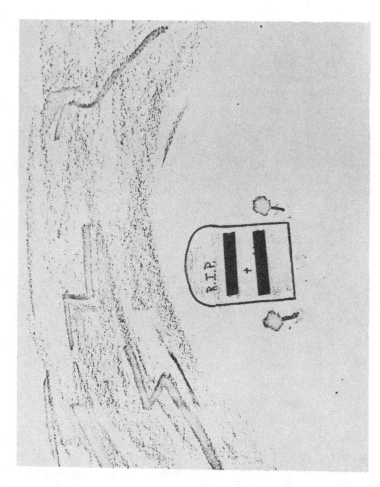

"I am afraid that my mom and dad are going to die before I get a chance
to clear things up with them and make it right between me and my mom so
I don't feel guilty any more."

"Me and my mom. I am caught in her pain over all this. And I don't want to lose my mom. I love my mom."

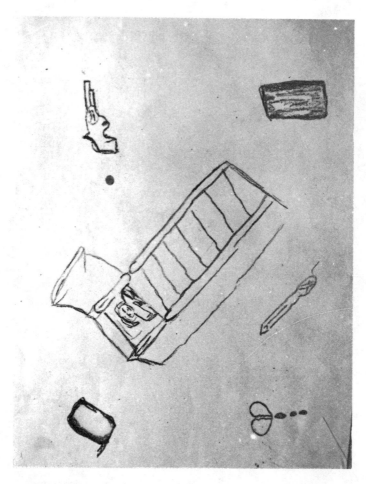

"The gun resembles of being scared of harm from someone and things happening to my body. It scares me. And losing my life. And for people seeing through me before I am getting a chance to explain. And I am scared to open up."

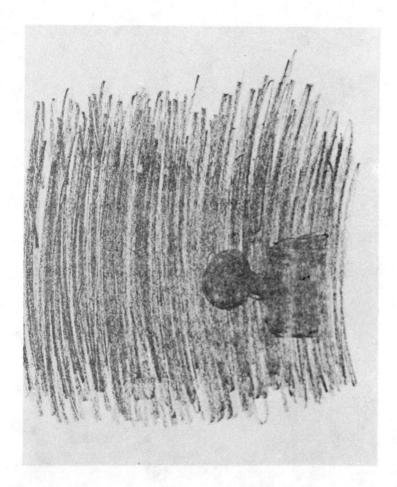

"The silhouette of a man. It's dark. I'm afraid of what it really is. What it symbolizes."

"I was very scared and I was lost because I didn't know what way to turn. In this picture there is a lot of blood because I will bleed to death. Thank you."

"I'm afraid and so I'm saying, 'Oh, my God.' He says, 'Ha, Ha!'"

"Being pulled into a pit of fire by something I don't understand."

"A man being stabbed and then sliced. It doesn't go through the whole process. In the end, he rips and turns inside out. That's bad. Ugg."

"When someone comes in that you don't know and it's dark."

23
WRITING TECHNIQUES

Writing techniques used with victims of sexual abuse include the unsent letter, the journal, sentence blanks, self-esteem rating scales, checklists and sociograms. The present chapter describes use of the first two methods. Remaining topics are treated in Chapter 24.

The Unsent Letter

The unsent letter is a standard technique for use with victims of sexual abuse. Children respond well to this exercise and require little direction. Specific instructions vary with individual situations but should include the following information:

1. I want you to relax and think about your father/stepfather for a few minutes.

2. Now I want you to write a letter to him, telling him how you feel about what happened between you. This is a real letter but it is between you and me (you and the group). Your dad/stepdad will never see it. Say anything you want in any way no matter how bad or vulgar you think it sounds. Use curse words if you want. Tell him everything you feel.

3. Sometimes it helps first to describe what happened between you — what sexual things he did to you. That helps you to express your feelings. Remember, the reason for the letter is for you to express your feelings.

After the letter is written, it is read aloud to the therapist or group. Feelings are clarified and validated. Afterwards, the child specifically is told that she can do as she wishes with her letter. (Interestingly, many children with whom I have worked do not destroy their letters but ask me to keep them instead.) With children, it is neither necessary nor advisable to use confrontation techniques or group coercion to stimulate catharsis. The letter by itself serves to clarify and condense feelings and is part of the over-all closure process for resolving feelings.

Examples of several types of unsent letters follow:

1. The first letter was written by a 13-year-old girl molested for one year by her stepfather.

    Dear Dad:

    You are dirty and fucked and I would shoot your balls off if I could. I'd like to see you get beaten up by some cowboys. You are an asshole. Dirty and fucken bastard. You put me through Hell. Go to Hell. Because of the abortion.

    Jane

2. Next is a letter by a 12-year-old girl to her mother after the disclosure of incest with her father.

    To Mom:

    I need you not be so angry. Rite now I regret you a lot because you graunched at me. I have asked you a lot and told you and every time I did you said no and I know what you told me. I need you to be more understanding on what I fele but you probally had a hard life.

    Stephanie

    (This child asked to share her letter with her mother during a therapeutic session.)

3. The third letter was written by an 18-year-old girl following disclosure of a ten-year incestuous relationship with her father. The girl suffered from migraine headaches and an ulcer. Her letter clearly reflects her initial inability to release anger during early therapeutic sessions.

Dear Dad:

I don't know if I can ever forgive you for the pain and hurt that you have caused me. I just hoe that someday we will or could be friends, because I will never love you, that much I do know. I really feel you should continue this counseling sessions. I think they will help solve your sickness and problems.

Jan

4. The final letter was written by a 12-year-old girl involved in father-daughter incest. At the last moment, the child decided not to testify against her father. She was asked to write to the judge for closure, advising him of her feelings about the court proceedings.

Dear Judge Jones:

I was raped by my father for four years. You are telling me I have to go to court. and testify. That my father raped me. I don't want to go to court. Because I am scared and I don't want to sit in front of alot of people and say my dad raped me. You should have parents go to court for kids. I hate this hole thing. I don't like the court at all. Insted of my father going to jail I just wanted him to get help. I have been through a lot. I had dreams that I was sitting in the court room and that the Lawyer were yelling at me and then the Judge and Lawyers were all arguing and then at the end he just got off free.

Sincerely,

Christie

The Journal—A Directed Assignment

Journal writing is another traditional tool for working with victims. With children and adolescents especially, it is important to be quite specific about the purposes of the journal and the expectations regarding content. If the therapist simply asks the child to keep a journal of her feelings she or he may be surprised to read endless accounts of school projects, the weather and favorite television programs. Incest is painful and unless the child specifically is guided in the process of working through her feelings, she will resist.

Sometimes it helps to have the child do her writing at specific times such as during part of the therapeutic session or while she is waiting for her appointment. Setting specific times is a stimulant for task accomplishment and helps the child limit the amount of time that she dwells on incest. Giving the journal a name also helps to orient the victim to the specific task at hand. One child called hers a "Rape Diary;" another, "My Story of Dad and Me."

Instructions should include the fact that the journal is to be a record of the child's feelings about incest. She can write anything she wants as long as it relates in some way to her relationship, past or present, to her father and to other members of the family.

An excerpt from the journal, "Dad and Me," follows. It was written by a 13-year-old victim of incest:

I went to court on this day to see if my father would get help. My father was dressed in a pair of pants and a shirt and some tennys. He looked like a raged dog but that happens when you are in jail. I love my father very much. He says he wants help and I really do believe him but I really think that he wants help. I love my father very much even though he did this.

24
SENTENCE BLANKS, RATING
SCALES, CHECK LISTS
AND SOCIOGRAMS

Sentence blanks, self-esteem rating scales, adjective check lists and sociograms are among the many excellent vehicles employed to encourage dialogue in family and group work. They are also useful in one-to-one therapy, especially when an impasse has been reached with traditional verbal methods of communication. These tools should not be used to diagnose or to intimidate the victim and her family. Their purpose, to aid in communication, should be explained fully before they are used.

Generally, any one of these tools can be of value if it measures what it is designed to measure, if the client gains insight or release from its use, and if dialogue is stimulated. The blanks, check lists and scales should be devised to suit individuals, bearing in mind the age and intellectual functioning of the client and her or his specific therapeutic needs. Simplicity in form, brevity and lack of repetition are important in the construction of useful tools. Examples of several types of assessment and communication vehicles follows:

1. *The Sentence Blank.* The sentence blank presented below is useful with pre-adolescent or adolescent victims in family work. Its purpose is to encourage communication between the child and her parents. Specifically, it affords the victim a vehicle to discuss her feelings about her parents and home life with the family.

The Sentence Blank

1. The thing I like best about Mom/Dad is _____.
2. The thing I like least about Mom/Dad is _____.
3. Mom/Dad feel that I am _____.
4. Mom/Dad treat me as if I were _____.
5. At home, the best/worst times are _____.
6. If I could change on thing about home/Mom/Dad, it would be

   _____.
7. My favorite time with my parents is _____.
8. Mom/Dad cares most about _____.
9. Mom/Dad is unhappy about _____.
10. Things at home would be nicer if _____.
11. Mom feels that Dad is _____.
12. Dad feels that Mom is _____.

The blank can be completed orally in the family's presence or answers can be written and later read aloud by the victim to her parents. A successful variation is to have the child's parents answer complete sentences as they believe their daughter would. The blank can be used in its entirety or in part, with the therapist encouraging dialogue after each or any of the questions. It is important to process feelings about the use of the sentence blank before proceeding to other issues.

A variation in format of the above sentence blank requires a simple "yes" or "no" responses from the victim as illustrated below:

1. Mom likes and respects me as a person.
2. Dad understands me.
3. I feel loved in my family.
4. My home life is not what it should be.
5. I seem to annoy Mom most of the time.

2. *The Self-esteem Rating Scale.* Self-esteem rating scales are used frequently in therapy with adults to increase insights and to highlight areas where growth is needed. These scales can be modified to suit various age groups. The abbreviated scale shown below is useful with young children and the results not only pinpoint therapeutic issues for the child but can be shared with parents and school personnel.

		YES	NO
1.	I generally do well in school.	___	___
2.	At home my family picks on me.	___	___
3.	I make lots of mistakes when I do my chores.	___	___
4.	I do well in my school work.	___	___
5.	Mom thinks I am a good person.	___	___
6.	Dad really likes me.	___	___
7.	I get along with my brother/sister.	___	___
8.	I am pretty/good-looking.	___	___
9.	It is easy for me to make friends.	___	___
10.	I am a leader.	___	___
11.	When I grow up, I will be famous.	___	___
12.	I have good ideas.	___	___
13.	I cause trouble to everyone.	___	___
14.	People are happy to be with me.	___	___
15.	I cause fights at home.	___	___
16.	I usually am happy.	___	___
17.	I am important.	___	___
18.	I do many bad things.	___	___
19.	When I grow up, I will be successful.	___	___
20.	I am alone alot.	___	___
21.	I get nervous easily.	___	___
22.	I do many good things.	___	___
23.	My parents are proud of me.	___	___
24.	I get sick alot.	___	___
25.	I am stupid	___	___
26.	I have trouble sleeping.	___	___
27.	Everyone likes me.	___	___
28.	I am always tired.	___	___
29.	I am clever.	___	___
30.	I have lots of bad thoughts.	___	___

A variation of the rating scale to measure self-esteem asks the child to list her qualities, i.e., talents, skills, accomplishments and admired traits.

3. *Adjective Checklists.* Adjective checklists are quick and easy to complete and therefore are quite useful in family or group work. They consist of lists of adjectives that measure various qualities-- negativity, high or low self-esteem, reality orientation, depression and the like. The client is asked simply to check off or circle those adjectives which she feels apply to her or to a relative who is being discussed. The following checklist, designed to measure negative traits, is useful for teenagers or adults.

DEPRESSED	TENSE	AGGRESSIVE
RIGID	INHIBITED	DOMINANT
GUILTY	COLD	UNFRIENDLY
ANGRY	BIGOTED	LONELY
UNTRUSTING	DEPENDENT	JUDGEMENTAL
SAD	INFANTILE	INEFFICIENT
HOSTILE	SICKLY	AIMLESS
SHY	SELF-CRITICAL	HOPELESS
UNASSERTIVE	MOODY	ACTING OUT
PASSIVE	UNHAPPY	OVERLY SENSITIVE
HELPLESS	NEEDY	IMPULSIVE
RASH	HYPOCRITICAL	DECEITFUL

OTHER:

4. *The Sociogram.* Sociograms are used informally in schools to measure peer relationships, particularly social choices and rejection. An adolescent victim and her parents should be advised that the purpose of the exercise is to examine their relationship with one another so that they can decide what changes might be in order. The client is given a blank sheet of paper and pencil and asked to place a circle representing the self in the center of the paper. Circles of various sizes and at various distances from the self-circle are drawn to represent family members and close friends so that each one reflects his or her position with regard to the client.

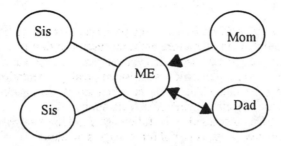

Arrows of various sizes point to (mutual) influences in the client's life. In the above sociogram, Mom exerts a non-reciprocal influence on the victim while she and Dad share a mutually influential relationship. In addition, Dad's size and proximity to the victim indicate that he plays an important role in her life.

Each relationship in the sociogram should be evaluated fully, with the following questions used as guidelines:

1. What relationship patterns are evident from your sociogram?
2. If you could, would you change these patterns? If so, how?
3. In your family, who understands you? Do you do the under-standing?
4. Are your relationships ones that give you happiness? Satisfaction? Discomfort? Joy? Pain? Anxiety?
5. Do you feel loved and supported in your family? Or do you provide the love and support for family members?
6. Are you needed in the family? If so, how? By whom? Whom do you need?
7. Who cares for you the most? In what way?

In evaluating each relationship, help the client to examine the concept of balance, self-growth, satisfaction and intimacy with a focus on insight and needed change.

25
DESENSITIZATION

Systematic or covert desensitization is a well-known technique for stress and anxiety reduction. Developed by Cautela (1966), desensitization involves two procedures—relaxation and counterconditioning—and is based on the principle that two antithetical responses cannot occur simultaneously. It is not possible for the body to experience relaxation and tension at the same time. In desensitization, the body first is relaxed through progressive deep muscle or autogenic relaxation. Following relaxation, the principles of counterconditioning are applied, based on the concept that fears are learned and, hence, can be unlearned by repeatedly associating the fear-producing, unpleasant stimulus with a pleasant one. The procedure involves deeply relaxing the client and then presenting a hierarchy of fear-producing stimuli, starting with the least threatening and proceeding gradually to the most threatening.

Relaxation Techniques

Relaxation, essential to the technique of desensitization, has numerous other benefits for victims of incestuous abuse. Relaxation techniques for children vary somewhat from those used with adults but the basic principles remain the same. Techniques vary largely because of children's shorter attention span and their less sophisticated use of vocabulary and imagery.

Relaxation in itself is helpful in counteracting anxiety. Once the child learns systematically to relax, she gains a sense of control of her body that enhances self-image and enables her to face difficult life experiences with a greater sense of confidence. Relaxation also is useful to alleviate psychosomatic symptoms, particularly those associated with muscle spasms such as the gastric distress often experienced by child victims.

Finally, relaxation is helpful as a prelude to various techniques that the therapist plans to use with the child, such as directed fantasy work, alternate story telling, dream work, meditation, systematic desensitization and coping self-statements.

All forms of relaxation follow similar principles, namely that relaxation can be learned, that individuals can gain control over autonomic reflexes, and that it is impossible for two antithetical bodily conditions (anxiety and a state of calm) to co-exist simultaneously. With children, techniques in deep muscle relaxation are particularly effective because they require the child actively to focus on bodily sensations.

An effective relaxation tool for use with children is guided imagery. Imagery (visualizing pictures in the mind's eye) is being used today increasingly for relaxation and to facilitate learning processes. Both applications, individually and combined, are useful for work with incest victims.

There are a number of centering and grounding exercises to use with both adults and children as part of the relaxation process. Children, however, seem to respond especially to abbreviated, guided visual journeys when they are geared toward their own experiences. The therapist can orient the imagery exercises to the particular child by obtaining answers to the following types of questions: What is your favorite, safest spot in the whole world? What do you think about in your quiet times? What do you dream about most often during happy times? What was the best trip that you ever took? What is your favorite daydream?

One nine-year-old male victim was obsessed with space travel. The following visual exercise helped to relax this youngster prior to the court experience:

> "First, I want you to lie down on the mat, close your eyes, and relax all of your muscles. Tell all of your muscles to let go and relax. Feel the mat underneath your body. Make contact with the mat with every part of your body. Relax. Breathe slowly and very deeply. Slowly and deeply. You feel calm and peaceful, totally relaxed. At peace. (Pause.) Now, I want you to imagine the light and warmth of the sun in the center of

your body. This is your center. This light and warmth. Feel the warmth inside of you. Picture what the light looks like. Now, this center of you takes a journey right out of the top of your head into outer space. You, your center, has left your body through the top of your head and is taking a journey deep into space. You are zooming a million miles away from earth into the darkness, past the stars, past the sun, past the moon, past the planets. You travel fast and far. Sometimes straight as an arrow. Sometimes in circles. (Pause.) Now, suddenly, you turn and begin your descent back to earth. Past the stars again, past the sun, past the moon, past the planets. Back to earth. Right back into the top of your head. Into your body once again. Once again the warmth and the light are back in the center of your body. (Pause.) Now, slowly open your eyes and tell me about your journey, all the things you saw and how you felt.

Another child, a five-year-old, gained the most comfort in life from two teddy bears, her sleeping companions. This victim's relaxation exercise focused on the image of floating on pink (the color of the girl's bedroom) clouds with two giant teddy bears.

Hierarchy for Systematic Desensitization of Court-related Anxiety

One of the most frightening aspects of disclosure for victims of incest is fear of court proceedings after charges have been filed against the offender. In many states, the reality is that child victims legally are treated as if they are the offenders. Such behavior on the part of the legal system is criminal. Apparently it stems from misplaced priorities in a male-dominated society, misperceptions about what constitutes the sanctity of the family, and from the basically fallacious concept of family "ownership" of children. In some legal interpretations, the betrayal of one's family (especially one's father) through disclosure of incest seems to be perceived as a sin meriting severe punishment.

The fact is that children rarely lie about incest. Yet in many cases each victim is subjected to rigorous and embarrassing physical examination and police interrogation. There are long, trumped-up delays in hearings and in some states children are forced to submit to lie detector tests. In the end, the victim must testify, sometimes in an open hearing, with her father present.

Such traumatic court experiences clearly are unjustifiable, especially when videotapes of private testimony exist and/or when surrogate witnesses for the child readily are available. It is no wonder that so many victims and their families refuse in the end to embark upon this emotionally-damaging and farcical procedure that ironically often results in freedom for the offenders. Because of the lack of humanity in the legal system and because of the lack of likelihood of progressive change, it is encumbent upon the therapist to devise methods to relieve court-related anxiety in child and adolescent victims.

Desensitization is an extremely effective technique to counteract court-related anxiety. To be effective, desensitization procedures require skill, patience and time. With children, modifications in both goals and procedures may be necessary. For example, the goal for desensitization for child victims often is to decrease, not eliminate, anxiety or fear. A second goal is to rehearse the key events involved in the court appearance in order to familiarize the child with the expected routine, thereby further decreasing anxiety. Procedurally, desensitization with children involves abridged methods of guided imagery and deep muscle relaxation suitable for young age groups.

The therapist begins systematic desensitization with several training sessions involving deep muscle relaxation. Once the child has mastered relaxation techniques, she can proceed to imagine scenes in the desensitization hierarchy while in the relaxed state. The instructions for the child begin with:

> "Keep your eyes closed, breathe deeply and remain relaxed. I am going to ask you to picture some scenes. Try to picture them very clearly in your minds-eye. As soon as the picture I suggest is clearly formed in your minds-eye, raise your index finger. First, I want you to picture seeing yourself dressing on the day you are to go to court."

After seeing the raised finger, the therapist then waits a few seconds and says, "Stop picturing the scene now. Did that scene make you anxious or scared?" The victim rates her fear on a simplified scale (alot, some, a little bit, not at all). The child then is asked to relax again for 30 seconds and picture the scene again until there is no anxiety. The therapist advances to scene #2 in the hierarchy, following the same procedure. Scenes introduced in this series of steps should include the following:

1. Seeing yourself dressing on the day you are to go to court.
2. Having breakfast before you are to go to court.
3. Driving to the courthouse.
4. Waiting outside the courtroom with your mother/counselor/lawyer.
5. Talking with your lawyer before the court hearing.
6. Entering the courtroom.
7. Seeing a picture of a courtroom in your minds-eye.
8. Seeing the judge presiding over the courtroom.
9. Seeing the courtroom filled with strange faces.
10. Being seated in the courtroom.
11. Taking the witness stand.
12. Being asked questions by your lawyer.
13. Being asked questions by your Dad's lawyer.
14. Seeing your Dad seated in front of the witness stand as you answer questions.

If the child is very anxious about testifying and if there is ample time, the therapist can devise gradients within the hierarchy. For example, the victim is asked if it matters whether the courtroom is large or small or whether the judge is male or female. It is helpful to add reinforcement to successful desensitization sessions with the young child. She should be rewarded with free time, a snack or a game after she has relaxed and imagined the scenes presented to her.

Relaxation, guided imagery and rehearsal of the court process can be combined as part of a desensitizing and centering process for the victim. A sample activity follows.

> The child is asked to sit in a comfortable chair in a relaxed position. She is told to close her eyes and breathe deeply for a few minutes, imagining a favorite activity or a pleasurable pursuit. Then, the following is recited to her in a slow, calm, monotone: "Now tense all of your muscles very, very tightly—all at the same time—your eyes, mouth, face, shoulders, chest, stomach, legs and feet. Hold that position while I count to three . . . One . . . Two . . . Three. Now, let go and feel the relaxation all over. (Pause.) Now, let's do that again. Tense every one of your muscles for a few seconds. (Pause.) Let go now. (Pause.) Feel the relaxation all over. Breathe slowly and deeply. Tell yourself to relax. Keep your

eyes closed and feel the relaxation all over your body. (Pause.) Now, I want you to imagine the day you are to go to court to testify. You are very relaxed and you feel confident. You feel energetic and capable. A good feeling. A feeling that you can do what you have set your mind to do. You and Mom see the courthouse in front of you. Picture what you imagine the building looks like. (Pause.) Now, you and Mom enter the building. You walk surely and confidently. What kind of doors do you pass through? Picture them. (Pause.) Remain relaxed and confident. Breathe deeply and slowly. Next, you find yourself seated outside the courtroom. Does anyone come to talk with you? Your lawyer? Picture the people you want to be with you. (Pause.) You feel good and safe with them. Still relaxed. Still breathing heavily, deeply. Confident. Full of energy. Now you enter the courtroom. There are many people there. Who are they? Who comes in? The judge? What does he look like? (Pause.) Is Dad there? Dad's lawyer? His family? You remain calm. You look into the faces of the people who care for you and with whom you feel safe. Now you are called to the witness stand, still confident, still feeling relaxed. Calm. You breathe deeply and slowly, telling yourself, 'I am O.K. I am relaxed and fine.' Now, people begin to question you. Your lawyer. Picture him. His face. Look at him directly. (Pause.) The questions are clear and all you must do is answer them as honestly as you can. And if you don't know an answer, you say, 'I don't know.' You continue to be calm and relaxed, breathing deeply, answering confidently. Now, Dad's lawyer asks you some questions. You know what to expect. You are confident and sure of yourself. Looking directly at his face, you answer each question truthfully. This is the hardest part of the court hearing and you are prepared. You conduct yourself beautifully. Breathing deeply, calmly. And then suddenly it is all over. You have done it! And you tell yourself how proud you are of the way you conducted yourself. It is over and you got through it calmly, confidently. You continued to breathe deeply and calmly. (Pause.) You feel energy and peace. (Pause.) Breathing deeply. Now, return to imagine a favorite activity as you did at the beginning of this exercise. Picture yourself doing something fun and enjoyable. Stay calm, relaxed, full of energy. And when you open your eyes as I count to three, you will continue to feel calm, relaxed, full of energy. One ... Two ... Three ..."

The clinician can be helpful also by accompanying the child to court and insuring that she is with a trusted ally during the proceedings. (A hostile paternal grandmother is not an appropriate companion for the victim about to testify against her father.)

It may be noted that the question of open versus closed courtrooms is of serious concern to therapists. Defense attorneys request open hearings to further intimidate young victims. Therapists are learning to retaliate by borrowing ideas from rape crisis counselors who have experience in coping with hostile attorneys. In the face of the threat of an open hearing, the therapist can suggest that she will advise representatives of women's organizations such as NOW or the League of Women Voters to send large numbers of their members to crowd the courtroom. The defense attorney undoubtedly will withdraw his request for an open hearing if he realizes that the courtroom may be filled with 50 antagonistic women. Such tactics may appear extreme but they could prove necessary for the protection of a child who needs to perceive the therapist as both helper and friend.

Desensitization Using Stories and Dreams

Story and dream telling are therapeutic in themselves as they allow for self-disclosure, catharsis and often sudden insights. Children sometimes can recount their deepest fears and concerns through dream telling, fears they otherwise would be unable to verbalize. The dream that follows, written by a nine-year-old female incest victim, provides an example:

> "I dreamed that he was hurting me. I was in the house and he had come in the door. I was yelling at him telling him that he had to get out. and then he kept on coming closer and closer to me. he had held me down and was beating me. he had slapped me and also cut me on the arm with a knife. Some people had heard me cry and screaming and they came in and saw him. He had ran out the door they didn't worry about that they had just got me and took me to the hospital. then I was under intinsive care. After that I woke up.
>
> The end."

The therapist can help the victim use dreams to decrease anxiety and as learning experiences. A ten-year-old male victim of homosexual incest recounted the following dream:

> "I was caught in a bad storm. I came to a man's house. There
> was no one there. It was wierd. I went in. The furniture was
> covered with white sheets. I thought there was a couch. It was
> really two chairs. One arm was missing on each. I sat down
> between them and the chairs broke. I saw a hand crawling on
> the floor. It was black and chased me through the house. I
> went to the top of the stairs. There was a monster with one
> hand off. Frankenstein. I jumped down three stories to a
> lagoon. The monster chased me. There were crocodiles and
> the monster threw them on the roof. I ran. He chased me. I
> found a wood cutter's axe and chopped off his head and then
> burned his house and went to my house."

By discussing the various elements of the dream along with his
accompanying fears, the boy was able to see that the monster represented
his father and that the boy, fearing mutilation through sodomy, projected
this fear onto his father. This youngster recorded his dream and was
instructed to relax and to play the tape until he no longer felt anxious.

Anxiety resulting from frightening dreams can be relieved in other
ways beside desensitization. A simple method is providing alternate
endings for painful dreams. For example, the girl who dreamed her father
was beating her and cutting her with a knife was instructed to think of an
alternate, less frightening, ending to her dream. When she was unable to
do so, I interactively assisted her by providing the following ending:

> "I was telling him to get out and then he kept on coming closer
> and closer to me. He had held me down but I managed to get
> free and called the police who came and helped me before he
> really could hurt me."

The ending helped this child to gain a sense of control over her own
welfare at a time when it was vitally important to help her understand that
the victim role was a position she could reverse with her own reasoning
power.

26
OTHER THERAPEUTIC MEDIA

There are a number of adjunctive tools and techniques that merit brief consideration as aids to the therapist attempting to help young victims work through the trauma of incestuous abuse. The clinician is encouraged to use these tools creatively to suit her or his own style of therapy.

Bibliotherapy

Even with young children, therapists can use bibliotherapy by selectively choosing passages from first-person accounts of incest victims. It also is useful for the clinician to keep a file of copies of writings from her or his own clients to refer to, and to use anonymously when appropriate.

Victims of all ages share common feelings and have very similar reactions to incest. Because of similarities in the incest experience, therapists can compose handouts, statements of rights, poems, passages and credos to be read or given to victims at appropriate times, always with consideration of the age of the victim. An example of one such handout follows:

Girls Who Are Sexually Abused by Adult Family Members Should Know:

1. Incest happens to thousands of girls every year.
2. No matter how you behaved or what you did *you are not responsible* in any way for the incest that occurred in your life. *Always* adults are responsible for what they do to children.
3. Incest is against the law and an adult who commits incest is breaking the law.

4. No matter how you felt (even if sometimes you enjoyed being touched or fondled sexually by your parent/step-parent), you should not feel guilty. Victims sometimes do enjoy incestuous experiences. Our bodies respond even when our minds tell us we don't like what is happening. You have done nothing wrong. The adult was wrong.

5. You may feel afraid but there are people who can help you—even if you have been threatened and told not to say anything to anyone.

6. Remember, you did the right thing by telling someone. If your parent is punished or if your family breaks up, it is not because you told. It is because your family has serious problems that they need to deal with and you helped them to face these problems by telling about the incest.

The O.K. Script

It is incumbent upon the therapist to alleviate unfounded but expected negative feelings that victims experience about themselves as a result of incest. Incest victims have a negative self-image. They do not understand what happened to them nor why.

Reassurances and a solid, trusting relationship with the therapist based on honest caring, empathy and an obvious desire to befriend the victim are invaluable, especially in the initial stages of therapy. Trust building cannot be emphasized too strongly because child victims of incest often never have had a trusting relationship with anyone. The father violated the child and the mother offered no protection. Silence and denial permeated the atmosphere of the home. Once self-esteem is improved and the crisis is alleviated, the therapist may begin deeper work, possibly involving confrontation related to anger releasing, covert manipulation of family roles and the like.

The O.K. Script, elaborated by Harris (1967), is a good tool for aiding self-image building. The script will vary depending on the age, experience and intellectual functioning of the child or adolescent. Nonetheless, the basic rationale for using the script remains the same. A written script cements and consolidates cognitive insights arising from the therapeutic process. Worded in the first person with the victim's name appearing in each statement or affirmation, it promotes a sense of ownership of thoughts and feelings and increases a sense of control over one's own destiny.

The script can be comprehensive, emphasizing, through wording and repetition, crucial areas of dissonance for the victim. It can be typed and hung in the victim's room, or written in total or in parts on index cards for the victim to carry with her.

Prepare the child or adolescent to use the script. Explain the rationale behind the use of affirmations: positive thoughts become part of us (of our consciousness) if we repeat them to ourselves a sufficient number of times and positive thoughts help us to feel better and to behave in ways in which we want to behave. Give the victim a cognitive basis for the script. Include the four basic Transactional Analysis positions, stressing that the healthiest posture for her to take is, "I'm O.K., You're O.K." Work on the script with the victim rather than use a standard one that may not fit her particular needs. Make her part of the process.

Finally, devise a brief contract together in the form of a statement or two for use with the script. For example, a sample contract for a pre-teen might state:

"I, _____, (victim's name) will read aloud my script every night for two weeks before I go to bed. I, _____, will make a check mark beside statements that are hard for me to accept so that I may discuss them with _____ (therapist's name)."

Have the contract signed, dated and witnessed for validation and to stress its importance. During therapy sessions, spend time discussing its efficacy, noting the client's progress or setbacks.

A sample O.K. Script called, "Declaration of Me and My Feelings" is presented below.

Sample O.K. Script
Me and My Feelings

1. I, _____, (victim's name) am a good person.
2. I, _____, am not responsible in any way for what happened sexually between me and my dad/stepdad.
3. I, _____, am a child/minor/adolescent and, rightfully trusted my dad/stepfather. He violated that trust. He is responsible.
4. I, _____, understand that I may feel guilty. I, _____, know that this feeling is natural because I am human. I also understand that I have no reason to feel guilty. What happened was not my fault.

5. I, _____, may feel afraid or angry. It's O.K. to have these feelings.
6. I, _____, may feel irritable or tense. It is O.K. to have these feelings.
7. I, _____, know that my (stomachaches, headaches, bedwetting) occur because I have been through a lot. I know that these problems will pass.
8. I, _____, am a unique person. I also am like everybody else in my humanness.
9. I, _____, forgive myself for mistakes I have made.
10. I, _____, had unpleasant/traumatic sexual experiences with my parent/step-parent. These experiences will not happen again.
11. I, _____, forgive my dad/stepdad.
12. I, _____, trust my myself.
13. I, _____, am proud of being me. I, _____, am O.K.

The Hand Test

The Hand Test (Bricklin, Piotrowski, Zygmunt and Wagner, 1978), which measures acting out tendencies, is another projective tool that consists of pictures of human hands in nine different poses. The subject is asked what she thinks the hand on each of the nine cards is doing. The tenth card is blank. The subject is asked to imagine a hand and then describe what that hand might be doing. As with The Most Unpleasant Concept Test, The Hand Test can be modified or used directly to elicit affect. It is particularly appropriate for assessment purposes with victims of incestuous abuse since many victims have experienced digital penetration, fondling and manual manipulation of the genitals by the offender.

One useful modification of this test involves asking the victim "to draw a hand doing something." On the following page is the drawing of a hand by a six-year-old male victim of incest. The phallic symbolism is evident. This youngster had been a victim of fellatio which was a traumatic preoccupation for him. It certainly is plausible to hypothesize that the faces depicted on each of the (phallic) fingers symbolize part of the conflict centering around the issue of fellatio.

As cards in the Hand Test were presented one-by-one, accompanied by the repeated question, "What is this hand doing?", a seven-year-old female victim gave the following series of responses.

1.   It's going to suck something.
2.   It's an old hand about to die.
3.   It's pointing at a little girl. It's going to stick her.
4.   It's going to pat a little girl on the shoulder and say, "Good girl."
5.   It's going to touch a little girl.
6.   It's going to punch someone — in the stomach. Omar (a class-mate).
7.   It's going to pat a stomach.
8.   It's going to snap its fingers.
9.   It going to reach for his toes so he can touch his penis—I mean, toes. Write down toes.

This test alone, without any background data, provided sufficient information from responses #1, 3, 4, 5, 7 and 9 to suspect the likelihood of sexual assault.

Puppets for Re-enactment

The use of puppets is an aspect of play therapy. Unlike art therapy where symbolic objects are created, play involves the use of objects that assume symbolic roles for the child.   Play is a spontaneous and self-expressive activity that is extremely useful in helping children in conflict reach resolution through the fantasized and symbolic interaction of objects.

Puppets can be used interactively, with the therapist and child engaged in role plays, or singly by the imaginative and expressive child. Activities can be directed, as in role plays, or spontaneous.   One incestuously abused five-year-old suffered from a repetition compulsion where over and over again he reenacted with puppets the abuse he had been sustaining for years.   Role plays involving thought, creativity and imagination could not begin until this youngster primitively and symbolically had worked through the initial trauma.

Another six-year-old followed a weekly ritual with all the puppets in the playroom before he would become engaged in role plays. He entered the room, picked up the puppets one by one, lifted their clothing and looked for their (nonexistent) genitals, repeating, "This one has a pussy, this one has a dick, this one has a pussy . . ." Such activities, which involve reality testing and re-enactment of trauma, are related to a need to alleviate anxiety and should be allowed without interference from the therapist. The key to successful play therapy always is related to the warm, trusting relationship with the therapist in a permissive setting.

Non-directed play therapy does, however, involve verbalizing on the part of the therapist who clarifies feelings and makes contact with the child by means of empathic, relevant statements such as, "You look concerned when you can't find the dick," or, "You really are looking for that pussy today. It must be important for you to find it." As always, use the vocabulary and phraseology of the particular child.

In role plays, the therapist interacts freely with the child and may be subtly directive. For example, the clinician may begin the role play by saying, "Let's let this puppet be a daddy. What should the other one be?" If role plays are used to re-enact incestuous abuse, the therapist should reassure the child, "These are just puppets and we can do anything we want with them. They aren't real people."

Puppets also can be used to teach alternative assertive responses and behaviors. For example, in one session with a child victim, I played Dad and she played the little girl. We re-enacted an episode of incestuous abuse as it had occurred in reality except that in the role play the little girl bitterly beat her father. When the role play was completed, I suggested that we replay the scene with the child practicing assertive responses to her manipulative father at the first sign of his approaching her for illicit purposes. Hence, in one session with puppets, trauma was re-enacted and alternate modes of responding were rehearsed.

The Playhouse and Use of Dolls

A potent vehicle to use for re-enactment of trauma is the playhouse equipped with three figures — a "Mom," "Dad" and child. It is wise first to familiarize the child with the playhouse in a non-directed way, having her play spontaneously with the figures and arrange the furnishings as she chooses. Later, some direction can be given, either openly or more subtly, through interactive role plays with the therapist. Sometimes the child provides direction by "ordering" the therapist to create certain scenes. Such play has several purposes in addition to re-enactment of painful past experiences:

1. The child has an opportunity to test reality in a fantasized setting.
2. A sense of control over the environment is enhanced through the child's manipulation both of the setting and of the key figures in her life.
3. Alternate, socially acceptable endings to traumatic episodes in the child's life can be enacted, thus affording an opportunity to learn that choices in behavior and affective responses are possible even in trying situations.

One five-year-old incest victim found the playhouse experience both enjoyable and compelling. For weeks, she chose this vehicle for self-expression, using her scenes to test reality, to release aggression and as an outlet for imaginative release. In one particularly intense session, she re-enacted the first episode of incest with her father, first tentatively, periodically looking at me for an anticipated negative response. Instead, I remained neutral, being careful only to reflect and clarify affect. For example, as the child figure backed off from "Dad," I remarked, "The little girl is acting scared. She wants to get away from her Dad." The child responded, "That's exactly right!" Re-enactment scenes proceeded until aggressive elements predominated as the father figure assaulted the child figure who retaliated by "beating him up." The scene ended with aggression turned to fantasized retaliation as imaginary snakes entered the room to destroy Dad. At this juncture, I clarified the child's desire for revenge, the notion that "anything is appropriate in play, which is not the real world," and the fact that play allows us to express many of our deepest feelings and desires in ways that will not harm others.

During later re-enactments, the child's desire for fantasized revenge dissipated as she and I interactively played scenes involving more reality-based endings. Among the various choices (drawing, clay, dolls, tape recordings) the playhouse was this child's chosen vehicle to work through trauma. Partly because of its availability and the victim's freedom to choose her own media for self-expression, therapy progressed quite rapidly.

Stuffed animals and larger dolls also can be used for re-enactments. Some police departments in the United States now are using anatomically correct Raggedy Ann and Raggedly Andy dolls to allow young children an opportunity to demonstrate sexual abuse incidents without the embarrassment of verbally recounting painful details or the difficulty of using correct terminology. The dolls being used by the police and in the courts have increased considerably the number of offender convictions.

The Sandbox

The Sandbox is a useful vehicle for non-verbal children and it has been used effectively with adults as well. It consists of a box, at least two by two, painted blue on the bottom (the sea) and filled approximately three quarters full with sand. The sand can be dry or wet. Wet sand allows for greater flexibility, molding and construction and generally is considered preferable to dry sand. Make available to the child a vast array of small toys and models (plastic or metal) for her to use as she constructs her "world" in the box. The models should include a variety of people and things found both in reality and fantasy, such as the following:

1. Figures representing adults and children of each sex.
2. Cars, trucks, ambulances, military and construction vehicles.
3. Domestic and wild animals.
4. Figures from both the world of reality and fantasy that carry symbolic significance for children (dragons, dinosaurs, witches and snakes).
5. Historical figures encouraging re-enactments of scripts and scenes from the past (military figures, pirates, cowboys and Indians).

Have the objects placed at random on a table or on shelves in the vicinity of the sandbox. Let the child work non-directively as she constructs her "world." Encourage her to make any changes that she wants until she is satisfied with her construction. Finally, allow her to describe her world in her own words by showing interest and making non-judgmental observations such as, "I see you have placed the dragon near the little boy," or, "Your world seems mostly peopled with soldiers."

The purpose of the sandbox is to help the child re-enact past conflict and trauma. In addition, sandbox constructions provide valuable insights and direction for the therapist.

APPENDIX A:
Suggested Books and Articles Regarding Child and Sexual Abuse (Annotated)

Adams, C. and Fay, J. *No More Secrets.* San Luis Obispo, CA: Impact Publishers, 1981.

> Sexual abuse prevention for parents to use with their children. Increases an understanding of molestation and the effects of victimization.

Adams, C.; Fay, J.; and Loreen-Martin, J. *No Is Not Enough: Helping Teenagers Avoid Sexual Assault.* San Luis Obispo, CA: Impact Publishers, 1984.

> Advice on talking to teens about sexual assault, acquaintance rape and sexual exploitation.

Allen, C.V. *Daddy's Girl.* N.Y.: Wyndham Books, 1980.

> Readable autobiography of a victim of ten years of father-daughter incest. Belongs to the first-person accounts useful for both therapist and victim for increasing awareness and empathic understanding.

Armstrong, L. *Kiss Daddy Goodnight: A Speak-out On Incest.* N.Y.: Pocket Books, 1978.

> Moving, poignant first-person accounts by the victims of incest. Strong, powerful and with much impact both for the therapist

attempting to gain empathic awareness of this formerly taboo topic and for the victim seeking understanding and release.

Bass, E. and Thornton, L. (Eds.). *I Never Told Anyone: Writings By Women Survivors Of Child Sexual Abuse.* N.Y.: Harper & Row, 1983.

Personal accounts by survivors; includes comprehensive resource lists.

Bass, E. *The Courage To Heal.* N.Y.: Harper & Row, 1988.

Stages of recovery, feelings associated with abuse, exercises and techniques; includes accompanying workbook.

Baxter, A. *Techniques For Dealing With Child Sexual Abuse.* Springfield, IL: Charles C. Thomas, Publisher, 1986.

Identification, intervention, effects and community resources.

Bear, E. *Adults Molested As Children: A Survivor's Manual For Women And Men.* Orwell, VT: The Safer Society Press. 1988.

Manual written by survivors to help others begin to deal with the trauma of child sexual abuse.

Berry, J. *Sexual Abuse: Alerting Kids To The Danger Zones.* Waco, TX: Word, Educational Products Division, 1984.

Advice to parents and teachers for educating children about sexual abuse.

Bloomfield, H.H. *Making Peace With Your Parents.* N.Y.: Ballantine Books, 1983.

Causes and management of unresolved anger. Presents sexual scripts and roles along with suggestions and exercises for reaching resolution with parents.

Blume, Sue, E. *Secret Survivors: Uncovering Incest And Its Aftereffects In Women.* N.Y.: Ballantine, 1991.

Aftereffects of incest including depression, sexual dysfunction, eating disorders, chemical abuse and so forth; includes resources and aftereffects checklist.

Brady, K. *Father's Days: A True Story Of Incest.* N.Y.: Seaview Books, 1979.

> Personal account detailing a ten year incestuous relationship between the author and her father. Provides valuable information regarding the extent and nature of the problem along with insights into the complicated family dynamics, pain and suffering involved.

Burgess, A.W., & Holmstrom, L.L. *Rape: Victims Of Crisis.* Bowie, MD: Robert J. Brady, 1974.

> Provides insights into the medical and emotional needs of rape victims. Details treatment implications and methods of treatment for both the crisis intervention worker and the on-going therapist. Gives a thorough and comprehensive discussion of the reactions of rape victims.

Burgess, A.W.; Groth, A.N.; Holmstrom, L.L.; & Scroi, S.M. *Sexual Assault of Children and Adolescents.* Lexington, MA: Lexington Books, D.C. Heath & Company, 1978.

> Very valuable sourcebook for the therapist. Comprehensive coverage of the subject including a wide range of topics from needs assessment, community involvement, court process, diagnosis, guidelines for intervention and assessment, interviewing techniques to patterns of offender behavior. Ample clinical case examples provided.

Butler, S. *Conspiracy of Silence: The Trauma of Incest.* San Francisco, CA: New Glide Publications, 1978.

> Based on thousands of hours of interviewing with hundreds of men and women. Covers the scope of the problem and the psychodynamic and social forces operating among members of the triad individually and as a unit. Stresses the traumatic effects of incest.

Byerly, C.M. *The Mother's Book: How to Survive the Incest of Your Child.* Dubuque, IO: Kendall/Hunt, 1985.

> Focuses on needs of mothers of young victims.

Carnes, P. *The Sexual Addiction.* Minneapolis, MN: Compcare Publications, 1983.

The addiction cycle, levels of addiction, co-addiction and the twelve-step recovery program.

Colao, F. and Hosansky, T. *Your Children Should Know.* NY: Harper & Row, 1987.

Guide for parents for helping their children following assault.

Crowley, P. *Not My Child: A Mother Confronts Her Child's Sexual Abuse.* N.Y.: Avon, 1990.

Covers investigation and effects of daycare abuse.

DeFrancis, V.J. *Protecting the Child Victim of Sex Crimes.* Denver, CO: The American Humane Association, 1969.

Detailed summary report citing the results of a three year study analyzing the dimensions of the problem, characteristics of family members, impact on the victim and community response and responsibility. Contains valuable data for the clinician despite the difficulties in forming valid generalizations due to socio-economic and geographical limitations posed by the sample used.

Dennison, S.T. and Glassman, C.K. *Activities for Children In Therapy: A Guide to Planning and Facilitating Therapy with Troubled Children.* Springfield, IL: Charles C. Thomas, Publisher, 1987.

Activities and exercises for professionals to use with children aged 5-12 in therapy; covers communication, self-awareness and social skills.

deYoung, M. *Incest: An Annotated Bibliography.* Jefferson, N.C.: McFarland & Co., Inc., 1985.

Over 400 annotated published references on incest.

Finkelhor, D. et al. *A Sourcebook on Child Sexual Abuse.* Beverly Hills, CA: Sage Publications, 1986.

Covers high-risk children, prevention, prevalence, abusers and effects.

Finkelhor, D. *Sexually Victimized Children.* N.Y.: The Free Press, 1979.

Comprehensive study covering varying aspects of sexual abuse including historical context, social reform, social and cultural forces, and theoretical considerations regarding motivations of the victim, offender and family. Includes a survey of child victims, a lengthy questionnaire on sexual abuse, and a comparison with other studies.

Fortune, M.M. *Sexual Abuse Prevention: A Study For Teenagers.* N.Y.: United Church Press, 1984.

Training guide with five-session course for teenagers.

Forward, S., & Buck, C. *Betrayal of Innocence: Incest and Its Devastation.* Los Angeles, CA: J.P. Tarcher, Inc., 1978.

Focuses on effects, psychological characteristics among members of the triad, motivations and symptomatology. Examines incest in detail and in the context of family pathology. Includes sound exposition on the different types of incestuous involvement. Considers treatment approaches.

Freeman, L. *It's My Body.* Seattle, WA: Parenting Press, 1986.

Prevention guide for pre-schoolers; includes accompanying parents' guide.

Giarretto, H. *Integrated Treatment of Child Sexual Abuse: A Treatment And Training Manual.* Palo Alto, CA: Science & Behavior Books, Inc., 1982.

Description and evaluation of Parents United and the Child Sexual Abuse Treatment Program in Santa Clara, California.

Gomes-Schwartz, B.; Horowitz, J.M.; and Cardarelli, A.P. *Child Sexual Abuse: The Initial Effects.* Newberry Park, CA: Sage Publications, Inc., 1991.

Data on nature and effects of abuse; effects of crisis intervention; and description of child abuse theory.

Hawkins, P. *Children At Risk: My Fight Against Child Abuse — A Personal Story And A Public Plea.* Bethesda, MD: Adler & Adler, 1986.

Personal experience of Senator Paula Hawkins who was a victim of child sexual abuse; includes recommendations for legislative changes and a listing of national and local services.

Helfer, R.E., & Kempe, C.H. (Eds.) *The Battered Child.* Chicago, IL: The University of Chicago Press, 1974, 2nd Ed.

> Scholarly and comprehensive study by two experts in the field. Designed for professionals from several disciplines. Includes detailed considerations of medical, psychiatric, social, and legal aspects. Contains psychiatric study of abusive parents.

Holder, W.M.,(Ed.) *Sexual Abuse of Children: Implications for Treatment.* Englewood, CO: Child Protection Division, the American Humane Association, 1980.

> Contains useful information on psychological assessment. Illustrated with victims' drawings used in evaluative interview. Includes a descriptive analysis of father-daughter incest. Extensive bibliography.

Justice, B., & Justice, R. *The Broken Taboo: Sex in the Family.* N.Y.: Human Science Press, 1979.

> Provides cues to identifying high-risk families. Elaborates on the long-term consequences and effects of incest. Gives useful information related to treatment including stress management. Includes guidelines for establishing appropriate parent-child behaviors.

Kempe, R.S. and Kempe, R.H. *The Common Secret: Sexual Abuse of Children And Adolescents.* N.Y.: W.H. Freeman & Co., 1984.

> An overview of child sexual abuse for professional and lay people.

Knopp, F.H. *Retraining Adult Sex Offenders: Methods and Models.* Syracuse, N.Y.: Safer Society Press, 1984.

> Description of ten adult sex offender treatment programs; components of sexual assault reduction model.

Kroth, J.A., *Child Sexual Abuse: Analysis of a Family Therapy Approach.* Springfield, IL: Charles C. Thomas, Publisher, 1979.

> Provides a thorough, empirical analysis of Henry Giarretto's humanistic family therapy model in use in the Child Sexual Abuse Treatment Program in San Jose, California. Useful for clinicians interested in research and sound methodology. Includes description

of computer based data system to report demographic data and an annotated listing of major sexual abuse treatment centers in the United States.

Laws, R.D. *Relapse Prevention with Sex Offenders.* NY: Guilford Press, 1989.

Treatment approaches and components of relapse prevention.

Lew, M. *Victims No Longer: Men Recovering from Incest and Other Sexual Child Abuse.* N.Y.: Neuvramont Publishing Co., 1988.

Trauma of child sexual abuse for male victims.

MacFarlane, K. and Waterman, J. *Sexual Abuse of Young Children.* NY: The Guilford Press, 1986.

Tools and techniques for treatment of young child victims; includes use of dolls, puppets, art, court testimony, videotaping and evidence gathering.

Maltz, W. and Holman, B. *Incest and Sexuality: A Guide to Understanding and Healing.* Lexington, MA: D.C. Heath, 1987.

Information for partners of victims.

Mann, E. and McDermott, Jr.,J.F. "Play Therapy for Victims of Child Abuse and Neglect." In (Ed.) Schaefer, C.E. and O'Connor, K.J. *Handbook of Play Therapy.* N.Y.: John Wiley & Sons, 1983.

Uses and approaches to play therapy.

Mayer, A. *Sexual Abuse: Causes, Consequences, and Treatment of Incestuous and Pedophilic Acts.* Holmes Beach, FL: Learning Publications, Inc., 1985.

Overview of child sexual abuse; includes treatment.

Morris, M. *If I Should Die Before I Wake.* L.A.,CA: J.P. Tarcher, Inc., 1976.

Powerful novel of incestuous abuse written in the first person.

O'Brien, S. *Child Abuse: A Crying Shame.* Provo, UT: Brigham Young University, 1980.

Action-oriented text focusing on the extent of child abuse in the
United States and ways that community leaders, educators and
parents can help to alleviate the problem.

Patton, M.Q.   *Family   Sexual   Abuse.*   Newberry Park, CA: Sage
Publications, Inc., 1991.

Results of eleven research studies covering family reunification,
removal of incest offenders from the home and prognoses for
offenders after treatment.

Plummer, C.A.   *Preventing Sexual Abuse: Activities and Strategies for
Those Working with Children and Adolescents.*   Homes Beach, FL:
Learning Publications, Inc., 1984

Curriculum guides for K-6, 7-12 and special populations.

Polese, C.   *Promise Not to Tell.*   N.Y.:   Human Sciences Press, 1985.

Prevention for child victims, aged 8-12.

Rush, F.   *The Best Kept Secret: Sexual Abuse of Children.*   Englewood
Cliffs, N.J.:   Prentice Hall, 1980.

Cogent and thoughtful exposition on the perpetuation of sexual abuse
of minors by history, religion, psychology and our cultural heritage.
Valuable contribution to increasing awareness about the urgency of
changing our perspective to protect the welfare of innocent minors.

Russell, D.   *The Secret Trauma: Incest in the Lives of Girls and Women.*
N.Y.:   Basic Books, 1986.

Eight years of comprehensive research on incest.

Schultz, L.D. (Ed.)   *The Sexual Victimology of Youth.*   Springfield, IL:
Charles C. Thomas, Publisher, 1980.

One of the most comprehensive studies addressing the problem from
a wide range of perspectives including medical, legal and psychiatric.
Contains articles by leading authorities dealing with diagnosis,
treatment implications and effects.   Also contains a section focusing
on incest and outlining Giarretto's humanistic treatment model
currently in use at the Child Sexual Abuse Treatment Program in San
Jose, California.

Sgroi, S.M. *Handbook of Clinical Intervention in Child Sexual Abuse.* Lexington, MA: D.C. Heath & Co., Lexington Books, 1982.

Comprehensive treatment manual including investigation, treatment, court preparation, agency coordination, art therapy and program evaluation.

Shengold, L. *Soul Murder: The Effects of Childhood Abuse and Deprivation.* N.Y.: Fawcett Columbine, 1989.

Psychological effects of childhood trauma.

Sonkin, D.J. and Durphy, M. *Learning to Live Without Violence: a Handbook For Men.* San Francisco, CA: Volcano Press, 1985.

Step-by-step program in workbook format to deal with anger, stress, chemicals, feelings, communication and assertiveness.

Soukup, R.; Wicker, S. and Corbett, J. *Three in Every Classroom.* Bemidji, MINN: Sexual Assault Program, 1984.

Resource for teachers to help in identifying and reporting child sexual abuse.

Terkel, S. and Rench, J. *Feeling Safe, Feeling Strong: How to Avoid Sexual Abuse and What to Do If It Happens to You.* Minneapolis, MN: Lerner Publications, 1984.

First-person fictional accounts of young people dealing with uncomfortable situations.

Walters, D.R. *Physical and Sexual Abuse of Children: Causes and Treatment.* Bloomington, IN: Indiana University Press, 1975.

Readable text focusing on diagnosis, treatment methods and cultural causation. Includes two chapters with detailed discussion of sexual abuse of children focusing on prevalent myths, scope of the problem, types and variations of abuse and treatment implications.

Ward, E. *Father-Daughter Rape.* N.Y.: Grove Press, 1985.

Analysis of interrelationship among sex, power, men and women.

APPENDIX B
References

Abel, G.G. et al. "The Components of Rapists' Sexual Arousal." *Archives of General Psychiatry,* 34: 895-903, 1977.

Aberle, D.R. et al. "A Biological Basis for the Incest Taboo." In: Goode, W.(Ed.) *Readings on the Family and Society.* Englewood Cliffs, NJ: Prentice-Hall, 1964.

Adams, C. and Fay, J. *No More Secrets.* San Luis Obispo, CA: Impact Publishers, 1981.

Adams, C.;Fay, J.; and Loreen-Martin, J. *No is Not Enough: Helping Teenagers Avoid Sexual Assault.* San Luis Obispo, CA: Impact Publishers, 1984.

Alberti, R.E. and Emmons, M.L. *Your Perfect Right: A Guide to Assertive Behavior.* San Luis Obispo, CA: Impact, 1970.

Allen, C.V. *Daddy's Girl: A Memoir.* N.Y.: Wyndham Books, 1980.

Altman, C. *Lovemaking: You Can Be Your Own Sex Therapist.* N.Y.: Berkeley Publishing Corp., 1977.

Amir, M. *Patterns in Forceable Rape.* Chicago, IL: The University of Chicago Press, 1971.

Apolinsky, S.R. and Wilcoxon, S.A. "Symbolic Confrontation With Women Survivors of Childhood Sexual Victimization." *The Journal for Specialists in Group Work,* Vol. 16, #2, 5-19, 85-90.

Armstrong, L. *Kiss Daddy Goodnight: A Speakout on Incest.* N.Y.: Pocket Books, 1979.

Assagioli, R. *Psychosynthesis: A Manual of Principles and Techniques.* N.Y.: Hobbs-Dorman and Co., 1965.

"Attacking the Last Taboo." *Time Magazine*, April 14, 1980.

Axline, V. *Play Therapy.* N.Y.: Houghton Mifflin Co., 1947.

Awad, G.A. "Single Case Study: Father-Son Incest, A Case Report." *Journal of Nervous and Mental Disease,* 162(2): 135-139, 1976.

Baily, J.F. and Baily, W.H. "Criminal or Social Intervention in Child Sexual Abuse: A Review and A Viewpoint," Denver, CO: *American Human Assoc.,* 1983, 16-19.

Barbach, L. *For Yourself, the Fulfillment of Female Sexuality.* N.Y.: Doubleday, and Co., 1975.

Barry, M.J. and Johnson, A.M. "The Incest Barrier." *Psychoanalytic Quarterly,* 27(4): 485-499, 1958.

Bass, E. and Thornton, L. (Eds.). *I Never Told Anyone: Writings by Women Survivors of Child Sexual Abuse.* N.Y.: Harper & Row, 1983

Bass, E. and Davis, L. *The Courage to Heal.* N.Y.: Harper & Row, 1988.

Baxter, A. *Techniques for Dealing with Child Sexual Abuse.* Springfield, IL: Charles C. Thomas, Publisher, 1986.

Bear, E. *Adults Molested as Children: A Survivor's Manual for Women and Men.* Orwell, VT: Safer Society Press, 1988.

Begart, A.M. "Isolation to Intimacy: Incest Survivors in Group Therapy." SOCIAL CASEWORK, 67, May 1986, 266-75.

Bender L. and Blau, A. "The Reactions of Children to Sexual Problems with Adults." *American Journal of Orthopsychiatry,* 8(4): 1937, 500-518.

Benson, H. *The Relaxation Response.* N.Y.: Avon Books, 1975.

Benward, J. and Densen-Gerber, J. *Incest as a Causative Factor in Anti-social Behavior: An Exploratory Study.* N.Y.: Odyssey Institute, 1975.

Berry, J. *Sexual Abuse: Alerting Kids to the Danger Zones.* Waco, TX: Word, Educational Products Division, 1984.

Betensky, M. *Self-discovery through Self-expression.* Springfield, IL: Charles C. Thomas, Publisher, 1973.

Bloomfield, H.H. *Making Peace With Your Parents.* N.Y.: Ballantine Books, 1983.

Blume, E.S. *Secret Survivors: Uncovering Incest and Its Aftereffects in Women.* N.Y.: Ballantine Books, 1991.

Bolton, F.G.; Morris, L.A.; MacEachron, A.E. *Males at Risk: The Other Side of Child Sexual Abuse.* Newberry Park, CA: Sage Publications, Inc., 1991.

Bower, S.A. and Bower, G.H. *Asserting Yourself: A Practical Guide for Positive Change.* Reading, MA: Addison-Wesley Publishing Company, 1976.

Bradford, J. "The Hormonal Treatment of Sex Offenders," *Bulletin of AAPL,* II, 163, 1983, 164-7.

Brady, K. *Father's Days: A True Story of Incest.* N.Y.: Seaview Books, 1979.

Branden, N. *The Disowned Self.* N.Y.: Bantam Books, 1979.

Brant, R.S.T. *Manual on Sexual Abuse and Misuse of Children.* Boston, MA: Judge Baker Guidance Center, New England Resource Center for Protective Services, N.D.

Braun, B.G. and Sachs, R.G. "The Development of Multiple Personality Disorder: Predisposing, Precipitating, and Perpetuating Factors," In (Ed.) Kluft, R.P. (Ed.) *Childhood Antecedents of Multiple Personality.* Washington, D.C., American Psychiatric Press, 1985.

Brecher, E.M. *Treatment Programs for Sex Offenders.* Washington, D.C.: U.S. Dept. of Justice, National Institute of Law Enforcement and Criminal Justice, January 1978, 9,10,85.

Bricklin, B.; Piotrowski, A.Z.; and Wagner, E.E. *The Hand Test: A New Projective Test with Special Reference to the Prediction of Overt Aggressive Behavior.* Springfield, IL: Charles C. Thomas, Publisher, 1978.

Brill, A.A. (Ed.) *The Basic Writings of Sigmund Freud.* NY: Random House, The Modern Library, 1938.

Bruckner, D.F. and Johnson, P.E. "Treatment for Adult Male Victims of Childhood Sexual Abuse." *Social Casework,* 68, 2-87, 81-87.

Bulkley, J. (Ed.). *Innovations in the Prosecution of Child Sexual Abuse Cases.* Washington, D.C.: American Bar Association, National Legal Resource Center for Child Advocacy and Protection, November, 1981.

Burgess, A.W. and Holmstrom, L.L. *Rape: Victims of Crisis.* Bowie, MD: Robert J. Bradley, 1974.

Burgess, A.W. et al. *Sexual Assault of Children and Adolescents.* Lexington, MA: Lexington Books, D.C. Heath & Company, 1978.

Burns, R.C. and Kaufman, S.H. *Kinetic Family Drawings (K-F-D): An Introduction to Understanding Children through Kinetic Drawings.* N.Y.: Brunner-Mazel, Inc. 1970.

Burton, L. *Vulnerable Children.* N.Y.: Schocken Books, 1968.

Butler, S. *Conspiracy Of Silence: Tthe Trauma of Incest.* San Francisco, CA: New Glide Publications, 1978.

Byerly, C.M. *The Mother's Book: How to Survive the Incest of Your Child.* Dubuque, IO: Kendall/Hunt, 1985.

Cappuzzi, D. and Hensley, A. "Rape: Relationships and Recovery." *The American Personnel And Guidance Journal,* October, 1979.

Carnes, P. *The Sexual Addiction.* Minneapolis, MN: CompCare Publications, 1983.

Cautela, J.R. "Covert Sensitization" In: Stumphauser, J.S. *Behavior Therapy With Delinquents.* Springfield, IL: Charles C. Thomas, Publisher, 1973.

Chappell, D.; Geis, R.; and Geis, G. (Eds.) *Forcible Rape, the Crime, the Victim and the Offender.* N.Y.: Columbia University Press, 1972.

Chase, N.F. *A Child is Being Beaten.* N.Y.: Holt, Rinehart and Winston, 1975.

Clyde, A. *A Child's Library Of Dreams.* Milbrae, CA: Celestial Arts, 1978.

Cohen, T. "The Incestuous Family Revisited." *Social Casework,* 64, 3-83, 154-61.

Colao, F. and Hosansky, T. *Your Children Should Know.* N.Y.: Harper & Row, 1987.

Comfort, A. *The Joy Of Sex: A Gourmet Guide to Love Making.* N.Y.: Simon and Schuster, 1972.

Courtois, C. *Healing the Incest Wound: Adult Survivors in Therapy.* N.Y.: W.W. Norton, 1988.

Courtois, C. and Watts, D.L. "Counseling Adult Women Who Experienced Incest in Childhood or Adolescence," *The Personnel And Guidance Journal,* 60, 1-82, 275-79.

Crewdson, J. *By Silence Betrayed: Sexual Abuse of Children in America.* N.Y.: Harper & Row, 1988.

Crootof, C. "Poetry Therapy for Psychoneurotics in a Mental Health Center." In : Leedy, J. (Ed.) *Poetry the Healer.* Philadelphia, PA: J.B. Lippincott, 1973.

Crowley, P. *Not My Child: A Mother Confronts Her Child's Sexual Abuse.* N.Y.: Avon, 1990.

D'Arcy, A.J. *One Woman's War On V.D. in the Nursery School.* Cincinnati, OH: Pamphlet Publications, 1978.

Davidson, T. *Conjugal Crime: Understanding and Changing the Wife Beating Pattern.* N.Y.: Hawthorne Books, Inc., Publisher, 1978.

De Courcey, P. and De Courcey, J. *A Silent Tragedy, Child Abuse in the Community.* Port Washington, N.Y.: Alfred Publishing Company, 1973.

De Francis, V. *Child Victims of Incest.* Denver: The American Humane Association, 1969.

De Francis, V. *Protecting The Child Victims of Sex Crimes Committed by Adults.* Denver: The American Humane Association, 1978.

De Francis, V. and Lucht, C.L. *Child Abuse Legislation in the* 70's. (Rev. Ed.) Denver: The American Humane Association, 1974.

Dennison, S.T. and Glassman, C.K. *Activities for Children in Therapy: A Guide for Planning and Facilitating Therapy with Troubled Children.* Springfield, IL: Charles C. Thomas Publisher, 1987.

de Young, M. *Incest: An Annotated Bibliography.* Jefferson, N.C.: McFarland & Co., Inc., 1985.

Diagram Group. *Man's Body: An Owner's Manual.* N.Y.: Paddington Press, Ltd., 1976.

Diagram Group. *Woman's Body: An Owner's Manual.* N.Y.: Paddington Press, Ltd., 1977.

Dietz, C.A. and Craft, J.L. "Family Dynamics of Incest:A New Perspective." *Social Casework,* 61, 12-80, 602-9.

Dinitz, S., Dynes, R.R., and Clarke, A.C. *Deviance: Studies in Definition Management And Treatment.* (2nd Ed.) N.Y.: Oxford University Press, 1975.

Dollard, J. and Miller, N.E. *Personality and Psychotherapy: An Analysis in Terms of Learning, Thinking And Culture.* N.Y.: McGraw Hill Book Company, Inc., 1950.

Durkeim, E. "The Nature and Origin of the Taboo". In: Sagarin, E., (Tr., Intro.) *Incest.* N.Y.: Lyle Stuart, Inc., 1963.

Eaton, A.P. and Vastbinder, E. "The Sexually Molested Child, A Plan of Management." *Clinical Pediatrics,* 8(8): 438-441, 1969.

Ebeling, N.B. and Hill, D.A. *Child Abuse: Intervention and Treatment.* Acton, MA: Publishing Sciences Group, Inc., 1975.

Eist, H. and Mandell, A. "Family Treatment of Ongoing Incest." *Family Press,* 7: 216-232, 1968.

Ellenson, G.S. "Detecting a History of Incest: A Predictive Syndrome." *Social Casework,* 66, 11-85, 525-32.

Ellenson, G.S. "Disturbances of Perception in Adult Female Incest Survivors." *Social Casework,* 67, 3-86, 149-59.

Ellis, A. "The Origins and Development of the Incest Taboo." In: Sagarin, E. (Tr., Intro.) *Incest.* N.Y.: Lyle Stuart, Inc., 1963.

Engel, B. *The Right to Innocence: Healing the Trauma of Childhood Sexual Abuse.* N.Y.: Ivy Books, 1989.

Engel, L. and Ferguson, T. *Hidden Guilt: How to Stop Punishing Yourself and Enjoy the Happiness You Deserve.* N.Y.: Pocket Books, 1990.

Erickson, E.L.; McEvoy, A.; and Colucci, N.D. *Child Abuse and Neglect: A Guidebook for Educators and Community Leaders.* Holmes Beach, FL: Learning Publications, Inc., 1979.

Fagan, J. and Shepherd, I.L. (Eds.) *Gestalt Therapy Now: Theory, Techniques, Applications.* N.Y.: Harper Colophon, 1971.

Faller, K.C. *Understanding Child Sexual Maltreatment.* Newberry Park, CA: Sage Publications, Inc., 1991.

Figley, C.R. (Ed.) *Trauma and Its Wake: The Study And Treatment of Post-traumatic Stress Disorder.* N.Y.: Brunner/Mazel Publishers, 1985.

Finkelhor, D. et al. *A Sourcebook on Child Sexual Abuse.* Beverly Hills, CA: Sage Publications, 1986.

Finkelhor, D. *Sexually Victimized Children.* N.Y.: The Free Press, 1979.

Fischoff, J. "The Role of the Parents' Unconscious in Children's Anti-Social Behavior." *Journal of Clinical Child Psychology,* 2(3): 31-33, Fall, 1973.

Flammang, C. "Interviewing Child Victims of Sex Offenders." In Schultz, L. *Rape Victimology.* Springfield, IL: Charles C. Thomas Publisher, 1975.

Fontana, V.J. *Somewhere a Child is Crying: Maltreatment Causes and Prevention.* N.Y.: New American Library, A Mentor Book, 1976.

Fortune, M.M. *Sexual Abuse Prevention: A Study for Teenagers.* N.Y.: United Church Press, 1984.

Forward, S. and Buck, C. *Betrayal of Innocence: Incest and Its Devastation.* Los Angeles: J.P. Tarcher, Inc. N.Y.: 1978.

Frankel, S. and Harrison, S. "Children's Exposure to Parental Intercourse." *Medical Aspects of Human Sexuality,* 115-117, September, 1976.

Franks, C.M. "Recidivism, Psychopathy and Personality," *The British Journal Of Delinquency,* #6, 1956.

Freed, A.M. *T.A. For Kids (and Grown-ups Too).* Los Angeles: Jalmar Press, Inc. Distributed by Price/Stern/Sloan Publishers, Inc., 1971.

Freeman, L. *It's My Body.* Seattle: Parenting Press, 1986.

Gager, N. and Schurr, C. *Sexual Assault: Confronting Rape In America.* Grosset and Dunlap, A Filmways Company, Publishers 1976.

Gagnon, H. and Simon, W. *Sexual Deviance.* N.Y.: Harper and Row, 1967.

Garret, C.A. and Ireland, M.S. "A Therapeutic Art Session with Rape Victims," *American Journal of Art Therapy,* 18, #4, 103-107, July 1979.

Geiser, R.L. *Hidden Victims: The Sexual Abuse of Children.* Boston: The Beacon Press, 1979.

Gelberman, J.H. and Komak, D. "The Psalms as Psychological and Allegorical Poems." In: Leedy, J.J.(Ed.) *Poetry Therapy.* Philadelphia: J.B. Lippincott, 1969.

Giarretto. H. "Humanistic Treatment of Father-Daughter Incest." *Journal of Humanistic Psychology,* 18(4): 17-21, December, 1968.

Giarretto, H. "Treating Sexual Abuse: Working Together." San Jose, CA: *Child Sexual Abuse Treatment Program,* N.D.

Giarretto, H. "Treatment of Father-Daughter Incest: A Psychosocial Approach." *Children Today,* July-August, 1976.

Giarretto, H. *Integrated Treatment of Child Sexual Abuse: A Treatment and Training Manual.* Palo Alto, CA: Science & Behavior Books, Inc., 1982.

Gibbens, T. and Prince, J. *Child Victims of Sex Offenses.* London: Institute for the Study and Treatment of Delinquency, 1963.

Gigeroff, A.K. et al. "Sexual Offenders on Probation: Heterosexual Pedophiles." *Federal Probation,* 33(4): 17-21, December, 1968.

Gil, D.G. *Violence Against Children: Physical Child Abuse in the United States.* Cambridge, MA: Harvard University Press, 1970.

Goldstein, M.J. and Kant, H.S. with Hartman, J. *Pornography and Sexual Deviance*. Berkeley, CA: University of California Press, 1973.

Goodenough, F.L. *Measurement of Intelligence by Drawings*. NY: Harcourt, Brace and World, Inc., 1926.

Goodman, G.S. (Ed.). "The Child Witness." *Journal of Social Issues,* Summer, 40(2), 1984.

Goodman, G. and Michelli, J.A. "Would You Believe a Child Witness?" *Psychology Today,* November, 1981, 15(11), 83-95.

Goodwin, J.; Sahd, D.; and Rada, R. "Incest Hoax: False Accusations, False Denials." In: Holder, W.M. (Ed.) *Sexual Abuse of Children: Implications for Treatment.* Englewood, CO: American Humane Association, Child Protection Division, 1980, 37-38.

Goodwin, J.; McCarthy, T.; DiVasto, P. "Prior Incest in Mothers of Abused Children." *Child Abuse and Neglect,* 5, 1981, 87-95.

Gordon, T. *P.E.T. Parent Effectiveness Training: The Tested Way to Raise Responsible Children.* N.Y.: New American Library, 1975.

Gottfredson, D.M. "Assessment Methods." In: Radzinowicz, L. and Wolfgang, M.E. (Eds.) *Crime and Justice, 3, The Criminal Under Restraint.* N.Y.: Basic Books, 1977, 97-100.

Gottlieb, B. "Incest: Therapeutic Intervention in a Unique Form Sexual Abuse." In: Warner, C.G. (Ed.) *Rape and Sexual Assault.* Germantown, MD: An Aspen Publication, Aspen Systems Corporation, 1980.

Gottlieb, B. and Dean, J. "The Co-Therapy Relationship in Group Treatment of Sexually Mistreated Adolescent Girls." In: Beezly-Mcazeh, P and Kempe, C. (Eds.) *Sexually Abused Children and Their Families.* N.Y.: Garland Press, 1979.

Gould, R. *Child Studies Through Fantasy: Cognitive-affective Patterns in Development.* N.Y.: Quadrangle Books, Inc., 1972.

Groth, A.N. *Men Who Rape: The Psychology of the Offender.* NY: Plenum Press, 1979.

Groth, A.N. "Patterns of Sexual Assault Against Children and Adolescents." In: Burgess, A.W.; Groth, A.N.; Holmstrom, L.L.; and

Sgroi, S.M. (Eds.) *Sexual Assault Against Children and Adolescents.* Lexington, MA: Lexington Books, D.C. Heath and Co., 1978.

Hobson, W.F. and Gary, T.S. "The Child Molester: Clinical Observations." In: *Social Work and Child Sexual Abuse.* N.Y.: Haworth Press, Inc., 1982, 134-6.

Haley, J. *Uncommon Therapy: The Psychiatric Techniques of Milton H. Erikson.* N.Y.: W.W. Norton and Company, Inc., 1973.

Halpern, S. *Rape: Helping the Victim — A Treatment Manual.* Oradell, N.J.: Medical Economics Company Book Division, 1978.

Hammer, E.F. *The Clinical Application of Projective Drawings.* Springfield, IL: Charles C. Thomas, Publisher, 1978.

Harris. T.A. *I'm O.K. — You're O.K.* N.Y.: Harper and Row, 1967.

Hawkins. P. *Children at Risk: My Fight Against Child Abuse — A Personal Story and a Public Plea.* Bethesda,MD: Adler & Adler, 1986.

Helfer, R.E. and Kempe, C. (Eds.) *the Battered Child.* (2nd Ed.) Chicago: University of Chicago Press, 1974.

Hendricks, G. and Wills, R. *The Centering Book: Awareness Activities for Children, Parents and Teachers.* Englewood Cliffs, N.J.: Prentice-Hall, Inc., 1975.

Heppner, P.P. "Counseling Men in Groups." *Personnel and Guidance Journal,* December 1981, 60 (4).

Herman, J. and Hirschman, L. "Father-Daughter Incest." In: Schultz, L.G. (Ed.) *The Sexual Victimology of Youth.* Springfield, IL: Charles C. Thomas, Publisher, 1980.

Holder, W.M. (Ed.) *Sexual Abuse of Children: Implications for Treatment.* Englewood, CO: The American Humane Association, 1980.

Holmes, R.M. *Sex Crimes.* Newberry Park, CA: Sage Publications, Inc., 1991.

Horton, A.L. and Johnson, B.L. *The Incest Perpetrator: A Family Member No One Wants to Treat.* Newberry Park, CA: Sage Publications, Inc., 1991.

Hopson, B. and Hopson, C. *Intimate Feedback: A Lover's Guide to Getting in Touch With Each Other.* N.Y.: Simon and Schuster, 1975.

Horn, P. "How to Enhance Healthy Sexuality: Behavior Mod in the Bedroom." *Psychology Today,* 94-95, November, 1975.

Hurt, M., Jr. *Child Abuse and Neglect: A Report in the Status of the Research.* Washington, D.C.: U.S. Government Printing Office, 1975.

Jenkins, J.L. et al. *Child Protective Services: A Guide for Workers.* Washington D.C.: Government Printing Office, August, 1979.

Justice, B. and Justice R. *The Broken Taboo: Sex in the Family.* NY: Human Science Press, 1979.

Kaplan, H.S. *Disorders of Sexual Desire and Other New Concepts and Techniques in Sex Therapy.* N.Y.: Brunner-Mazel Publishers, 1979.

Kaplan, H.S. *The New Sex Therapy: Active Treatment of Sexual Dysfunctions.* N.Y.: Brunner-Mazel Publishers, 1974.

Karpman, B. *The Sexual Offender and His Offenses.* N.Y.: Julian Press, 1954.

Kempe, C. and Helfer, R. (Eds.) *Helping the Battered Child and His Family.* Philadelphia: J.B. Lippincott Company, 1972.

Kempe, R.S. and Kempe, C.H. *Child Abuse.* Cambridge, MA: Harvard University Press, 1978.

Kempe, R.S. and Kempe, R.H. *The Common Secret: Sexual Abuse of Children and Adolescents.* N.Y.: W.H. Freeman & Co., 1984.

Kinkead, G. "The Family Secret." *Boston Magazine,* October, 1977.

Kinsey, A.C. *Sexual Behavior in the Human Female.* Bloomington, IN: University of Indiana Press, 1948.

Kittrie, N.N. *The Right To Be Different: Deviance and Enforced Therapy.* Baltimore: Penguin Books, Inc., 1974, 1971.

Kluft, R.P. (Ed.) *Childhood Antecedents of Multiple Personality.* Washington, D.C., American Psychiatric Press, 1985.

Konopka, G. *The Adolescent Girl in Conflict.* Englewood Cliffs, N.J.: Prentice-Hall, Inc., 1966.

Knopp, F.H. *Retraining Adult Sex Offenders: Methods and Models.* Syracuse, N.Y.: Safer Society Press, 1984, 16.

Kroth, J.A. *Child Sexual Abuse: Analysis of a Family Therapy Approach.* Springfield, IL: Charles C. Thomas, Publisher, 1979.

Kubler-Ross, E. *On Death and Dying.* N.Y.: MacMillan, 1969.

Ladner, J. and Hammond, B. "Socialization into Sexual Behavior." *Society for the Study of Sexual Problems,* 1967.

Landis, J. "Experiences of 500 Children with Adult Sexual Deviation." *Psychiatric Quarterly Supplement,* 30: 91-109, 1956.

Langevin, R. *Sexual Strands: Understanding and Treating Sexual Anomalies in Men.* Hillsdale, N.J.: Lawrence Erlbaum Associates, Publishers, 1983, 50-53, 58, 163, 293.

Laws, D.R. *Relapse Prevention with Sex Offenders.* NY: Guilford Press, 1989.

Leavitt, J.E. *The Battered Child: Selected Readings.* Morristown, N.J.: General Learning Corporation, 1974.

Leedy, J. (Ed.) *Poetry the Healer.* Philadelphia: J.B. Lippincott, 1973.

Leedy, J.J. (Ed.) *Poetry Therapy.* Philadelphia: J.B. Lippincott, 1969.

Lester, D. *Unusual Sexual Behavior: The Standard Deviations.* Springfield, IL: Charles C. Thomas, Publishers, 1975.

Lew, M. *Victims No Longer: Men Recovering from Incest and Other Sexual Child Abuse.* N.Y.: Neuvramont Publishing Co., 1988.

Lewinsohn, R. *A History of Sexual Customs.* N.Y.: Harper, 1959.

Lewis, H.A. *Self-hypnosis Dynamics.* Oak Park, Michigan: The Lewis Hypnosis Training Center, 1962.

Lewis, M. and Sarrel, P.M. "Some Psychological Aspects of Seduction in Incest, and Rape in Childhood." *Journal of American Academy of Child Psychiatry,* 8:606-619. October 1969..

Lipkin, K.M. and Daniels, R.S. "The Role of Seduction in Interpersonal Relationships." *Medical Aspects of Human Sexuality,* 79-88, 1969.

Litin, M. et al. "Parental Influences in Unusual Sexual Behavior in Children." *Psychoanalytic Quarterly,* 25:37, 1956.

LoPiccolo, J. and LoPiccolo, L. *Handbook of Sex Therapy.* N.Y.: Plenum Press, 1978.

Lustig, Captain N. et al. "Incest: A Family Group Survival Pattern." *Archives of General Psychiatry,* Vol. 14, January, 1966.

McCord, W. and McCord, J. *The Psychopath: An Essay on the Criminal Mind.* Princeton, N.J.: Van Nostrand, 1964.

McGuire,I.S. and Wagner, N.N. "Sexual Dysfunction in Women Who Were Molested As Children: On Response Patterns and Suggestions for Treatment." *Journal of Sex and Marital Therapy,* 4, 1978, 11-15.

McWilliams, P. *Surviving the Loss of a Love.* Allen Park, MI: Versemonger Press, 1971.

MacDonald, J.M. *Rape: Offenders and Their Victims.* Springfield, IL: Charles C. Thomas, Publisher, 1971.

Macfarlane, K. "Sexual Abuse of Children." In: Chapman, J.R. and Gates, M. (Eds.) *The Victimization of Women,* Vol 3, Beverly Hills, CA: Sage Publications, Sage Yearbooks in Women's Policy Studies, 1978.

MacFarlane, K.; Waterman, J.; Conerly, S.; Damon, L.; Durfee, M; and Long, S. *Sexual Abuse of Young Children: Evaluation and Treatment.* N.Y.: Guilford Press, 1986.

MacFarlane, K. "The Young Witnesses in the McMartin Sexual Abuse Case Undergo a Legal Battering in Court." *People,* July 8, 1985, 24 (2), 26.

Machover, K. *Personality Projection in the Drawing of the Human Figure.* Springfield, IL: Charles C. Thomas, Publisher, 1949.

Maddox, B. *The Half Parent: Living With Other People's Children.* N.Y.: M.Evans and Company, Inc. 1975.

Maletzky, B.M. *Treating the Sexual Offender.* Newberry Park, CA: Sage Publications, Inc., 1991.

Maltz, W. and Holman, B. *Incest and Sexuality: A Guide to Understanding and Healing.* Lexington, MA: Lexington Books, 1987.

Mann, E. and McDermott, Jr., J.F. "Play Therapy for Victims of Child Abuse and Neglect." In: (Ed.) Schaefer, C.F. and O'Connor, K.J. *Handbook of Play Therapy.* N.Y.: John Wiley & Sons, 1983.

Masters, R. *Patterns of Incest.* N.Y.: Basic Books, 1963.

Masters, W.H. and Johnson, V.E. "Incest: The Ultimate Sexual Taboo." *Redbook Magazine,* 54-59, 1976.

Mathis, J.D. *Clear Thinking about Sexual Deviations: A New Look at an Old Problem.* Chicago: Nelson-Hall Company, 1972.

Mayer, A. *Sexual Abuse: Causes, Consequences, and Treatment of Incestuous and Pedophilic Acts.* Holmes Beach, FL: Learning Publications, Inc., 1985.

Mayer, A. *Sex Offenders: Approaches to Understanding and Management.* Holmes Beach, FL: Learning Publications, Inc., 1988.

Mayer, A. *Child Sexual Abuse and the Courts: A Manual for Therapists.* Holmes Beach, FL: Learning Publications, Inc., 1990.

Meares, A. *Shapes of Sanity: A Study in the Therapeutic Modeling in the Waking and Hypnotic State.* Springfield, IL: Charles C. Thomas, Publisher, 1960.

Meichenbaum, D. and Turk, D. "The Cognitive Behavioral Management of Anxiety, Anger and Pain." In: Davidson, P.O. (Ed.) *The Behavioral Management of Anxiety, Depression and Pain.* N.Y.: Brunner-Mazel Publishers, 1976.

Meiselman, K.C. *Incest.* San Francisco: Jossey-Bass, 1978.

Middleton-Moz, J. *Children of Trauma: Rediscovering Your Discarded Self.* Deerfield, MA: Health Communications, 1989.

Miller, A. *For Your Own Good: Hidden Cruelty in Childrearing and the Roots of Violence.* N.Y.: Farrar, Straus & Giroux, 1983.

Mohr, J.W. "A Child Has Been Molested." *Medical Aspects of Human Sexuality.* 43-50, November, 1968.

Moll, A. *The Sexual Life of the Child.* N.Y.: Emerson, 1962.

Morneau, R. and Rockwell, R. *Sex, Motivation and the Criminal Offender.* Springfield, IL: Charles C. Thomas, Publisher, 1980.

Morris, M. *If I Should Die Before I Wake.* Los Angeles, CA: J.P. Tarcher, Inc., 1982.

Nadelson, C.C. and Notman, M.T. "Emotional Repercussions of Rape." *Medical Aspects of Human Sexuality,* 16-33, March, 1977.

"National Analysis of Official Child Neglect and Abuse Reporting." Denver: American Humane Association, 1978.

Nelson, J. "A New Look at Incest." *Forum: The International Journal of Human Relations.* 9(11), 41-45, August, 1980.

Nelson, M. and Clark, K. (Eds.) *The Educator's Guide to Preventing Child Sexual Abuse.* Santa Cruz, CA: Network Publications, 1986.

Norwood, R. *Women Who Love Too Much.* N.Y.: Pocket Books, 1985.

Oates, K. *Child Abuse: A Major Concern of Our Times.* Secaucus, N.J.: Citadel Press, 1986.

O'Brien, S. *Child Abuse: A Crying Shame.* Provo, UT: Brigham Young University, 1980.

Palm, R. and Abrahamsen, D. "A Rorshach Study of the Wives of Sex Offenders." *Journal of Nervous and Mental Diseases,* 119:167, February, 1954.

Parker, R.S. "Poetry as a Therapeutic Art in the Resolution of Resistance in Psychotherapy." In: Leedy, J.J. (Ed.) *Poetry Therapy.* Philadelphia: J.B. Lippincott, 1969.

Parker, T. *Hidden World of Sex Offenders.* In: Bobbs-Merrill, 1969.

Patton, M.Q. *Family Sexual Abuse: Frontline Research and Evaluation.* Newberry Park, CA: Sage Publications, Inc., 1991.

Paul, J. et al. *Child Advocacy Within the System.* Syracuse, N.Y.: Syracuse University Press, 1977.

Paulson, M. and Chaleff, A. "Parent Surrogate Roles: A Dynamic Concept in Understanding and Treating Abusive Parents." *Journal of Clinical Child Psychology,* 2(3):38-40, Fall, 1973.

Peele, S. *Love and Addiction.* N.Y.: New American Library/Signet Books, 1976.

Pekhanen, J. *Victims: An Account of Rape.* N.Y.: The Dial Press, 1976.

Peters, J.J. "Children Who Are Victims of Sexual Assault and the Psychology of Offenders." *American Journal Of Psychotherapy,* 30(3), 398-421, July, 1976.

Pietropinto, A. "Exploring the Unconscious Through Nonsense Poetry." In: Leedy, J. (Ed.) *Poetry The Healer.* Philadelphia: J.B. Lippincott, 1973.

Pitcher, E.G. and Prelinger, E. *Children Tell Stories: An Analysis of Fantasy.* N.Y.: International Universities Press, Inc., 1963.

Plummer, C.A. *Preventing Child Sexual Abuse: Activities and Strategies for Those Working With Children and Adolescents.* Holmes Beach, FL: Learning Publications, Inc., 1984.

Polese, C. *Promise Not To Tell.* N.Y.: *Human Sciences Press,* 1985.

Pomeroy, W.B. *Dr. Kinsey and the Institute for Sex Research.* N.Y.: A Signet Book, New American Library, 1973.

Porter, E. *Treating the Young Male Victim of Sexual Assault: Issues and Intervention Strategies.* Syracuse, N.Y.: Safer Society Press, 1986.

Powell, J. *The Secret of Staying in Love.* Niles, IL: Argus Communications, 1974.

Powers, M.E. *A Practical Guide to Self-hypnosis.* Hollywood, CA: Wilshire Book Company, 1961.

Poznanski, E. and Blos, P.,Jr. "Incest." *Medical Aspects Of Human Sexuality,* 46-79, October, 1975.

Radzinowicz, L. *Sexual Offenses.* N.Y.: MacMillan, 1957.

Raths, L.E. et al. *Values and Teaching: Working With Values in the Classroom.* Columbus, OH: Charles E. Merrill Publishing Company, 1966.

Ray, S. *I Deserve Love: How Affirmations Can Guide You to Personal Fulfillment.* Milbrae, CA: Les Femmes Publishing, 1976.

Raybin, J.B. "Homosexual Incest." *The Journal of Nervous and Mental Disease,* 148(2), February, 1969.

Reich, W. "The Origin of Clan Division and the Incest Taboo." In: *The Invasion of Compulsory Sex-morality.* N.Y.: Farrar, Strauss, and Giroux, 1971.

Reid, W.H.; Dorr, D.; Walker, J.I.; and Bonner, J.W. (Eds.) *Unmasking The Psychopath: Antisocial Personality and Related Syndromes.* N.Y.: W.W. Norton, 1986.

Reik, T. *The Many Faces Of Sex.* N.Y.: Farrar, Strauss, and Giroux, 1966.

Retzinger, S.M. *Violent Emotions.* Newberry Park, CA: Sage Publications, Inc., 1991.

Rhyne, J. "The Gestalt Art Experience." In: Fagan, J. and Shepherd, I.L. (Eds.) *Gestalt Therapy Now — Theory, Techniques, Applications.* N.Y.: Harper and Row, 1970.

Rogers, C.M. and Terry, T. "Clinical Interventions With Boy Victims of Sexual Abuse." In (Eds.): Stuart, I.R. and Greer, J.G. (Eds.) *Victims of Sexual Aggression: Men, Women and Children.*

Rogers, C.R. and Stevens, B. *Person to Person: The Problem of Being Human.* N.Y.: Pocket Book, 1972.

Rosenfeld, D.L. and Garcia, C.R. "Injuries Incurred During Rape." *Medical Aspects of Human Sexuality,* 77-78, March, 1976.

Rothchild, E. "Answering Young Children's Sex Questions." *Medical Aspects of Human Sexuality,* 23-24, December, 1975.

Rubin, T.I. *The Angry Book.* N.Y.: Collier Books, 1978.

Ruitenbeek, H.M. (Ed.) *Varieties of Personality Theory.* NY: E.P. Dutton and Company, Inc., 1964.

Rush, F. "The Sexual Abuse of Children: A Feminist Point of View." In: Connell, N. and Wilson, E. (Eds.) *Rape: The First Sourcebook for Women By New York Radical Feminists.* N.Y.: New American Library, A Plume Book, 1974.

Rush, F. "The Sexual Abuse of Children: Recommendations and Proposals for Victims of Child Abuse." In: Connell, N. and Wilson, C.

(Eds.) *RAPE: The First Sourcebook for Women by New York Radical Feminists.* N.Y.: New American Library, A Plume Book, 1974.

Rush, F. *The Best Kept Secret: Sexual Abuse of Children.* Englewood Cliffs, N.J.: Prentice-Hall Book Company, 1980.

Russell, D. *The Secret Trauma: Incest in the Lives of Girls and Women.* N.Y.: Basic Books, 1986.

Salter, A.C. *Treating Child Sex Offenders and Victims: A Practical Guide.* Newberry Park, CA: Sage Publications, Inc., 1991.

Saltman, V. and Soloman, R. "Incest and the Multiple Personality." *Psychological Reports,* 50, June 1982, 1127-41.

Schildkrout, M.S.; Shenker, I.R.; and Sonnenblick, M.S. *Human Figure Drawings in Adolescence.* N.Y.: Brunner-Mazel, Inc., 1972.

Schofield, M. *The Sexual Behavior of Young People.* Boston: Little Brown, 1967.

Schultz, L.G. "The Child Sex Victim: Social Psychological and Legal Perspectives." *Child Welfare,* 52(3): 147-157, March, 1973.

Schultz, L.G. (Ed.) *The Sexual Victimology of Youth.* Springfield, IL: Charles C. Thomas, Publisher, 1980.

Scrignar, C. "Sex and the Underage Girl." *Medical Aspects of Human Sexuality,* 2:34-39, 1968.

Sgroi, S.M. *Handbook of Clinical Intervention in Child Sexual Abuse.* Lexington, MA: D.C. Heath & Co., Lexington Books, 1982.

Shamroy, J.A. "A Perspective on Childhood Sexual Abuse." *Social Work,* National Association of Social Workers, Inc., March 1980.

Sheldon, W.H. "Constitutional Factors in Personality." In: Ruitenbeek, H.M. (Ed.) *Varieties of Personality Theory.* N.Y.: E.P. Dutton and Co., Inc., 1964.

Shengold, L. *Soul Murder: The Effects of Childhood Abuse and Deprivation.* N.Y.: Fawcett Columbine, 1989.

Slager-Journe, P. "Counseling Sexually Abused Children." *Personnel and Guidance Journal,* October, 1978.

Slaughter, C. *Relations.* N.Y.: Pocket Books, 1976.

Smith, G.W. and Phillips, A.I. *Couple Therapy.* N.Y.: Collier Books, 1973.

Smith A.B. and Berlin, L. *Treating The Criminal Offender.* Englewood Cliffs, N.J.: Prentice-Hall, Inc., 2nd Ed., 1981.

Sonkin, D.J. and Durphy, M. *Learning to Live Without Violence: A Handbook for Men.* San Francisco: Volcano Press, 1985.

Soukup, R.; Wicker, S; and Corbett, J. *Three in Every Classroom.* Bemidji, MN: Sexual Assault Program, 1984.

Spaks, A. "The End of the Ride: Analyzing a Sex Crime." *Mother Jones,* 5(111), 34-44, April, 1980.

Sparks, L. *Self-hypnosis: A Conditional-response Technique.* Hollywood, CA: Wilshire Book Company, 1962, 1968.

Steele, B. and Alexander, H. "Long-Term Effects of Sexual Abuse in Childhood." In (Eds.): Mrazek, P and Kempe, H. *Sexually Abused Children in Their Families.* N.Y.: Pergamon Press, 1981.

Stein, F. *Guilt Theory and Therapy.* London: Allen and Unwin, 1969.

Stein, R. *Incest and Human Love: The Betrayal of the Soul in Psychotherapy.* Baltimore, MD: Penguin, 1974.

Stoller, R.J. *Perversion: The Erotic Form of Hatred.* NY: Pantheon Books, Division of Random House, 1975.

Stuart, I.R. and Greer, J.G. (Eds.) *Victims of Sexual Aggression: Treatment of Children, Women and Men.* N.Y.: Van Nostrand Reinhold Co., 1984.

"Study Discovers Unhappy Hookers in San Francisco." *Arizona Republic,* June 28, 1980.

Summit, R. and Kryso, J. "Sexual Abuse of Children: A Clinical Spectrum." *American Journal of Orthopsychiatry.* 48, 4-78, 237-51.

Swanson, D.W. "Adult Sexual Abuse of Children." *Diseases of the Nervous System,* 29:677-683, 1968.

Swerdlow, H. "Trauma Caused by Anal Intercourse." *Medical Aspects of Human Sexuality,* 93-98, July, 1976.

Talent, N. "Sexual Deviation As A Diagnostic Entity: A Confused and Sinister Concept." In: Smith, S. (Ed.), *Bulletin of the Menninger Clinic,* 41(1), January, 1977, 52.

Taylor, R.L. "Marital Therapy In the Treatment of Incest." *Social Casework,* 65, 4-84, 195-202.

Terkel, S. and Rench, J. *Feeling Safe, Feeling Strong: How to Avoid Sexual Abuse and What to Do If It Happens to You.* Minneapolis, MN: Lerner Publications, 1984.

Tormes, Y.M. *The Victim: Child Victims of Incest.* Washington: U.S. Children's Bureau, 1968.

Tormes, Y.M. *Child Victims Of Incest.* (2nd Ed.) Denver: The American Humane Association, 1978.

Trainer, R. *The Lolita Complex.* N.Y.: Paperback Library, 1966.

U.S. Department of Health, Education and Welfare. *Special Report from The National Center on Child Abuse and Neglect: Child Sexual Abuse-incest, Assault and Sexual Exploitation.* Washington: Government Printing Office, August, 1978.

U.S. Department of Health, Education and Welfare. *Resource Materials: A Curriculum of Child Abuse and Neglect.* Washington: Government Printing Office, 1979.

U.S. Department of Health, Education and Welfare. *Child Abuse And Neglect, the Problem and Its Management, Vol. 1, An Overview of the Problem.* Washington: Government Printing Office, 1974, 1975.

U.S. Department of Health, Education and Welfare. *Child Abuse and Neglect, the Problem and Its Management, Vol.2., The Roles and Responsibilities of Professionals.* Washington: Government Printing Office. 1974, 1975.

US. Department of Health, Education and Welfare. *The Role of the Mental Health Professional in the Prevention and Treatment of Child Abuse and Neglect.* Washington: Government Printing Office, August, 1979.

U.S. Department of Health, Education and Welfare. *The Role of Law Enforcement in the Prevention and Treatment of Child Abuse and Neglect.* Washington: Government Printing Office, 1979.

U.S. Department of Health, Education and Welfare. *Child Protective Services: A Guide for Workers.* Washington: Government Printing Office, August, 1979.

Walker, G. with Smith, A.P. *Me, You and Us.* N.Y.: Peter H. Wyden, Inc., 1971.

Walters, D.R. *Physical and Sexual Abuse of Children: Causes and Treatment.* Bloomington, IN: Indiana University Press, 1975.

Ward, E. *Father-Daughter Rape.* N.Y.: Grove Press, 1985.

Weeks, R.B. "Counseling Parents of Sexually Abused Children." *Medical Aspects of Human Sexuality.* 43-81, August, 1976.

Weinberg, S.K. *Incest Behavior.* N.Y.: Citadel Press. 1955.

Weiss, J.; Rogers,E.; Darwin, M.R.; and Dutton, C.E. "A Study of Girl Sex Victims." *Psychiatric Quarterly,* 29:1, 1955.

Wiessberg, M. *Dangerous Secrets: Maladaptive Responses to Stress.* N.Y.: W.W. Norton & Company, 1983.

Westman, J.C. "Telling Children About Sexual Molestation." *Medical Aspects of Human Sexuality.* 53-61. August, 1975.

Wheeler, B. and Walton, E. "Personality Disturbances of Adult Incest Victims." *Social Casework,* 68, 12-87, 597-602.

Wolfe, D.A. *Child Abuse: Implications for Child Development and Psychopathology.* Newberry Park, CA: Sage Publications, Inc., 1991.

Wood, W. and Hatton, L. *Triumph Over Darkness: Understanding and Healing the Trauma of Childhood Sexual Abuse.* Hillsboro, OR: Beyond Words Publishing, Inc., 1988.

Wyatt, G.E. and Powell, G.J. (Eds.) *Lasting Effects of Child Sexual Abuse.* Newberry Park, CA: Sage Publications, Inc., 1991.

Yorukoglu, A. and Kemph, J.P. "Children Not Severely Damaged by Incest with a Parent." In: Schultz, L.G. (Ed.) *The Sexual Victimology of Youth.* Springfield, IL: Charles C. Thomas, Publisher, 1980.

Zaphiris, A.G. "Incest: The Family With Two Known Victims." Denver: *The American Humane Association.* 1978.

Zeig, J.K. (Ed.) *A Teaching Seminar with Milton H. Erikson.* N.Y.: Brunner-Mazel, 1980.

Zuger, B. "Children Who Wear Clothing of the Opposite Sex." *Medical Aspects Of Human Sexuality,* 79-80, May, 1976.

Index

Active Listening, 172, 206
Affirmations, 87, 90, 91-94, 127, 129
Aggressor (Identification with), 128
Alberti, R. E. and Emmons, M. L., 69
Alcoholism (See Chemical Abuse)
American Humane Association, 54
Art Therapy, 49, 51, 149
Assertiveness Training, 135, 151, 152, 167, 173-180, 188
    Contractual Agreement, 73-74, 175
    DESC Script, 72, 174
    Downer Detours, 72, 179
    Role Plays, 71-74, 180
Auto-suggestion, 87, 89
Battered Wives, 30
Behavior Modification, 113, 116, 133-135
    Contractual Agreement, 112, 116, 136
    Learning Theory, 125-127
    Shaping, 232-233
Bender, L. and Blau, A., 13, 16
Benson, H. and Klipper, M.Z., 89-90
Benward, J. and Densen-Gerber, J., 15
Bibliotherapy, 50, 116, 135, 149, 157
Bower, S. A. and Bower, G.H., 72, 90
Branden, N., 48
Bricklin, B. et al., 268
Burgess, A. W. and Holmstrom, L. L., 6, 34, 35
Burns, R. C. and Kaufman, S. H., 218
Burton, L., 13, 16
Butler, S., 14, 23, 24, 27, 30
Case History (Outline), 105-106
Catharsis, 46, 49, 51, 146, 152, 227, 248-249, 263
Cautela, J. R., 257
Chemical Abuse (Alcohol and Drugs), 27, 29, 31, 50, 84, 104, 105, 108, 112,
    120, 121, 127
Child Protective Services, 63, 85, 203
Cognitive Dissonance, 13
Compulsion, Chronic, 98

Confidentiality, 146, 147, 165
Conflict
    Approach-Avoidance, 64, 79
    Reactivation of, 35, 128, 149, 236, 270-273
Court (Process), 34-36, 69, 203, 207, 214, 230, 250, 259-263
Crisis Centers, 17
Crisis (Resolution of), 64-65, 203-204, 205
CSATP (Child Sexual Abuse Treatment Program), 18
Data
    Collection of, 6, 11, 14
    Distortions, 13
Daughters and Sons United, 18
DeFrancis, V., 4, 10, 15, 16, 34, 97
Denial, 6, 11, 29, 30, 41, 77, 78,79, 81, 82, 84, 88, 99, 100, 101, 102,
    103, 107, 109, 110, 115, 122, 138, 139, 140-141, 142, 151, 152, 201, 206
Densen-Gerber, J., 15
Development (Psychosexual), 17
DHEW, 4, 11
Dollard, J. and Miller, N.E., 45
Dolls (Raggedy Ann and Raggedy Andy), 272
Double-bind (Paradox), 138
Draw-A-Person Test (D-A-P), 123
    Interpretation, 124
Drug Abuse (See Chemical Abuse)
Emotional Constriction, 22, 31, 32
Enmeshment, 22
Exhibitionism, 5
Feedback, 189
Feminists, 11, 14
"Fight or Flight" (Reaction), 98, 128
Finkelhor, D., 3, 6, 7, 8, 13, 14, 17, 24
Fontana, V. J., 15
Forward, S. and Buck, C., 4, 23, 24, 30, 34
Freud, S., 6, 14
Gelberman, J. H. and Komak, D., 51
Generational Blurring, 24
Gestalt Therapy, 47, 52-53, 149, 152, 204
Giarretto, H., 15, 18, 97
Goodenough, F. L., 212
Gottlieb, B., 3, 22, 23, 27, 31, 32
Groth, A. N., 98, 99, 125
Guided Imagery, 258-259, 261-262

Hammer, E. F., 211, 235
Harris, T. A., 266
Herman, J. and Hirschman, L., 15
Holmes-Rath Triggering Events Rating Scale, 128, 176-177
Holmstrom, L. L., 34, 35
Iatrogenesis, 17
"I-Messages," 116, 136, 171, 174, 184, 188, 189
Incest (Types of), 22
Incestuous Assault (Types), 5
Institute for Sex Research, 160
Isolation (Social), 22, 24, 28, 81, 83, 105, 111, 115, 116, 126, 133, 134, 151
Interviewing (Techniques), 53, 202-208
Journal Writing, 47-48, 55, 183
Justice, B. H. and Justice, R., 7, 8, 27
Kinsey, A. C. 4, 13
Kroth, J. A., 9, 10, 17
Kubler-Ross, E., 78, 79
Landis, J., 16
Law (See Court)
League of Women Voters, 263
Learned Helplessness (Theory), 154
Learning Theory (See Behavior Modification)
Leedy, J., 50
Legal Aid, 83
Litin, M., 23
Lustig, N., 23, 24
MacDonald, J. M., 30
Machover, K., 212
Mandala, 191, 194
Meares, A., 235
Meichenbaum, D. and Turk, D., 126
Methodology
    Frequency of Incest, 7
    Research, 8, 9, 10-17
Minnesota Multiphasic Personality Inventory, 98
National Analysis of Official Child Neglect and Abuse Reporting, 4
National Committee for Prevention of Child Abuse and Neglect (DHEW), 11
Nonverbal Behaviors, 71, 152, 190, 207
NOW, 263
Oedipus Complex, 14
Offenders (Characteristics of), 29-30
Parents Anonymous, 149

Parents United, 18
Parker, R. S., 51
Passive Aggressiveness, 27, 29, 83, 134, 140
Pedophile, 27, 98, 110, 157, 158
    Types, 98, 125, 158
Personality (Antisocial), 15, 29, 36, 98, 99, 100, 106, 158
Peters, J. J., 16, 23
Physical Examinations, 6
Phobia (School), 31, 35
Pietropinto, A., 51
Poetry Therapy, 50, 61-62
Police (Reports), 6
Pornography, 8
Projection, 11, 29, 88, 100, 102, 103, 104, 109, 128, 141
Pseudo-maturity, 32
Psychoanalytic Theory, 15
Psychosis, 16, 21, 22
Questionnaires (Assessments, Exercises), 48-49, 55, 56, 57-60, 101-104, 105-106, 107, 108, 111-112, 121-122, 136, 154-155, 162-163, 170, 175, 180-182, 183, 185-187, 193, 194, 214, 217, 222, 252-255, 267-268
Rape, 5, 11
    Crisis Centers, 54, 149, 153
Ray, S., 90, 91-92
Reaction Formation, 137
Recidivism, 63, 98, 110
Rene Guyon Society, 11
Relaxation
    Autogenic, 116, 135
    Deep Muscle, 258-259, 260-262
Rogers, C., 85, 113, 116
Role Plays, 147, 148, 149, 207, 270
Role Reversal, 21, 24, 25, 67, 133, 142, 202
Rush, F., 11
Sampling, 10
Sensate Focus, 116
Sexual Dysfunction, 15, 23-24, 31, 86, 111, 135, 140, 157, 159-160
Sexual History, 162-163
Schizophrenia, 16, 50
Schultz, L. G., 4, 9, 16, 17
Slager-Jorne, P., 7, 22
Stress Management (Alternate), 126, 128
"The Victim No One Believes", 54

Therapeutic Silence, 152
Transactional Analysis, 266-267
Turk, D., 126
Venereal Disease, 6
Victim Precipitation (Theory of), 13-14, 31, 139
Victims (Characteristics of), 31-32
Victim Witness Program, 34
Voyeurism, 5
Walters, D. R., 27
Weinberg, S. K., 4
Weiss, J. et al., 13, 14
Wives of Offenders (Characteristics of), 30, 81-82
Women's Movement (See Feminists), 8
Writing Techniques (See Journal Writing), 47-49
Yorukoglu, A. and Kemph, J. P., 15, 16
Zaphiris, A. G., 27, 30